Ethical and legal debates in Irish healthcare

Manchester University Press

IRISH SOCIETY

The Irish Society series provides a critical, interdisciplinary and in-depth analysis of Ireland that reveals the processes and forces shaping social, economic, cultural and political life, and their outcomes for communities and social groups. The books seek to understand the evolution of social, economic and spatial relations from a broad range of perspectives, and explore the challenges facing Irish society in the future given present conditions and policy instruments.

SERIES EDITOR
Rob Kitchin

ALREADY PUBLISHED

Ireland and the Freedom of Information Act: FOI@15
Edited by Maura Adshead and Tom Felle

Public private partnerships in Ireland: Failed experiment or the way forward for the state? *Rory Hearne*

Migrations: Ireland in a global world
Edited by Mary Gilmartin and Allen White

The economics of disability: Insights from Irish research
Edited by John Cullinan, Seán Lyons and Brian Nolan

The domestic, moral and political economies of post-Celtic tiger Ireland: What rough beast? *Kieran Keohane and Carmen Kuhling*

Challenging times, challenging administration: The role of public administration in producing social justice in Ireland
Chris McInerney

Corporate and white-collar crime in Ireland: A new architecture of regulatory enforcement *Joe McGrath*

Management and gender in higher education *Pat O'Connor*

Defining events: Power, resistance and identity in twenty-first-century Ireland
Edited by Rosie Meade and Fiona Dukelow

Ethical and legal debates in Irish healthcare

Confronting complexities

Edited by Mary Donnelly and Claire Murray

MANCHESTER UNIVERSITY PRESS

Published by Manchester University Press
Altrincham Street, Manchester M1 7JA
www.manchesteruniversitypress.co.uk

British Library Cataloguing-in-Publication Data
A catalogue record for this book is available from the British Library

Library of Congress Cataloging-in-Publication Data applied for

ISBN 978 0 7190 9946 5 hardback

First published 2016

Typeset by
Servis Filmsetting Ltd, Stockport, Cheshire
Printed in Great Britain by
CPI Group (UK) Ltd, Croydon CR0 4YY

Contents

Contributors

Louise Campbell is a Clinical Ethicist and a Lecturer in Medical Ethics at National University of Ireland, Galway and co-author of *End-of-Life Care: Ethics and Law* (Cork: Cork University Press, 2011).

Mary Donnelly is a Professor of Law at University College Cork. Her books include *Healthcare Decision-Making and the Law: Autonomy, Capacity and the Limits of Liberalism* (Cambridge: Cambridge University Press, 2010) and she is co-author of *End-of-Life Care: Ethics and Law* (Cork: Cork University Press, 2011).

Heike Felzmann is a Lecturer in Ethics at the National University of Ireland, Galway. Her research interests are in healthcare ethics, research ethics and information ethics. She has contributed to several European and national research projects on bioethical and research ethical issues and was a member of national working groups that developed Irish research ethics guidance documents.

Ruth Fletcher is a Senior Lecturer in Medical Law at Queen Mary, University of London. She is Academic Editor of *Feminist Legal Studies* and has published widely in the area of reproductive rights. She leads the ReValuing Care network, an international, interdisciplinary network which aims to create spaces for dialogue about care across a range of contexts.

Brendan D. Kelly is Associate Clinical Professor of Psychiatry at University College Dublin and Editor-in-Chief of the *Irish Journal of Psychological Medicine.* Recent books include *Custody, Care and Criminality* (Dublin: The History Press), *Ada English: Patriot and Psychiatrist* (Dublin: Irish Academic Press) and *'He Lost Himself Completely': Shell Shock and its Treatment at Dublin's Richmond War Hospital (1916–1919)* (Dublin: Liffey Press).

Mary Keys is a Lecturer in Law at National University of Ireland, Galway and has published widely on mental health and mental capacity law. She is a member of the Mental Health Commission and is involved in a number of non-governmental organisations.

Barry Lyons is a Consultant Anaesthetist at Our Lady's Hospital for Sick Children, Crumlin and a Lecturer in Medical Ethics at Trinity College Dublin. He holds a PhD in Bioethics from the University of Manchester and has published extensively in the fields of parental rights, children and bioethics.

Deirdre Madden is a Professor of Law at University College Cork. Her books include *Medicine, Ethics and the Law* (Dublin: Bloomsbury, 2nd edn, 2011) and *Medical Law* (Alphen aan den Rijn: Kluwer, 2010). She was Chair of the Medical Council's Ethics Committee from 2006–2012 and is a member of the National Advisory Committee on Bioethics.

Joan McCarthy is a College Lecturer in Healthcare Ethics in the School of Nursing and Midwifery, University College Cork. She is the author of *Dennett and Ricoeur on the Narrative Self* (New York: Humanity Books, 2007) and co-author of *End-of-Life Care: Ethics and Law* (Cork: Cork University Press, 2011) and *Nursing Ethics, Irish Cases and Concerns* (Dublin: Gill and MacMillan, 2nd edn, 2012).

Claire Murray is a Lecturer in Law at University College Cork. She researches in mental health law and feminist theory and is the author of *A Feminist Analysis of Mental Health Law: Reconceptualising Rights* (London: Routledge, 2016 forthcoming). She has been a Visiting Scholar at the Vulnerability and the Human Condition Initiative, Emory University.

Shaun T. O'Keeffe is a Consultant Geriatrician at Galway University Hospital and an Honorary Personal Professor of Medicine at National University of Ireland, Galway. His interests include patient preferences, ethical issues for older people and delirium. He was a member of the HSE National Consent Policy Advisory Group and the Medical Council of Ireland Ethics Working Group.

Asim A. Sheikh is a practising barrister, specialising in medical negligence and medical law and Lecturer in Legal Medicine at the School of Medicine, University College Dublin. He is Editor of the *Medico-Legal Journal of Ireland* and has published various articles on medical law. He is a member of the National Advisory Committee on Bioethics and the European Association of Healthcare Law.

Ciara Staunton, Irish Research Scholar, works at the Centre for Medical Ethics and Law at the University of Stellenbosch, South Africa where she is Researcher on the Social and Ethical Aspects of HIV Cure Project and Co-ordinator of the Advancing Research Ethics Training in Southern Africa programme. She is the Chief Legal Officer of the Irish Stem Cell Foundation.

Katherine Wade is a Post-Doctoral Research Associate at the Centre of Medical Law and Ethics at King's College London. She undertook her PhD entitled 'Medical Research with Neonates: A Children's Rights Approach' at the School of Law, University College Cork. She was a visiting scholar in the Brocher Foundation, Geneva, St Louis Law School and Emory Law School.

Tom Walker is a Senior Lecturer in Ethics at the School of Politics, International Studies and Philosophy at Queen's University Belfast. He has published extensively on issues of autonomy, consent and resource allocation

Darius Whelan is a Senior Lecturer in Law at University College Cork. He is author of *Mental Health Law* (Dublin: Round Hall, 2009) and is expert in both civil and criminal aspects of mental health law. He is currently President of the Irish Mental Health Lawyers Association.

Series editor's foreword

Over the past twenty years Ireland has undergone enormous social, cultural and economic change. From a poor, peripheral country on the edge of Europe with a conservative culture dominated by tradition and Church, Ireland transformed into a global, cosmopolitan country with a dynamic economy. At the heart of the processes of change was a new kind of political economic model of development that ushered in the so-called Celtic Tiger years, accompanied by renewed optimism in the wake of the ceasefires in Northern Ireland and the peace dividend of the Good Friday Agreement. As Ireland emerged from decades of economic stagnation and The Troubles came to a peaceful end, the island became the focus of attention for countries seeking to emulate its economic and political miracles. Every other country, it seemed, wanted to be the next Tiger, modelled on Ireland's successes. And then came the financial collapse of 2008, the bursting of the property bubble, bank bailouts, austerity plans, rising unemployment and a return to emigration. From being the paradigm case of successful economic transformation, Ireland has become an internationally important case study of what happens when an economic model goes disastrously wrong.

The Irish Society series provides a critical, interdisciplinary and in-depth analysis of Ireland that reveals the processes and forces shaping social, economic, cultural and political life, and their outcomes for communities and social groups. The books seek to understand the evolution of social, economic and spatial relations from a broad range of perspectives, and explore the challenges facing Irish society in the future given present conditions and policy instruments. The series examines all aspects of Irish society including, but not limited to: social exclusion, identity, health, welfare, life cycle, family life and structures, labour and work cultures, spatial and sectoral economy, local and regional development, politics and the political system, government and governance, environment, migration and spatial planning. The series is supported by the Irish Social Sciences Platform (ISSP), an all-island platform of integrated social science research and graduate education focusing on the social, cultural and economic transformations shaping Ireland in the twenty-first century. Funded by the Programme for Research in Third Level Institutions, the ISSP brings together leading social science academics from all of Ireland's universities and other third-level institutions.

Given the marked changes in Ireland's fortunes over the past two decades it is important that rigorous scholarship is applied to understand the forces at work, how they have affected different people and places in uneven and unequal ways, and what needs to happen to create a fairer and prosperous society. The Irish Society series provides such scholarship.

Rob Kitchin

Introduction

Mary Donnelly and Claire Murray

At the heart of the Irish health system, there is an interplay between ethics, law and medicine. Every day in Irish hospitals and clinics, decisions are made which have profound effects on individual lives, and deaths. More broadly, these decisions and the manner in which we make them are the building blocks for the kind of healthcare system we operate, which in turn reflects the kind of society we have constructed. Yet, beyond the 'headline' issues, our understanding of how decisions in healthcare are made is partial, at best, and the normative foundations for decisions remain largely unexplored.

The stifling impact of religious ethos, in particular that of Catholicism, is often cited as an explanation for the lack of debate around ethical issues in healthcare in Ireland in the past (McDonnell and Allison, 2006). However, given the increasingly secularised nature of contemporary Irish society (Inglis, 1998), it is no longer feasible to attribute an ongoing lack of debate to this source. Moreover, simple stereotyping based on conceptions of Catholicism or secularism is largely unhelpful. Legitimate differences exist within both religious (McDonagh and MacNamara, 2013) and secular traditions (Turner, 2003), and ascribing positions simply on the basis of religious affiliation/non-affiliation stifles dialogue.

There has tended to be limited political appetite for discussion of ethical issues in healthcare. This derives in part at least from political timidity, which was perhaps an inevitable response to the polarised nature of debates around the introduction of the Eighth Amendment to Bunreacht na hÉireann in 1983 (Hesketh, 1990). Because of this timidity, Ireland has not signed or ratified the Oviedo Convention for the Protection of Human Rights and Dignity of the Human Being with regard to the Application of Biology and Medicine 1997 (Convention on Human Rights and Biomedicine) and expert reports, such as the Report of the Commission on Assisted Human Reproduction (2005) and the Irish Council for Bioethics Opinion on Stem Cell Research (2008), were allowed to remain dormant. This inaction has negative consequences not just for bioethical standards but also for the broader Irish scientific research agenda (Barrington, 2002). It also leaves important areas without legislative clarification. Political disregard for these issues was evident also in the decision to cease funding for the Irish Council for Bioethics in 2010, leaving Ireland as 'the sole country in the EU without an effective bioethics organization' (Lyons, 2012: 382). Although a National Advisory Committee on Bioethics was established by the Minister for Health in 2012, this Committee has a limited public profile and a more restricted membership and its terms of reference are notably more constraining than those of the Council.

In spite of these limitations, there are several positive indicators of greater public engagement with questions of health ethics and law. The Oireachtas hearings which preceded the introduction of the Protection of Life During Pregnancy Act 2013 showed the potential for a less polarised and more grounded discussion around women's healthcare during pregnancy (O'Sullivan et al., 2013: 9). The extent to which this approach informed the legislation as enacted is open to question. Nonetheless, by providing space for the contributions of medical experts, ethicists and lawyers, as well as special interest groups, the Oireachtas hearings enabled not just legislators but also members of the public to evaluate contributions and to form their own views on the issues discussed. Subsequent public hearings, including those on palliative and end-of-life care and organ donation, suggest a new openness to discussion although, of course, it is only when the task of legislating is embarked upon that the real impact of this approach can be assessed. It is also positive that, although the Irish courts have sometimes been slow to provide written judgments in cases of ethical complexity, a body of jurisprudence is gradually growing and this helps to provide a context for informed, critical engagement with the legal positions adopted.

This book contributes to these emerging conversations and reflects our view that reasoned discussion is essential in developing appropriate responses to difficult questions about health ethics and law and that such discussion must be informed by the perspectives of the range of stakeholders in the decision-making process. Sharing differing perspectives facilitates the exchange of knowledge and expertise and it allows the creation of a more nuanced understanding of complex issues and the development of more sophisticated ways of addressing these.

The book developed from a two-day interdisciplinary workshop, entitled 'Emerging Issues in Irish Healthcare,' funded by the University College Cork Strategic Research Fund, which was held in University College Cork in April 2014, with contributors drawn from academic and practice backgrounds in ethics, law and medicine. From these conversations, it became clear that the Irish health system is confronted by a range of challenges, both emerging and recurring, and that, because the system is fluid and dynamic, these cannot be resolved by simple or one-dimensional solutions. This understanding informs the chapters in this book.

The book has four parts, organised around four interlinking themes: context and care; rights and responsibilities; regulating research; and oversight of decision-making. The chapters in Part I adopt a contextual approach to three situations of contemporary significance. Joan McCarthy draws out the power differentials in operation in two high profile medical cases. These are the medical practices of Michael Neary in Our Lady of Lourdes Hospital, Drogheda between 1974 and 1998 and the death of Savita Halappanavar in University College Hospital Galway in 2013. By placing these cases within this broader context, she shows why, in both situations, women were conceptualised not as individual rights subjects but rather as means towards an end, resulting in blatant violations of bodily integrity and autonomy. Ruth Fletcher addresses the issue of conscientious objection, arguing that individuals who are conscientious objectors ought to be respected in some circumstances but that organisations should not. Recognising the context in which conscientious objection in respect of lawful abortion takes place, she adopts a harm reduction approach, seeking to address both the harm to those who would have to act against their most intimate convictions in providing abortion and to women whose lawful right to abortion may be restricted by the actions of conscientious objectors. Claire Murray sets out the reasons why health law and policy should take account of the position of carers. Drawing on arguments grounded in ethics of care and relational autonomy and using the context of Irish mental health law to provide a basis for her analysis, she emphasises the importance of caring about carers but also that this must be achieved in a manner which continues to respect the distinct individual rights of each of the parties to the caring relationship.

Part II – Rights and Responsibilities – explores the role of rights in health ethics and law, with several of the chapters engaging with issues of autonomy and liberty. Louise Campbell shows that, while the principle of autonomy is frequently referenced in debates around assisted suicide, to date there has been limited engagement with what this principle actually means. She presents different perspectives on autonomy within bioethics literature and argues that, in order to ground a right to assistance in dying, it is necessary to draw on a richer understanding of autonomy than has been the case to date. Tom Walker continues the interrogation of autonomy in healthcare decision-making, with a particular focus on the refusal of medical treatment by young people, aged 16 and 17 years. He argues that the recognition of a right to consent to treatment (as set out in the Non-Fatal Offences Against the Person Act 1997) does not require the recognition of an equivalent right to refuse treatment. He also challenges the widely accepted position that it is always morally wrong to give an adult treatment that he or she refuses.

Asim Sheikh looks at autonomy from a different perspective, exploring the possible imposition of legal responsibilities on patients arising from the legal recognition of the right of autonomy. He notes that healthcare practice is slowly moving away from the paternalistic model of dealing with patients and explores the possible consequences of this in the context of medical negligence litigation, including the possibility that patients may be liable for contributory negligence. Both Mary Keys and Shaun O'Keeffe address the position of older people, with a focus on the rights to autonomy and liberty. Keys presents the case for a coherent approach to the human rights of older people. She shows that the current framework is fragmented and that it fails to meet the specific needs of older people. She identifies the establishment of legal frameworks around decision-making as central to the protection of older people and she discusses some of the law and policy reforms necessary to ensure that older people's choices are respected and not ignored. O'Keeffe makes a strong argument in favour of a rights-based approach to admission of older people to long-term care. He asserts that healthcare professionals have a duty to ensure that all admissions to a nursing home against the wishes of the person admitted can only occur through a legal mechanism, even if this is inconvenient to others or expensive for the healthcare system.

Part III moves the focus of analysis to regulation, addressing bioethical issues in research. All three chapters in this part identify the need for legislative intervention to provide a robust grounding for medical research in Ireland. Deirdre Madden considers tensions between data protection and the facilitation of clinical research in the context of the retention and use of human biological samples, with particular reference to the controversy surrounding new-born screening cards (Guthrie cards). Madden argues that legislation should be introduced to exempt the collection of new-born screening cards from data protection legislation and to put in place a clear and robust governance framework. Ciara Staunton outlines shortcomings in the regulatory framework in respect of embryonic stem cell research. She identifies a need for enhanced debate on the status of the embryo as a prelude to the development of a regulatory framework that both protects the embryo and accommodates embryonic stem cell research. The lack of legislative clarity in respect of non-therapeutic clinical trials involving children is central to Katherine Wade's chapter. She argues that the state should ratify the Oviedo Convention on Human Rights and Biomedicine (1997) and its Additional Protocol and that the Convention's definition of minimal risk and minimal burden should be incorporated into new Irish legislation which would apply to all interventional clinical trials with children.

The focus of the final part of the book is on oversight of decision-making, with the chapters investigating different forms of oversight in operation. Heike Felzmann draws on literature on organisational clinical ethics and business ethics to provide a framework for thinking about the wider ethical responsibilities of healthcare organisations. As with McCarthy, Felzmann uses the Neary and Halappanavar cases to explore the ways in which organisational structures can contribute to the facilitation of ethical actions by members of the organisation. Brendan Kelly's chapter shows the importance of the form of oversight provided by empirical research and data collection in developing informed national health policies. Kelly's chapter is grounded in a study of admission to inpatient mental health services and it highlights different patterns of help-seeking depending on an individual's country of origin. Kelly relies on this finding to advocate the development of increased cultural competence among mental health care providers. Mental health is also the subject of Darius Whelan's chapter, which analyses the oversight of the operations of mental health tribunals provided by the courts. Whelan argues that the courts have not engaged in robust supervision of tribunals and that the judicial approach has been to endorse tribunal decisions which deprive people of liberty and to limit interventions by the courts to the most serious violations of procedural rights. Whelan expresses disappointment with this in light of the supposed rights-based focus of the Mental Health Act 2001.

The book concludes with two chapters about the role of oversight of decisions at the end of life. Mary Donnelly argues that the dying process is likely to become increasingly subject to legal oversight and identifies both benefits and dangers in this for dying patients. She advocates a patient-centred approach to dying but questions the capacity of an adversarial court process to deliver this and suggests that other oversight mechanisms need to be developed. Barry Lyons identifies the lack of oversight of decisions to withdraw or withhold therapies in intensive care units. Lyons emphasises the social and political dimensions to decisions about the withdrawal of life-sustaining therapies and calls for public discourse and the development of public policy on the subject. Lyons also questions the suitability of courts as the forum to determine the dilemmas that arise in ICU care. He proposes that the question of the appropriate use of scarce resources should be placed squarely in the political process and, in order to maintain a fair system, there must be a form of social contract with distributive justice as the dominant underlying value.

This book does not purport to address all the challenging issues in health ethics and law, nor, in keeping with its underlying ethos, to provide definitive solutions to the complex ethical questions raised. Rather, its contribution is to offer diverse entry points and different perspectives on some of the most important challenges confronting the Irish health system. By doing this, we hope to encourage conversations which we believe can ultimately influence the development of more considered and ethically informed laws, policies and practices.

References

Barrington, R. (2002) 'Terrible beauty or Celtic mouse? The research agenda in Ireland', *New Hibernia Review*, 6: 138.

Hesketh, T. (1990) *The Second Partitioning of Ireland?: The Abortion Referendum of 1983*. Dublin: Brandsma Books.

Inglis, T. (1998) *Moral Monopoly: The Rise and Fall of the Catholic Church in Modern Ireland*, 2nd edn. Dublin: University College Press.

Lyons, B. (2012) 'The Irish Council for Bioethics: an unaffordable luxury?', *Cambridge Quarterly of Healthcare Ethics*, 21: 375.

McDonagh, E. and MacNamara, V. (2013) *An Irish Reader in Moral Theology: The Legacy of the Last Fifty Years: Volume III: Medical and Bioethics*. Dublin: Columba Press.

McDonnell, O. and Allison, J. (2006) 'From biopolitics to bioethics: church, state, medicine and assisted reproductive technology in Ireland', *Sociology of Health & Illness*, 28: 817.

O'Sullivan, C., Schweppe, J. and Spain, E. (2013) 'Article 40.3.3° and the Protection of Life during Pregnancy Bill 2013: the impetus for, and process of, legislative change', *Irish Journal of Legal Studies*, 3: 1.

Turner, L. (2003) 'Zones of consensus and zones of conflict: questioning the "common morality" presumption in bioethics', *Kennedy Institute of Ethics Journal*, 13: 193.

I
CONTEXT AND CARE

1

Reproductive justice in Ireland: a feminist analysis of the Neary and Halappanavar cases

Joan McCarthy

Introduction

This chapter analyses two Irish case studies concerning reproductive justice and maternal health that raise serious ethical and legal concerns. These are, first, unnecessary hysterectomies that were carried out at Our Lady of Lourdes Hospital, Drogheda; and second, the case of Savita Halappanavar whose 17-week pregnancy ended in miscarriage and her death in University College Hospital Galway (UCHG) on the 28 October 2012. Even though these cases are very different from one another in many respects, they also share important similarities. They provide evidence of not only a profound unease with women's reproductive capacity but also the influence of Catholic norms on healthcare practice, and the denigration of women's moral authority, agency and professional credibility (sometimes by women themselves). These are two examples among many in recent times where these kinds of factors have led to the abuse and deprecation of women in Ireland (McAleese, 2013; Walsh, 2013).

My feminist reading of these different situations draws attention to the power and power differentials inherent in moral relationships at individual, organisational and societal levels and adopts Margaret Urban Walker's feminist ethics perspective, which she summarises in the following way:

> We welcome all relevant scientific data but believe that the social situations of both science and morals must be kept in view, paying attention to differences of social and institutional position, perspective, and power that determine which voices and whose interests and experiences are audible and authoritative in ethics as elsewhere (Walker, 2009: 5)

Key to my analysis is a desire to understand the mechanisms by which the voices and concerns of the women at the centre of these two cases were ignored, marginalised and trivialised. I address each case in turn, paying particular attention to the way in which an excess of moral authority was vested in religious leaders, religious doctrine and doctors and a correlated lack of authority was invested in women patients and midwives.

Unnecessary hysterectomies at Our Lady of Lourdes Hospital

When a small number of young and newly trained midwives in Our Lady of Lourdes Hospital Drogheda brought their concerns about the high rate of hysterectomies being carried out in their maternity unit to the attention of authorities in the hospital and the Irish Health Board in 1998, they initiated a course of events that eventually led to the suspension and deregistration of Michael Neary, the consultant obstetrician/gynaecologist responsible for the bulk of these hysterectomies. The government-appointed inquiry, undertaken by Justice Maureen Harding Clark, subsequently determined that many of Neary's gynecological patients as well as his obstetric patients were subjected to unnecessary hysterectomies and/or oophorectomies (McCarthy et al., 2008). A brief excerpt from the Report describes the experience of one woman and draws attention to the normalisation of surgical hysterectomies in the maternity unit:

> Dr Neary asked her to attend as a day patient for a D&C. She was aware of the routine involved in a diagnostic D&C procedure .... When she woke in pain she knew something had happened. She learned that she had undergone a total abdominal hysterectomy with removal of her ovaries and fallopian tubes. Dr Neary informed her that he had to carry out a hysterectomy, as he 'could not stop the bleeding'. Later she was told that she did 'not have any cancer'. This was not a possibility that had ever been discussed with her. The histology reported no disease but rather 'degenerate products of conception and a collection of endometrial polyps'. The operation notes and the request for histology indicate that Dr Neary believed when he carried out the hysterectomy that she had advanced uterine cancer. (Harding Clark, 2006: 159–60)

Women's bodies, fertility and well-being

Evidence from several sources: the Harding Clark Report (2006); the transcripts from the Irish Medical Council Fitness to Practice Committee (2000) and the court cases taken against Michael Neary paint a grim picture of the maternity services that were provided to many women up to and including Neary's tenure at the hospital (1974–98). The Report notes how habituated health professionals had become to the hysterectomies themselves – one incident is recounted where a junior anaesthetist and midwife talked about a TV programme while a bucket with a uterus in it was carried past – '[t]he normal curiosity for reasons why unusual outcomes happened simply did not occur' (Harding Clark, 2006: 160). The Report also refers to outdated practices such as midline instead of bikini line incisions, putting birthing women into the lithotomy position and rectal rather than vaginal examinations. The Fitness to Practice Committee of the Irish Medical Council cite one witness who alleges that in his response to her query as to why he had to remove one of her ovaries, Neary responded, 'I did not like your bloody ovary anyway' (Irish Medical Council, 2000: 144). The same witness notes elsewhere that Neary compared her to a car that breaks down and told her 'that if [she were] to see the bloody mess inside [her] he had to clean up' (Irish Medical Council, 2000: 146).

This attitude towards women was not exceptional. Discomfort and unease with women's embodiment and reproductive capacity is evidenced in the broader culture of the time as well as in the practices of Neary's colleagues. For example, in the 1970s and 1980s, Gerard Connolly, the senior obstetrician in Our Lady of Lourdes Hospital prior to Neary, carried out the highly painful and traumatic symphysiotomy procedure, which involved enlarging the capacity of the pelvis by cutting through the pubic bone in cases where labour was obstructed, long after medical evidence demonstrated that a caesarean section was a safer clinical alternative. One of the reasons that caesarean sections were not favoured by Catholic-run hospitals was because repeated caesarean sections were considered dangerous for women. Therefore, repeated pregnancies would be dangerous and would have to be avoided, prompting the need to use artificial methods of birth control. In short, many symphysiotomies were carried out in order to meet religious, not clinical, imperatives (Institute of Obstetricians and Gynaecologists, 2012; Morrissey, 2012; Walsh, 2013).

Moral authority as religious authority

The proliferation and continuance of such harmful practices as symphysiotomies was due, in part, to the historical and ongoing influence of Catholic doctrine and authority on Irish law, education and medical practice. In the years after Ireland succeeded in gaining independence from Britain, the legislature, dominated by members who adhered to a Roman Catholic moral code, banned divorce (1925), prevented the dissemination of literature on contraception (1929) and the import and sale of contraceptives (1935). As Oaks (1999) points out, the focus of Irish legislation in this regard has been on women's reproductive not productive lives evidenced by the marriage ban in the civil service (eventually removed in 1973). In practice, these restrictions meant that many thousands of Irish women were, effectively, forced to have large families until the (restricted) legalisation of contraception in 1980.

The Harding Clark Report indicates that the Catholic religious sisters, the Medical Missionaries of Mary (MMMs), who ran Our Lady of Lourdes Hospital until 1997, regularly appealed to Church laws and doctrine and consulted various clergymen on clinical issues that raised moral worries for them. On the matter of hysterectomies, they were, in fact, out of step with other Catholic hospitals in that their hospital code of ethics did not permit sterilisation – tubal ligation – even if it was indicated on medical grounds for a serious pathological condition of the uterus. Only 'indirect' sterilisation, a hysterectomy that removed the 'diseased organ', was the accepted practice (Harding Clark, 2006: 42).

In one case recounted by Michael Neary to the Harding Clark inquiry, a patient asked him to carry out a medically indicated tubal ligation at the same time as a caesarean section. The patient had herself, prior to this, sought the views of a moral theologian who had advised that, in her case, tubal ligation was permitted as the primary intention was to prevent her death or serious ill health in a future pregnancy. Neary consulted the matron on the matter, who in turn consulted the MMMs. Unhappy with the advice of the theologian the sisters sought the opinion of a cardinal and a bishop. Both men argued that the tubal ligation should be refused. According to the bishop:

> [t]he Church's thinking regarding this operation is very clear. It does not depend on circumstances nor on certain thinking among some theologians. One must seek the solution outside of direct sterilisation which can only be wrong in itself … If we had exceptions we would not maintain Catholic standards. No diversity of opinion can be permitted. (Harding Clark, 2006: 244)

Consultant authority

While religious leaders were vested with moral authority to grant or refuse permission to clinicians to act on patient requests or their own clinical judgement, consultants too were able, within limits, to exercise their moral agency. In the situation, referred to above, Neary vehemently defended the woman's medical need for a tubal ligation. Further, in another testimony to the Fitness to Practice Committee, one of Neary's patients reports that remarking on her RC (Roman Catholic) status at the top of her chart, he admitted that 'according to Church law he should never have laid a finger on me. He had a pile of books on the desk. Slapping his hands on them he said "I did an abortion for you". He went on to say that I was ungrateful' (Irish Medical Council, 2000: 146). In both of these cases, Neary appears to regard himself as acting on the basis of his moral conviction to benefit two of his patients. Moreover, one of the justifications that he offered the Inquiry for the significant number of hysterectomies that he carried out was that they were prompted by medical concerns in relation to further pregnancies. These are described as 'indirect sterilisation' or 'compassionate hysterectomies' (Harding Clark, 2006: 236, 244).

The moral authority of women patients and midwives

The question remains, what of the moral authority of the women patients[1] and of the midwives? The evidence demonstrates that the requests of the patients (some of whom, as Catholics themselves, appealed to the authority of some theologians) were ignored in favour of either Church law or leaders, or the occasional intervention by their doctor. Their questions about their 'treatment' were not answered; their concerns were trivialised; their voices were silenced (Irish Medical Council, 2000; Harding Clark, 2006).

Within such a system, the midwives were also constrained by predetermined gender-roles/scripts that they were assigned and were expected to conform to, and by the power structures within which they operated. In contrast to the MMMs and the consultants in Our Lady of Lourdes Hospital, the midwives and nurses seemed to have little or no moral authority or space for raising moral concerns. Harding Clark notes:

> The sisters belonged to an era when nurses were efficient, ordered and respectful. They carried out orders and did not question consultants. Matron maintained a formal, distant authority over nurses. The nuns who had set the practices and protocols for training nurses and midwives in the hospital in the 50s thus produced suitable nurses who fitted their mould – hardworking, respectful, Catholic nurses who were well trained, knew their place, trusted the consultants and suspended their critical or questioning faculties. They were trained to certain tasks – and to those tasks only. (Harding Clark, 2006: 41)

The Report notes that, in reality, the Matron of the maternity unit did not have any power or authority to question the consultants. This lack of power meant that many midwives believed, rightly, that 'there was no point in complaining to her' (Harding Clark, 2006: 157).

Harding Clark describes a minority of the midwives in the unit as having no concerns about the consultants' activities and the rate of hysterectomy. They saw themselves as 'disempowered' by the consultants and in the role of 'handmaidens to the consultants'; their job was to 'anticipate the consultants' needs' (Harding Clark, 2006: 190). A second group, in the majority, were described as 'decent, hard-working caring women' who were 'deeply shocked', tearful when giving testimony, and blamed themselves for not suspecting anything. They knew and liked Neary, found him to be far more personable and approachable than others and believed that 'he never deliberately meant to harm anyone' (Harding Clark, 2006: 190). A third group of mainly junior midwives and a newly appointed part-time practice development nurse and midwifery tutor were more critical, according to the Report. They believed that peripartum hysterectomies were unnecessary in certain cases but they were not confident that their concerns were well-founded because other senior midwives and even newly appointed doctors had made no complaint. This third group found no support among their colleagues – in fact they were admonished when they did raise concerns:

> Ann made her concerns regarding a caesarean hysterectomy carried out by Dr Neary known to her colleagues immediately after an incident in theatre, where she questioned why she should 'fetch the hysterectomy clamps'. Her colleagues either did not wish to countenance such criticisms, or found reasons to disprove her perceptions. (Harding Clark, 2006: 188–9)

The events at Our Lady of Lourdes Hospital raise serious questions about the lack of moral authority vested in women patients and midwives. A second case which highlights ongoing failures in relation to reproductive justice in Ireland is that of Savita Halappanavar.

The unnecessary death of Savita Halappanavar

Savita Halappanavar died in UCHG on 28 October 2012 following a miscarriage after a 17-week pregnancy. Ms Halappanavar self-referred to the gynaecology ward of UCHG on 21 October 2012. Initial assessment concluded that Ms Halappanavar was suffering from lower back pain and she was sent home. However, later in the day, she returned and reported 'unbearable pain' and medical records after clinical examination noted a diagnosis of 'an inevitable/ impending pregnancy loss'. She was admitted to the hospital for the management of the inevitable miscarriage.

Ms Halappanavar's membranes spontaneously ruptured very early on 22 October 2012. She asked the health professionals caring for her if she could be induced in order to avoid waiting for the inevitable but she was told that nothing could be done as long as there was a foetal heartbeat. Her condition continued to deteriorate over the next two days and she was diagnosed with sepsis on 24 October. She was then moved to the High Dependency Unit with the intention of inducing labour. However, on admission it was determined that she had already miscarried minutes before she arrived. During that night, her condition deteriorated and she was transferred to the ICU early in the morning of 25 October where she was immediately intubated and mechanically ventilated. Despite all efforts, her condition further deteriorated over the next few days and she died in the early hours of Sunday 28 October (MacLoughlin, 2013).

To date there have been three separate reports into the circumstances that lead to the tragic death of Savita Halappanavar: the post-mortem inquest report of Dr Ciaran MacLoughlin (2013); the Health Service Executive (HSE) Report carried out under the chair of Sir Sabaratnam Arulkumaran (HSE, 2013a); and the Health Information and Quality Authority (HIQA) Report (HIQA, 2013).

Gross inadequacies in basic care

All three reports point to gross inadequacies in the basic elements of Ms Halappanavar's care. The results of the post-mortem found that Ms Halappanavar's death was caused by septic shock associated with a miscarriage and chorioamnionitis and the inquest subsequently concluded that she had died as a result of 'medical misadventure' (MacLoughlin, 2013). The HSE Report identified causal factors that contributed to the adverse outcome, including inadequate assessment and monitoring and non-adherence to clinical guidelines related to the prompt and effective management of sepsis. The HIQA Report concluded that there was 'general lack of provision of basic, fundamental care, for example, not following up on blood tests; a failure to recognise that Ms Halappanavar was at risk of clinical deterioration and a failure to act or escalate concerns to an appropriately qualified clinician when Ms Halappanavar was showing the signs of clinical deterioration' (HIQA, 2013: 10).

As important as it is to identify the many failures of care that Ms Halappanavar received, it is also profoundly important not to overlook the crucial fact that, as stated by the Clinical Director of the National Maternity Hospital, Dr Peter Boylan, in his report to the coroner, had Ms Halappanavar's pregnancy been terminated within the first two days of her hospitalisation, 'it is highly likely, on the balance of probabilities, that she would not have died' (Boylan, 2013: 18). The fact that her membranes ruptured early on Monday 22 meant that her chances of developing sepsis increased exponentially and her continued dilation over the next two days practically ensured that would happen.

The Coroner's Report, the HSE Report and the HIQA Report all acknowledge that the lack of intervention was of serious concern. The HSE Report concluded that one of the key causal factors that effected the adverse outcome was the failure to offer all management options to a patient experiencing inevitable miscarriage of an early second trimester pregnancy where the risk to the mother increased with time, from the time that membranes were ruptured (HSE, 2013a: 13). Specifically, the Report concluded that 'there was an apparent over-emphasis on the need not to intervene until the fetal heart stopped together with an under-emphasis on the need to focus appropriate attention on monitoring for and managing the risk of infection and sepsis in the mother' (HSE, 2013a: 73).

The law on abortion: the price of uncertainty

In order to understand the circumstances that led to delays in Ms Halappanavar's treatment, one must understand the legal position in Ireland in relation to abortion. Two legal provisions are directly relevant to understanding what happened. The first is Article 40.3.3 of the Constitution (added as the 8th Amendment to the Constitution in 1983) which states that:

> The State acknowledges the right to life of the unborn and, with due regard to the equal right to life of the mother, guarantees in its laws to respect, and, as far as practicable, by its laws to defend and vindicate that right.

This constitutional provision was interpreted by the Supreme Court in *Attorney General* v. *X and Others* [1992] 1 IR 1 (the 'X case'). The case concerned a 14-year-old girl who had become pregnant as result of rape. The Attorney General applied to the High Court for an injunction preventing the girl from travelling to England for an abortion. In the High Court, a psychologist testified that the girl might commit suicide if she was refused an abortion. The High

Court granted the injunction but its decision was overturned on appeal by a majority of the Supreme Court. Finlay CJ laid down the test to be applied in such cases as follows:

> I, therefore, conclude that the proper test to be applied is that if it is established as a matter of probability that there is a real and substantial risk to the life, as distinct from the health, of the mother, which can only be avoided by the termination of her pregnancy, such termination is permissible, having regard to the true interpretation of Article 40, s. 3, sub-s. 3 of the Constitution. (1992: 53–4)

In brief, the Supreme Court found that abortion is legal in limited cases where there is a real and substantial risk to the life, as distinct from the health, of the pregnant woman, which can only be avoided by the termination of her pregnancy. The critical question for health professionals is how to determine what comprises 'a real and substantial risk'. For over 20 years, up until and including the death of Ms Halappanavar, successive governments failed to bring forward legislation to give effect to the Supreme Court ruling.

The patient's voice

Ms Halappanavar, with the support of her husband, asked for a termination of her non-viable pregnancy on a number of occasions. When and how often she made this request is in dispute. The evidence of the inquest, the HSE Report and interviews with her husband, friends and some of the staff, suggests that she first asked for a termination on Monday 22 October and repeated the request on each of the following two days. The HSE Report states that Dr Katherine Astbury acknowledged that, on 23 October Ms Halappanavar's husband had enquired about the possibility of inducing labour in order to avoid a protracted waiting time for an inevitable miscarriage. She also reported that she had advised him that this was not possible under Irish law. She indicated to the HSE investigation that the law was such that '[i]f there is a threat to the mother's life you can terminate. If there is a potential major hazard to the mother's life the law is not clear … [t]here are no guidelines for inevitable miscarriages' (HSE, 2013a: 72). Dr Astbury's claim that the law was unclear was also supported by Dr Peter Boylan, who told the inquest, '[t]ermination of pregnancy at that time [on 22 or 23 October] was not a practical proposition because of the law' (Boylan, 2013: 18). The HSE Report concluded that the law as it stood needed clarification as to what constitutes sufficient risk to warrant a termination:

> There is difficulty in interpretation of law in relation to 'what constitutes a potential major hazard or threat to mother's life'. This needs clarification. The consultant clearly thought that the risk to the mother had not crossed the point where termination was allowable in Irish law on the morning ward round on the 24th. (HSE, 2013a: 72)

Moreover, the Report concluded that the investigation team 'were satisfied that concern about the law, whether clear or not, impacted on the exercise of clinical professional judgement' (HSE, 2013a: 76).

Moral authority: the rights of pregnant women and the rights of everyone else

In recent years, Irish healthcare providers and health professionals have become more sensitive to the values and preferences of patients and service users. This is reflected in government policy documents, professional codes of conduct as well as (draft) legislation on capacity, advance directives and case-law. Specifically, where there is any medical uncertainty in relation to the possible outcomes of interventions, the obligation on doctors is to acknowledge this uncertainty and to seek the views of the patients whose lives are at risk. The HSE National Consent Policy, for example, obliges doctors in situations where they are unsure of the outcome of resuscitation measures to seek the views of patients as to whether or not they want the intervention:

> In some cases, the health professional may be uncertain whether the potential benefits of CPR outweigh the risks. In these situations, the preferences and values of the individual are of paramount importance, and the health professional should acknowledge the uncertainty, outline the benefits and risks of each option, and assist the individual in coming to a decision. (HSE, 2013b: para. 6.2)

Not so with pregnant women whose lives are at risk because of their continuing pregnancy. Even when there is a great deal of uncertainty, as in Ms Halappanavar's case, and the risk is very grave, pregnant women's assessment of the uncertainty and their view of how much of a risk they are willing or able to take counts for nothing as against, supposedly, objective statistical probabilities and clinical judgement.

The lack of authority vested in pregnant women prompts an important ethical and legal question: what is the morally significant difference (if any) between pregnant women and other people that would justify treating them differently? The obvious difference is that a pregnant woman carries a human foetus in her womb and it could be argued that this relationship places a particular kind of moral duty on her which would justify treating her differently. The warrant for treating her differently however, would hinge on determining the scope of this 'moral duty'. Laura Purdy puts it thus:

> The question before us is a special case of the most general moral question: what do we owe others? ... Several different levels of obligation are recognized, depending on the nature of the relationship between the individuals in question. Various types of agreements (marriage, for instance), as well as biological relationships (such as parenthood) raise our expectations of what is morally owed; the law tends to reflect this understanding. (Purdy, 1990: 278)

Purdy suggests that the closest analogy to the relationship between a woman and a foetus is that between relatives. However, she points to several cases where the law has asked less of relatives and parents of born children than it does of pregnant women, including the case of *McFall* v. *Shimp* 10 Pa. D & C3d. [C.P. 1978] where a court refused to order involuntary bone marrow surgery on Shimp in order to increase the probability of his leukemic cousin McFall's survival. In a similar vein, Annas points out, '[n]o mother has ever been legally required to undergo surgery or general anesthesia (e.g. bone marrow or kidney transplant) to save the life of her dying child. It would be ironic, to say the least, if she could be forced to submit to more invasive surgical procedures for the sake of her f[o]etus than for her child' (Annas, 1982: 17).

In short, even if one were to grant the foetus the same moral status as a born child, a pregnant woman's obligations towards her foetus should be no more demanding than a parent's duty towards her child. And, if one holds, as many people do, that foetuses are not yet persons, then *a fortiori*, the demands on pregnant women should be significantly less than the duties we expect of parents of born children. Refusing Ms Halappanavar her request for a termination and forcing her to continue her pregnancy is an extreme example of the differential treatment of pregnant women. It is a particularly tragic one given that her foetus was not viable and the continuation of the pregnancy posed a serious threat to her health and, ultimately, her life.

New legislation: old ambiguities

Savita Halappanavar's death and the argument made by the health professionals charged with her care – that they were bound by the legal position set out in Article 40.3.3 and the X case – caused a national and international outcry and put pressure on Irish legislators to clarify the precise scope of the law in circumstances such as Ms Halappanavar's. Ironically, in the same week that Ms Halappanavar was in the Galway hospital, an expert group appointed by the government was finalising its recommendations in response to the European Court of Human Rights judgment in *A, B, and C* v. *Ireland* (2011) 53 EHRR 13 that required the state to clarify by law and/or regulation when it would be permissible for a woman whose life was at risk to avail of an abortion in Ireland. The publication of the Report of the Expert Group, combined with the general public's repugnance at what had befallen Ms Halappanavar, assured the introduction of legislation that specified more clearly the implications of Article 40.3.3 and the X case in determining access to abortion in certain circumstances. In brief, the Protection of Life During Pregnancy Act 2013 provides that, in cases where a woman's life is at risk, it is lawful for health professionals:

> [T]o carry out a medical procedure in respect of a pregnant woman … in the course of which, or as a result of which, an unborn human life is ended where … there is a real and substantial risk of loss of the woman's life from a physical illness, and in their reasonable opinion (being an opinion formed in good faith

which has regard to the need to preserve unborn human life as far as practicable) that risk can only be averted by carrying out the medical procedure (section 7(1))

While this legislation represents a long-awaited gesture towards recognising the obligation of the state to protect the lives of pregnant women, many argue that it does not go far enough. It fails to include circumstances where the foetus is not viable or where the woman has become pregnant through rape or incest. The legislation also patently fails to acknowledge pregnant women's rights to bodily integrity and autonomy and requires significantly more of them than other people. However, even if one were satisfied with the narrow scope of the legislation, it is extremely doubtful that it will succeed in addressing concerns about women's safety. As a number of obstetricians have already pointed out, how a 'real and substantial risk' is quantified remains problematic and very few seem willing to acknowledge that the pregnant woman should be key to that determination (Joint Committee on Health and Children, 2013: 160–1, 515). Finally, it is possible that any ambiguity in the legislation may be availed of by some healthcare practitioners for ideological reasons to justify withholding a legally permissible abortion and that it will paralyse others from acting and/or prompt 'wait and see' care plans such as that which prevailed in UCHG.[2]

That health professionals can be very sensitised to the association between abortion legislation and Catholic ideology was made clear in another dimension to Ms Halappanavar's story that is considered in the final section – the 'Catholic country' remark.

The 'Catholic country' remark

In his account of events given to the Gardaí and, subsequently, to the inquest, Ms Halappanavar's husband, Praveen Halappanavar, mentioned that a number of the health professionals (at least one doctor and one midwife) had justified the refusal of a termination on the grounds that Ireland was a Catholic country (Holland, 2013a; Holland, 2013b). Global interest in the case included shock and outrage at the thought that religious ideology, not evidence-based medicine, had influenced clinical decisions. However, none of the health professionals who had either said this, or witnessed it being said, had come forward until the coroner's inquest. At the inquest, Ms Halappanavar's consultant confirmed that she had referred to Irish law but denied any reference to Catholicism. However, a senior midwife, Ann Maria Burke, admitted that she had suggested that the rationale for why the hospital could not provide Ms Halappanavar with an abortion was because Ireland was a 'Catholic country' (Holland, 2013b).

When Ms Burke told the inquest that she had made the comment to Ms Halappanavar, the coroner told her that her remarks had 'gone around the world', that the abortion had been refused on legal, not religious, grounds, and that neither religious dogma nor tenet influenced clinical practice in Irish public hospitals (Cullen, 2013). However, while in one way, the coroner is clearly correct – the law and the consultant's interpretation of it led to the refusal of a termination – it could also be argued that the law itself is religiously based. The history of the origins of Article 40.3.3, some 30 years ago, demonstrates that the law on abortion in Ireland is firmly embedded in Catholic ideology. In a statement issued in November 2012, the Irish Catholic Bishops' Conference distinguish between 'abortion' or the '*direct* and *intentional* destruction of an unborn baby', which they claim is always immoral, and 'medical treatments which *do not directly and intentionally* seek to end the life of the unborn baby'. This distinction appeals to what is known as the 'doctrine of double effect', a Catholic theory that has long been strongly debated and contested in the philosophical literature (Foot, 1967; Kamm, 1991; Clarke, 2013). Whatever its merits or demerits, this kind of thinking would explain why health professionals might be concerned about the timing and appropriateness of medical interventions where a foetal heartbeat was present and also provide a rationale for clinical care pathways that in Ms Halappanavar's case involved 'wait and see what happen[s] naturally' (HSE, 2013a: 73). It is beyond the scope of this chapter to discuss this at length, but at the very least, it indicates that Ms Burke may have been explaining the 'logic' behind the law as she understood it to Ms Halappanavar and her husband (O'Toole, 2013). In Ms Burke's testimony to the inquest, she expressed regret and stated that the remark had been made in a particular context and 'had not been meant in a hurtful way' (Holland, 2013b).

To conclude, instead of being castigated, it could be argued that Ms Burke should be praised, not just for her testimony to the inquest, but also for her sensitive response to Ms Halappanavar's puzzlement. On the other hand, the fact that none of Ms Halappanavar's requests for a termination, nor any of the conversations that Dr Astbury and Ms Burke acknowledge having had with her about an abortion, were documented in the medical or midwifery notes indicates an uneasiness about discussions involving abortion and a lack of respect for, and inability to respond appropriately to, a woman's request for an abortion. It also raises a more general worry about how health professionals view their role and ethical and legal obligations in relation to women who seek legally permitted abortion. The evidence of witnesses to the Hearings of the Joint Committee on Health and Children (2013) suggest a wide range of views on abortion among Irish health professionals. However, it is unclear what impact these views have on decision-making in maternity units around the country and independent empirical research on the impact of religious and cultural beliefs on clinical practices in Ireland is long overdue. Moreover, Dr Peter Boylan raises the worry that some midwives may, on occasion, neglect their duty of care to pregnant women and delay an emergency (and therefore legal) termination because of their objection to abortion. Boylan remarked, in his report to the inquest of Savita Halappanavar, that her transfer and termination was in part, 'dependent on the midwives in the delivery unit accepting care of Ms Halappanavar when it was known the foetal heartbeat was still present' (Boylan, 2013: 15). He later reported to Holland that the previous year, a colleague of his, in similar circumstances in another hospital in Dublin, had been told by a senior midwife on the labour ward, 'You're not doing a termination in this hospital'. According to Boylan, his colleague 'had to pull rank and say, "Then I'm getting agency nurses in," and it was only when a non-national nurse came forward [that the termination could proceed]' (Holland, 2013a: 223).

Conclusion

The cases discussed in this chapter are examples of the way in which women's bodies in the Irish state have become the site of various battles waged in relation to sexuality, reproduction and moral and religious authority. The first part of the chapter drew attention to the cultural unease with women's embodiment and reproductive capacity that permeated Irish society and culture until at least the final decades of the twentieth century. It also outlined the unnecessary suffering visited on many hundreds of women in Our Lady of Lourdes Hospital, which derived from the Catholic ethos of the hospital and the adherence of a significant number of the medical, nursing and midwifery professionals there to Catholic authority and doctrine. It observed that the unequal distribution of moral authority was also keenly felt by many female patients and midwives whose concerns were trivialised and whose voices were, for the most part, silenced. Finally, it indicated the ways in which some midwives used what authority they had to control dissenting voices and maintain the status quo while others raised their voices in resistance.

The second part of the chapter highlighted how clinical decision-making in relation to women's reproductive choices can be infused by Catholic ideology – this time through the ambiguity and interpretation of Irish laws on the permissibility of abortion. It also pointed to the marginalisation of the views, values and preferences of pregnant women in decisions that impact on their lives and the excessive obligations that pregnant women in Ireland are legally required to meet compared with other people.

While it is clear that the Catholic Church continues to cast a long shadow on Irish laws and medical practice, it is also clear that many health professionals, legislators and the general public are increasingly anxious to see a genuine separation between the Church and the functions and services of the state. The insights, conclusions and recommendations of the various reports on the tragedies discussed in this chapter send a strong signal to health professionals, allied professionals and healthcare organisations that they must set their moral compass to reflect the norms of a civil, egalitarian and pluralist society. They must focus, proactively, on fostering a maternity environment that consults with and encourages pregnant women to voice their experiences, concerns and preferences; one that is more open about the level of clinical, moral and legal uncertainty inherent in the practice of medicine and the need for that uncertainty to be made more explicit. It remains to be seen how much time, and what personal toll individual women, and those who love them, will have to pay before that cultural and ideological transformation is to take place.

Notes

1 It could be argued that the failure to recognise the moral authority of patients (male and female) was (and is) a more general issue; one that current HSE documents and policies as well as professional codes (Irish Medical Council, 2009 and Nursing and Midwifery Board of Ireland, 2014) are attempting to address.

2 It is evident from the HSE Report (2013a: 73) that a 'wait and see' approach was adopted from Sunday 21 October 14.20, 'wait and see what happened naturally'; Monday 22 October 08.20am, 'await events'; Tuesday 23 October before 6.00am, 'await events'.

References

Annas, G.J. (1982) 'Forced caesareans: the most unkindest cut of all', *Hastings Center Report*, 12: 17.

Boylan, P. (2013) 'Medical Report, Ms Savita Halappanavar', in C. MacLoughlin, *The Coroner's Report of the Inquest on the Death of Savita Halappanavar*. Clifden.

Clarke, D. (2013) 'Arcane principle behind traditional teaching on gynaecology and ethics is bad philosophy', *Irish Times*, 7 June.

Cullen, P. (2013) 'Ann Maria Burke says remark was intended to be broad and explanatory', *Irish Times*, 11 April.

Foot, P. (1967) 'The problem of abortion and the doctrine of double effect', *Oxford Review*, 5: 5.

Harding Clark, M. (2006) *The Lourdes Hospital Inquiry: An Inquiry into Peripartum Hysterectomy at Our Lady of Lourdes Hospital, Drogheda*. Dublin: The Stationery Office.

HIQA (Health Information and Quality Authority) (2013) *Investigation into the Safety, Quality and Standards of Services Provided by the Health Service Executive to Patients, Including Pregnant Women, at Risk of Clinical Deterioration, Including those Provided in University Hospital Galway, and as Reflected in the Care and Treatment Provided to Savita Halappanavar*. Dublin.

Holland, K. (2013a) *Savita*. London: Transworld Ireland.

Holland, K. (2013b) 'Husband relieved truth about Savita's death emerging', *Irish Times*, 12 April.

HSE (Health Service Executive) (2013a) *Final Report: Investigation of Incident 50278 from Time of Patient's Self-referral to Hospital on the 21st of October 2012 to the Patient's Death on the 28th of October 2012*. Dublin.
HSE (Health Service Executive) (2013b) *National Consent Policy*. Dublin.
Institute of Obstetricians and Gynaecologists (2012) *Walsh Report on Symphysiotomy in Ireland: Statement by the Institute of Obstetricians and Gynaecologists*. Dublin.
Irish Medical Council (2000) *Transcript of Fitness to Practice Inquiry into Michael Neary*. Dublin.
Irish Medical Council (2009) *Guide to Professional Conduct and Ethics for Registered Medical Practitioners*. Dublin.
Joint Committee on Health and Children (2013) *Report on Public Hearings on the Implementation of the Government Decision Following the Publication of the Expert Group Report on A, B, & C vs Ireland*. Dublin.
Kamm, F.M. (1991) 'The doctrine of double effect: reflections on theoretical and practical issues', *Journal of Medicine and Philosophy*, 16(5): 571.
MacLoughlin, C. (2013) *The Coroner's Report of the Inquest on the Death of Savita Halappanavar*. Clifden.
McAleese, M. (2013) *Report of the Inter-Departmental Committee to Establish the Facts of State Involvement with the Magdalen Laundries*. Dublin
McCarthy, J., Murphy, S. and Loughrey, M. (2008) 'Gender and power: the Irish hysterectomy Scandal', *Nursing Ethics*, 15(5): 643.
Morrissey, J. (2012) '"The murder of infants"? Symphysiotomy in Ireland, 1944–66', *History Ireland*, 20(5): 44.
Nursing and Midwifery Board of Ireland (2014) *Code of Professional Conduct and Ethics*. Dublin.
Oaks, L. (1999) 'Irish trans/national politics and locating fetuses', in L. Morgan and M. Michels (eds), *Fetal Subjects: Feminist Positions*. Philadelphia: University of Pennsylvania Press.
O'Toole, E. (2013) 'The midwife who told the truth in the Savita Halappanavar abortion case', *Guardian*, 19 April.
Purdy, L.M. (1990) 'Are pregnant women fetal containers?', *Bioethics*, 4(4): 273.
Standing Committee of the Irish Catholic Bishops' Conference (2012) *Statement on the Equal and Inalienable Right to Life of a Mother and Her Unborn Child*. Maynooth.
Walker, M.U. (2009) 'Introduction', in H. Lindemann, M. Verkerk and M.U. Walker (eds), *Naturalised Bioethics: Toward Responsible Knowing and Practice*, Cambridge: Cambridge University Press.
Walsh, O. (2013) *Report on Symphysiotomy in Ireland from 1944 to 1984*. Dublin: Department of Health.

2

Conscientious objection, harm reduction and abortion care

Ruth Fletcher

Introduction

The scope of any legal right to refuse to provide abortion care merits particular consideration following the introduction of the Protection of Life During Pregnancy Act 2013 (PLDPA). Irish health scholarship and practice may benefit from an account of conscientious objection (CO) that clarifies when CO is legitimately engaged by a refusal to provide care and whether CO is limited given its potential effect as a barrier to women's lawful access to abortion. This chapter responds to these concerns by arguing for a harm reduction approach to conscientious objection. Those who wish to refuse provision of healthcare in spite of a legal obligation, and those who wish to provide healthcare in spite of a legal prohibition, may be harmed by having to act against their most intimate convictions. Moreover, public reasoning about the proper scope of healthcare provision could be disadvantaged by a failure to recognise a space for critical consciousness. The need to reduce the risk of harm to women, whose lawful entitlement to access abortion has been hard-won, also animates the justification for legal limits on CO. In arguing for a harm reduction approach, the account offered here draws on, but distinguishes itself from, those who have relied on public obligations to refute CO and those who have relied on an individual right to moral integrity to ground CO.

Conscientious objection and critical consciousness

Some believe that healthcare professionals should not be able to refuse healthcare on grounds of conscience (Savulescu, 2006; Kelleher, 2010; Gallagher et al., 2013: 6; Fiala and Arthur, 2014) and that CO operates simply as an obstacle to women's access to healthcare (Thomson, 2013). Their argument is that the duty to provide public healthcare requires that providers put their personal views and opinions to one side. If acting on one's personal views in refusing to provide healthcare is done for discriminatory or otherwise harmful reasons, I agree that this is not acceptable. But it is obviously not unacceptable in itself to act on one's personal commitments in the context of providing healthcare (Dickens, 2014: 212). Second, requiring health professionals to act against their conscience when another alternative is available, risks taking much of the good out of the duty to care. If, as Campbell (2011a) notes, the effect of this is that the genuine objector leaves the healthcare sector, the complete rejection of CO may be counterproductive. Third, it is not good for those receiving healthcare to have to worry about the commitment of their healthcare provider to the healthcare sought. It would be better if the question of CO were openly addressed. As I argue below, there are considerable limits on CO. But any legal test for the scope of CO ought to recognise that its objective is to prevent any psychological harm to healthcare providers that may occur if they are required to act in a way that goes against their moral choices and intimate convictions.

Others argue that CO in a healthcare context is a right which results from respect for the moral integrity of the individual (Campbell, 2011a; Wicclair, 2011). On this understanding, CO arises when preserving an individual's moral integrity requires the breaking of a legal norm. This is why the right to CO may be narrowly drawn. Everyone is under a duty to abide by legal norms and any derogation from a legal obligation to provide healthcare has to be restrictive (see further Montgomery, 2015). This approach to CO is important in identifying a violation of an individual's moral integrity as the harm which CO addresses and in implying a narrow scope for CO given its location as dissent within a framework of lawful norms. Scholars such as Dickens, Cook and Joffe have done important work in reminding us that conscientious responses in healthcare are not always *refusals* to provide healthcare and are not always motivated by a conservative or 'sanctity of life' approach to ethical questions (Joffe, 1996; Dickens, 2006; Dickens and Cook, 2011; Dickens, 2014: 233–8). As Murphy (2014) noted recently in an Irish context, healthcare professionals also act out of a conscientious commitment to the provision of abortion care. Pro-choice doctors see the harm which abortion restrictions have on women's lives and challenge legal failures to endorse abortion provision (Doctors for Choice, 2014). In this chapter, I draw these different threads together to argue for a reframing of CO as an exercise in critical consciousness within a harm reduction framework. I reflect on the European Convention on Human Rights (ECHR) and comparative jurisprudence and policy in fleshing out a framework for interpreting the section 17 right in the PLDPA not to 'carry out, or to assist in carrying out, any medical procedure referred to in section 7(1) or section 9(1)' on grounds of CO. Both sections refer to medical procedures 'in the course of which, or as a result of which, an unborn human life is ended'.

Bearers of critical consciousness

The grounding of the right to CO in critical consciousness is an important factor in understanding why CO usually ought not apply to corporate persons (Sepper, 2012; 2013; Corbin, 2014). Although institutions may indeed have an ethos or a code of ethics, this is a matter of fact and results from a group's adoption of certain principles and values as that ethos. Ethos in this descriptive sense is qualitatively distinct from the consciousness which is part of the individual's critical and psychological being. Asking hospitals or corporate persons to act against their collective ethos or policy means asking those institutions to act against a rule they have adopted in a law-like process. It does not entail asking them to act against an intimate, psychological commitment because institutions cannot have that critical faculty. As Sepper (2012) notes, the effect of asserting an institutional ethos will often be to downgrade the consciences of individuals providing care within that institution. For Corbin (2014) the idea that corporations could be exempt from the provision of lawful abortion care on grounds of conscience is part of 'abortion exceptionalism', and should not be legally accepted.

The PLDPA frees medical practitioners, nurses and midwives from the obligation to provide lawful abortion care on grounds of CO, and does not refer explicitly to hospitals. The exclusion of hospitals as corporate persons from the category of conscientious objectors has some support in ECHR jurisprudence as companies and associations cannot usually rely on the right to freedom of thought, conscience and belief under Article 9 (*Company X* v. *Switzerland* (1979) 16 DR 85; *Verein Kontakt-Information-Therapie* v. *Austria* (1988) 57 DR 81). Campbell (2011a: 293) suggests that this limit should be read literally and that it does not mean that hospitals (as distinct from companies) are excluded. Rather, he suggests that the test is whether the state can organise the health service is such a way as to accommodate institutional CO. However, I think that his interpretation goes to a different point about CO concerning the significance of its limitations. Here I make a prior point that institutions are generally not the kind of legal person who has a critical consciousness and that is why they should not fall within the scope of Article 9 in the first instance. This approach is supported by the reasoning of the Colombian Constitutional Court in Decision T-388/2009 (2014), on the grounds that hospitals cannot experience intimate and deeply rooted convictions and might limit the freedom of individual employees (2014: 44). But it is not supported by the reasoning of the majority in the US Supreme Court decision in 'Hobby Lobby' (*Burwell, Secretary of Health and Human Services et al.* v. *Hobby Lobby Stores Inc. et al.* 573 US__ (2014)), nor by the European Parliamentary Assembly resolution 1763 (2010). 'Hobby Lobby' concerned a decision that corporate employers could 'engage in religious exercise' under the First Amendment's guarantee of freedom of religion. The capacity of corporate persons to so engage was crucial to deciding that they had a right to be exempt from providing health insurance coverage to employees in relation to certain contraceptives. Resolution 1763 protects hospitals and institutions, as well as individuals, against discrimination or coercion because of a refusal to perform an abortion (see further Campbell, 2011b). But the reasons for the Colombian Constitutional Court's position are more persuasive in my view (see further Melling and Lee, 2014).

When corporate persons such as religiously run hospitals have considerable institutional power, it is even more important to interrogate any claim that they are justified in refusing provision of lawful healthcare on grounds of conscience. The Irish legal context is complicated by the fact that Article 44.2.5 of the Constitution protects the right of every religious denomination to manage its own affairs. Some commentators have argued that this denominational autonomy might apply to voluntary hospitals operating under a religious ethos (Coen, 2013; Whyte, 2013). Coen has argued that *requiring* the hospitals to perform abortions under the 2013 Act could be open to a constitutional challenge. He believes that publicly funded religious hospitals do not have to act in a manner which conflicts with their ethos (Coen, 2013). But Daly has argued that this interpretation 'is based on an implausibly broad interpretation of religious freedom and denominational autonomy' (Daly, 2013). According to Daly, denominations have the right to maintain institutions, but that does not make them immune from public regulation (see further Daly, 2012). Daly is concerned with the limits imposed on hospitals through their public obligations to provide healthcare, an issue I take up below. But as the Colombian ruling helps make clear, there is a prior point: hospitals as a whole should not be recognised as the bearers of CO in the first place, and 'denominational authority' covers the management of a hospital's affairs according to a descriptive account of its ethos. The legal interest in denominational authority under the Irish Constitution does not justify the legal recognition of institutional CO since CO is not the kind of practice that fits within such a descriptive understanding of ethos. Moreover, recognising institutional conscience could undermine protection of the consciences of individual employees within that institution.

This issue has become more concrete in Ireland in the wake of the passing of the PLDPA. Two prominent Catholic hospitals, the Mater and St Vincent's, are named in the Act as hospitals authorised to provide terminations. One of the Board members of the Mater, Fr Doran, stated publicly that he was concerned about the possibility of the Act requiring the Mater to perform abortions, as this would breach their ethos. In September 2013, the Mater announced that it would be complying with the terms of the PLDPA (Holland, 2013; O'Carroll, 2013b). Fr Doran subsequently resigned from the Board. It would seem that the hospital has agreed to abide by the terms of the Act in its provision of public and private healthcare, and not to invoke some kind of collective CO to the performance of life-saving terminations which may not conform with Catholic doctrine. But the issue is bound to continue to be contested and has generated a great deal of media coverage and public commentary, including from an anti-choice campaigner who has called for the nuns in the Mater to take a test case (O'Brien, 2013). An understanding of CO as an exercise in critical consciousness may contribute to this debate by explaining why hospitals with a religious ethos are unlikely to qualify for CO.

Good faith, non-discriminatory claimants

Two other sets of issues to do with the nature of the claim to CO have arisen in an Irish context. The first concerns the genuineness of the objection. The second concerns whether non-direct participation in abortion care amounts to the carrying out, or the assistance in carrying out, of abortions under the PLDPA, and gives rise to a right to CO. In this section, I review how these concerns may play out. I argue that the best way to frame such concerns about legitimacy is by asking whether refusers of care are invoking a good faith, non-discriminatory objection.

Genuineness of CO

Usually the 'genuineness' of a refusal to provide abortion care is not scrutinised in itself, but refusers are asked to identify themselves and to give reasons so that arrangements to accommodate the conscientious refusal can be made. Conscientious refusers may be distinguished from 'obstructors' or those whose objection falls more readily within the category of civil disobedience. If someone wants to obstruct the provision of the lawful service by ostensibly participating in it but refusing to authorise abortion on the legal grounds available, then this is not conscientious refusal as normally understood. Rather the intention is to frustrate the system and the normal expectation is that this person would be held to account. Since civil disobedience is about drawing attention to an objection with a particular law by disobeying it and inviting the consequences, obstruction is closer to civil disobedience in kind than it is to CO. The obstructor is not a 'genuine' conscientious objector because they do not wish to withdraw from the healthcare provision to which they object. This distinction may be relevant in responding to any possibility that medical professionals may 'obstruct' the delivery of legal abortion care by participating while having no intention of approving abortion care in individual cases (see further Casey, 2013).

As Raz has pointed out, recognising a right to object 'involves sanctioning some degree of public intrusion into the private affairs of individuals' (2009: 287–8) because the genuineness of a conscientious objector needs to be assessed to prevent abuse (see also Campbell, 2011a: 287). If someone is seeking to rely on CO in order to lessen their workload or because they would rather do something else, then they are not objecting as an exercise in critical consciousness and do not have a legitimate claim. Some objectors will want to be freed of a range of activities which they associate with an immoral purpose on grounds of complicity (Campbell, 2011a: 300). This will be the case even if others think that associated actions are not necessary for abortion care and ought not be objectionable to the objector. In a sense, Glasgow midwives Doogan and Wood asked the UK Supreme Court to take the genuineness of their objection to being complicit in abortion care seriously when they supervise, delegate and support abortion care (*Greater Glasgow Health Board* v. *Doogan and Wood* [2014] UKSC 68: para. 12; Neal, 2014; see further Dickens, 2014: 229–30). They were unsuccessful because they were not participating in a 'hands-on capacity' when engaged in managerial and supervisory tasks. However, the genuineness of such a sense of complicity is not the only factor in deciding whether CO is legitimately engaged.

Non-direct participation

The legal distinction between direct and indirect participation in healthcare is also relevant to considering the legitimacy of a claim to CO. Law has often excluded indirect participants from claiming CO on the basis that their participation in something they find morally objectionable has to be direct (Fletcher, 2014: 130–2). As Sepper explains, 'across philosophical traditions, the necessity and proximity of the objector for the alleged bad act and the severity of the consequences of the act are central to moral responsibility' (2014: 726). Direct participants have a legal right to CO because they are proximate and necessary to the activity, and because the consequences of denying them that right would be serious. This distinction has also informed professional regulation. The British Royal College of Nursing's Framework on the Termination of Pregnancy currently provides:

> This right is limited only to the active participation in the termination of pregnancy where there is no emergency with regard to the physical or mental health of the pregnant woman ... Nurses and midwives who have a conscientious objection must inform their employer at the earliest opportunity. Under the 1990 legislation, nurses cannot refuse to provide nursing care for women, before or after the termination of the pregnancy. (2013: 7)

On this view, indirect participation does not give rise to a 'genuine' objection because the objector is not proximate enough to the relevant act in order to be responsible for it. However, this legal and policy distinction has been coming under pressure internationally as those who believe themselves complicit in the provision of something morally objectionable have challenged the exclusion of indirect participation. Sepper (2014) distinguishes between what she calls first and second generation conscience clauses in the US, where the first are narrowly focused on certain professions and acts and the second concern broader protection of pharmacists and of information and referral activities. In a European context, this legal distinction has recently been considered by the Supreme Court in the UK in the context of the Glasgow midwives case *Greater Glasgow Health Board* v. *Doogan and Wood* [2014] UKSC 68 (Doogan and Wood). Irish law and policy has not explicitly considered the relevance of this distinction to any great extent yet (Medical Council, 2009: 16). But it informed the controversy surrounding the alleged right of pregnancy counsellors, working in state-funded services contracted out to Catholic organisations, not to provide clients with information about abortion services abroad (Fletcher 2013: 172).

Glasgow hospital appealed against the decision by the Inner House of the Scottish Court of Session that indirect participation in the form of supervision, delegation and support of staff providing abortion care did give rise to a right to CO under section 4 of the Abortion Act, 1967. Baroness Hale, delivering the unanimous judgment for the Supreme Court, identified the key legal issue as a specific one of statutory interpretation, rather than human rights or employment equality analysis (see further Montgomery, 2015). Ultimately she ruled that participation under section 4 would not on any view cover things done before the course of treatment began, such as the booking before the first drug is administered. Moreover a narrow meaning of actually taking part in a 'hands-on capacity' was more likely to have been in contemplation by Parliament when the 1967 Act was passed (para 38). Therefore managerial and supervisory tasks, including delegation, will not usually be covered by 'participation'. Support tasks will not be covered unless they involve assistance which entails actual hands-on participation in the termination.

In other words, this Supreme Court decision is authority for the proposition that the legal distinction between direct and indirect participation cannot be considered solely from the subjective perspective of the conscientious objector. The question of participation ought to be decided objectively in terms of whether an action is actual, hands-on participation in termination of pregnancy. This approach is consistent with a court having regard to the proper objectives underpinning the lawful recognition of CO, that is the legal protection of critical consciousness within a harm prevention framework.

The question of whether indirect participants merit recognition as conscientious objectors is best decided first, in terms of the good faith genuineness of their claim and second, in terms of its reasonableness in the sense of being non-discriminatory. Some kinds of indirect abortion care (e.g. making arrangements for a woman who has decided to terminate her pregnancy, or handling foetal remains) may legitimately give rise to a CO because the objector genuinely believes that they would be complicit in something morally objectionable and may suffer a psychological harm as a result. This could be a belief that while a woman is entitled to make reproductive decisions and is entitled to reproductive healthcare, that professional does not want to be involved in the destruction of embryonic or foetal life because they believe that life has moral value from conception. As Kantymir and McLeod (2014) argue, however, genuineness should not be a sufficient condition because reasons although genuine may be based on false information or they may be normatively problematic. As a matter of law, we should respond to this concern by adopting the regulatory assumption that a claim to CO is genuine, unless there is evidence to suggest otherwise. The belief that indirect forms of abortion care would make the carer complicit may be unreasonable, and if so they ought not be recognised as grounding a CO in law. Even if the objection is reasonable in the sense of being non-discriminatory, another question (discussed below), is whether other interests such as the needs of the woman limit the genuine and reasonable objection either by trumping it or by imposing conditions on its execution.

Objections to the provision of abortion information or genetic testing to a pregnant woman on grounds that it may contribute to an abortion decision and render the provider complicit in that decision should not stand because that may be an empirically false claim. For example, where an abortion decision has not been made, the objection to the test on the grounds that it could lead to abortion is arguably factually incorrect. Results of a genetic test provide a woman with information about her pregnancy. This information may contribute to an abortion decision, but it is equally possible that it may not. Legal support for this approach can be found in the Colombian Court's opinion that indirect participation cannot ground CO 'because of the difficulty in determining how their work interferes with legitimate moral, philosophical or religious convictions' (para. 5.1). Before an abortion occurs, or before an abortion decision is made, we cannot know if care which provides a woman with information about her pregnancy, and which has abortion as one possible outcome, will contribute to abortion or not, and we cannot say as a matter of fact if the objector is complicit or not.

The issue arose in *RR* v. *Poland* (2011) 53 EHRR 31, but was not definitively addressed by the European Court of Human Rights (ECtHR). The applicant argued that a refusal to provide a diagnostic test because that test might lead to abortion was not justified by CO. In particular her lawyers argued that:

> [U]nder the established medical doctrine of informed consent, patients should be informed of all risks, benefits and alternatives to treatment in order to make a free and informed decision in their best interest. Refusing to diagnose a potentially serious illness on the basis that the diagnosis might subsequently lead to a therapeutic act to which the doctor concerned objected on grounds of conscience was incompatible with the very concept of conscientious objection. (para. 174)

In other words, patients who may be considering abortion are lawfully entitled to information and diagnostic tests about their pregnancy. Refusing to provide such information on the grounds that it is an aspect of abortion care is more than is necessary to protect the care provider's conscience. At the moment, pregnant women receiving care in Irish hospitals and crisis pregnancy centres may not be getting full information about their pregnancy options. The women and couples of Termination for Medical Reasons have discussed 'feeling abandoned' by the Irish healthcare system on discovery that there were serious anomalies with their pregnancies (O'Carroll, 2013a). Good quality information about pregnancy options, including the availability of abortion care abroad, is provided in a variety of cases (Fletcher, 2013a). In other instances, women's access to abortion information is impeded either by the chilling effect of restrictions under the Regulation of Information (Services Outside the State for Termination of Pregnancies) Act, 1995, or because relevant professionals are exercising a version of CO. I cannot review the issue in detail here, but the point I want to make for the purposes of this chapter is that if professionals are denying or delaying women's access to information about their pregnancies out of a CO to abortion, that is unlikely to be a legitimate claim to CO because it makes incorrect assumptions about what women will do with that information.

Some forms of pre-abortion care ought not to give rise to CO because it will be unreasonable to deny pregnant women health information to which pregnant women are normally entitled. Denying such information amounts to treating women who are contemplating abortion as if they are not entitled to basic healthcare information, information which other patients receive. Objections that refuse to provide care for discriminatory or other normatively problematic reasons should not be legally recognised as engaging a right to CO (Medical Council, 2009: 16; GMC, 2013b: para. 8). Post abortion care is particularly likely to fall into this category because here the objector wants to withhold the care on the grounds that the woman has had an abortion. At this point it is not reasonable to understand this care as complicit in the provision of abortion because the abortion has happened. Rather here the refusal would be unjustifiably discriminatory because it is denying healthcare to women who have had abortions because of who they are, and not because of the action they may take. This might be the best interpretation of national laws in the UK and Italy which have, to date, explicitly excluded indirect involvement from the scope of CO (Doogan and Wood, 2014; European Committee of Social Rights, 2014). They are seeking to exclude those actions such as the non-provision of post-abortion care which amount to discrimination against women who have had abortions as less worthy of healthcare than other women or men. Some refusals of abortion care, however, such as the supervision of abortion care in the Doogan and Wood case, are forms of indirect participation which are not obviously excluded as direct discrimination, but may have to be legally limited in order to avoid harm to pregnant people.

Harm reduction as a limit on conscientious objection

CO is a limited and not an absolute right (*Pichon and Sajous* v. *France* (2001) App. No. 49853/99, ECtHR; Lamacková, 2008; Daly, 2013). Most legal rights are limited by reference to the rights of others and public interests, but more extensive limitations are probably justifiable in the case of CO. This is because CO arises out of a context where there is usually a lawful obligation on the objector to provide a form of healthcare, which conflicts with their conscience. Even though it is trite law that CO is a limited right, in practice healthcare professionals have been known to act as if their CO is absolute. The ECtHR felt the need to criticise the doctors in *P and S* v. *Poland* (2012) App. No. 57375/08 for effectively assuming an absolute right to CO (para. 108). A more contested legal issue is not the fact of limitations *per se*, but the scope of such limitations and the kinds of harms that count in limiting CO. I will first examine the legal meaning of harm in this context (see further Erdman, 2011; Women's Link Worldwide, 2012) before considering the kinds of limits on CO that harm prevention entails.

The scope of harms

Most CO laws, including section 17 of the PLDPA, specify that healthcare professionals cannot rely on CO to deny a woman emergency life-saving abortion care (see further Department of Health, 2014: 40). Most CO laws also require timely referral to another provider if CO is being claimed in non-emergency situations. I argue that these kinds of legal limits on CO imply a recognition that CO could harm pregnant women in a variety of ways. How do we decide which harms count when considering the justifiable limits on CO? When abortion law recognises interests which may justify a termination of pregnancy it is recognising interests which may be harmed by the exercise of CO. Therefore, the criteria for harms which limit CO are provided by the criteria for lawful termination. These will vary between legal regimes but typically range over women's interests in life, health, well-being, self-determination, dignity, freedom from degrading treatment and equality. If abortion laws recognise grounds for lawful abortion such as risk of injury to a woman's health and well-being, or a compromising of her self-determination and dignity, then these are legally recognised harms which limit the exercise of CO (see further *IPPF-En* v. *Italy*, Complaint No. 87/2012). The harms which should count legally in calculating whether CO is limited in a particular case are all the harms anticipated by the legal measure permitting abortion and CO, not just the harm that is a life-threatening emergency. In an Irish context the harm of risk to life, including suicide risk, is recognised as a harm which grounds a legal right to abortion by the PLDPA, and operates to limit the objections of those who disagree with abortion being provided on such grounds (see further Murray, 2013). Those who object to the provision of abortion on grounds of suicide risk do not have an absolute right to conscientiously object to such provision. Rather, legal recognition of suicide risk as a ground for abortion means that any relevant CO has to be managed without becoming a barrier to lawful access on this ground.

A second issue is that the scope of abortion law may not be settled in relation to particular kinds of harms. At present the only harm, which is *explicitly* recognised as justifying lawful abortion in Ireland, is the harm of a real and substantial risk to a woman's life including the risk of self-destruction. However, it is arguable that the Irish courts have not fully considered the impact of women's ECHR rights, which now inform Irish domestic law (Egan et al., 2014); the proper scope of the legal term 'unborn' in the Constitution; the meaning of Article 40.3.3's reference to equality between woman and 'unborn'; or, the usual legal limits on the right to life. Although I cannot elaborate the argument fully here (see Fletcher, 1998; 2008; 2013b), it is possible that a court could expand the categories of lawful abortion in a particular fact situation and in light of lawful interests which were not in play when *Attorney General* v. *X* (1992) 1 IR 1 was decided. For example, it is not settled yet whether carrying a foetus with a fatal abnormality against a woman's better judgement is the kind of harm which could justify abortion. It is possible that the 'right to life of the unborn' may not be engaged in such circumstances (Schweppe and Spain, 2013). It is possible that carrying such a pregnancy against one's will is a form of inhumane and degrading treatment justifying access to lawful abortion (*RR*; *KL* v. *Peru* (UNHCR) CCPR/C/85/D/1153/2003; Centre for Reproductive Rights, 2014a; Centre for Reproductive Rights, 2014b). This means that it is also possible to invoke these harms as harms which *may* legally limit CO when contributing to the development of law and policy on CO in Ireland.

Harms which are explicitly recognised as legally justifying abortion ought to be recognised as harms which limit the exercise of CO. Given that the boundaries of legally recognised harms shift through argument and contestation, it is always possible that the category of harm that legally limits CO will be expanded or restricted. Even if the issue of what counts as harm is answered, there is still a question about the kind of limit such a harm may put on CO. In the section that follows I distinguish between legal recognition of harm reduction as a trump on CO and as a condition on CO. Harm reduction operates as a trump on CO when the right to CO is outweighed by the right underpinning access to abortion. Harm reduction imposes conditions on the exercise of any right to CO by requiring the objector to observe certain obligations, e.g. referral that arises from the refusal to provide care.

Limits on CO as trumps or conditions

When a CO law, such as section 17 of the PLDPA, specifies that health professionals cannot rely on CO to deny a woman emergency life-saving abortion care, it is recognising that any *prima facie* right to CO will be trumped by the duty to reduce an imminent threat to the woman's life. It is not that the *only* harm which limits CO is a threat to a woman's life. Rather the *effect* of this threat of substantial harm is to act as a trump. The circumstances which trigger such a trumping of CO will usually be rare given that there must be no other way to accommodate the woman's interest in survival. In many circumstances, harm prevention will operate to impose conditions (rather than trumps) on CO so that the objector may only object or commit conscientiously when certain conditions are met.

Referral obligations, including those within section 17 of the PLDPA, are best understood as conditions that are put on CO in order to prevent harm to the woman by delaying or inhibiting her access to lawful healthcare. In this way, the limiting of CO may translate into a series of standards and obligations, which objectors and the public health authorities which employ them must meet (see further Campbell, 2011a: 293; Dickens, 2014: 229). In effect, they should show that they are only breaching their duties to provide healthcare as far as is necessary in order to protect their critical consciousness. The emphasis on the need to guarantee access and eliminate any additional barriers that may arise in the exercise of CO (or its equivalent) is evident in the ECtHR's approach. This means that it is for the physician and not the patient to meet the conditions. Recognised conditions, which implement the duty to provide unobstructed access to lawful abortion care, include referral, timeliness, adequate staffing and procedural regularity.

National laws and policies commonly recognise an objector's obligation to refer the patient to another professional who will treat her (GMC, 2013a: para. 52; T-388/2009, 2014: 34; Doogan and Wood, 2014: para. 40). Westeson (2013) argues that a European regulatory standard of requiring the securing of referrals has been established as a result of the ECtHR decisions in *RR* and *P and S*. In *RR* the failure to refer for genetic testing, which was required under domestic legislation, gave rise to a breach of the applicant's rights to freedom from inhuman and degrading treatment (protected by Article 3) and to private and family life (protected by Article 8). In *P and S* the failure to provide a referral for abortion was part of the applicants' evidence that they had not been provided with an effective means to exercise their rights under Articles 8 and 3 (para. 81). Moreover, these failures to refer occurred in a context where domestic law imposed 'on the doctor an obligation to refer the patient to another physician competent to carry out the same service' (para. 107). The Health Service Executive has an obligation to ensure that objectors do refer women who have a lawful right to abortion on to other professionals in a timely manner.

The delays experienced by *RR* and by *P and S* in trying to claim a lawful right to abortion were clear breaches of the standard of timeliness in access that is also required as a consequence of CO. In *RR*, it was eight weeks after the request, and beyond the lawful time period for abortion, before the applicant received the genetic test results. Second, the court clearly saw the 'procrastination, confusion and lack of proper counselling and information given to the applicant' in determining whether she should have access to genetic testing (para. 153) as unnecessary barriers to access. Similarly in finding that *P and S*'s ECHR rights were breached, the court stated:

> The events surrounding the determination of the first applicant's access to legal abortion were marred by procrastination and confusion. The applicants were given misleading and contradictory information. They did not receive appropriate and objective medical counselling which would have due regard to their own views and wishes. No set procedure was available to them under which they could have their views heard and properly taken into consideration with a modicum of procedural fairness. (para. 108)

The court also noted that timeliness in the delivery of lawful healthcare was even more important in the context of pregnancy (para. 111). The need to provide lawful abortion care in a timely manner operates as another reason why it may be illegitimate for hospitals, rather than individuals, to refuse the provision of abortion care on grounds of their institutional ethos. In order to meet a timeliness requirement, the hospital would have to show that another care provider at another institution could provide the lawful abortion without undue delay. In the Irish context where abortion is only lawful when it is life-saving, it will be very difficult for a hospital to show that transfer to another hospital meets the appropriate standard of timeliness.

The complaint against Italy raised a different kind of condition – adequate staffing – on the practice of CO (IPPF-EN, 2012; European Committee of Social Rights, 2014). The successful argument here was that the state was failing to deliver appropriate standards of safe and lawful abortion because there was a dearth of personnel willing to provide abortion care in public hospitals. As a result the Committee decided that Italy had breached Article 11 of the European Social Charter, which protects the right to protection of health, in conjunction with the right to non-discrimination, protected by Article E. The failure to regulate CO had contributed to the low number of abortion providers, which put a barrier in the way of women's access to lawful abortion, making the whole safe and timely service unsustainable. As Raz observes, '[t]he conscientious exemption from a duty to participate in administering the right is allowed because, and so long as, it does not threaten the provision of the service' (2013: 3). This understanding is also supported by the reasoning of the Colombian Constitutional Court in Decision T-388/2009 (2014). The court was unequivocal in stating that the rights of pregnant women were not protected when the state or the governmental system responsible for healthcare insurance (EPS) fails to ensure the presence of a sufficient number of healthcare professionals (section 5.1).

The need to prevent harm places formal as well as substantive limits on CO. Regulators need to ensure that proper procedures are in place in order to guide the exercise of CO and allow objectors protection of their critical consciousness while ensuring that public health and women's interests are appropriately protected. Westeson (2013) argues that a European regulatory standard of requiring refusals in writing has been established as a result of the ECtHR decisions in *RR* and *P and S*. This documentation should include the reasons for the refusal and an appropriate referral. The Colombian Constitutional Court provided some further guidance on the standard required of refusals when it specified that the objector must explain why 'performing the abortion in this specific case goes against her most intimate convictions' and notes that 'general language presented on behalf of a group will not suffice, nor objections presented by any person other than the person who is conscientiously objecting' (T-388 /2009, 2014: 43). This provides a procedural means for enabling regulators to check for bad faith and discriminatory reasons.

Conclusion

Struggles for social justice in neighbourhoods the world over have emphasised the need to differentiate between claims to freedom and conscience. A hospital's public statement that it will not allow abortion to be performed on its premises is not the same claim as that of the individual midwife who refuses to perform an abortion, but continues to care for her patients otherwise. Moreover if that hospital takes public funding on the one hand but asserts the private values of a particular religion or secular ethos on the other, this is not the critical expression of moral freedom, but a kind of macho politics. Such a hospital is saying that it is entitled to public funding and state support, but is not publicly accountable. Institutional power needs to be revealed for what it is, not accepted on its own terms. Similarly, the articulation of a doctrinal religious viewpoint, which has long been institutionalised, is not the same as the expression of a critical moral view which stands against the legal status quo perhaps at some personal cost. We do a disservice to the many moral and religious traditions which have struggled against disadvantage with few resources if we accept dominant religious powers' efforts to characterise themselves as marginal and weak. Conscientious objectors ought to be recognised, but do need to be held accountable to public obligations to prevent harm. This is part of the struggle to preserve critical spaces against institutional power in its new and varied forms.

References

Campbell, M. (2011a) 'Conscientious objection, health care and Article 9 of the European Court of Human Rights', *Medical Law International*, 11: 284.

Campbell, M. (2011b) 'Conscientious objection and the Council of Europe', *Medical Law Review*, 19: 467.

Casey, P. (2013) *Submission to the Public Hearings on the Implementation of the Government Decision following the publication of the Expert Group Report into matters relating to A, B, C, vs Ireland, 8 January*. Dublin.

Centre for Reproductive Rights (2014a) *Abandoned and Stigmatised: The Impact of the Irish Abortion Law on Women.* Available at: http://reproductiverights.org/sites/crr.civicactions.net/files/documents/AbandonedAndStigmatized_ImpactOfIrishAbortionLaw.pdf.

Centre for Reproductive Rights (2014b) *Centre for Reproductive Rights Brings Second Case Against Ireland's Abortion Laws to United Nations.* Available at: http://reproductiverights.org/en/press-room/CRR-brings-second-Ireland-case.

Coen, M. (2013) 'Abortion law may run counter to Constitution', *Irish Times* 8 August.

Corbin, M. (2014) 'Abortion distortions', *William and Lee Law Review*, 71: 1175.

Daly, E. (2012) *Religion, Law and the Irish State.* Dublin: Clarus Press.

Daly, E. (2013) 'Religious freedom arguments in the abortion debate', *Human Rights in Ireland Blog*, 12 August.

Department of Health (2014) *Implementation of the Protection of Life During Pregnancy Act 2013: Guidance Document for Health Professionals.* Dublin.

Dickens, B. (2006) 'Conscientious objection: a shield or a sword?', in S.A.M. McLean (ed.), *First Do No Harm: Law, Ethics and Healthcare.* Aldershot: Ashgate, pp. 337–51.

Dickens, B. (2014) 'The right to conscience' in R. Cook, J. Erdman and B. Dickens (eds) *Abortion Law in Transnational Perspective.* Philadelphia: University of Pennsylvania Press, pp. 210–38.

Dickens, B. and Cook, R. (2011) 'Conscientious commitment to women's health', *International Journal of Gynaecology and Obstetrics*, 113(2): 163

Doctors for Choice (2014) *Submission to the UNHRC for Ireland's Review under the ICCPR.* Available at: www.ccprcentre.org/doc/2014/06/INT_CCPR_CSS_IRL_17440_E.pdf.

Egan, S., Thornton, L. and Walsh, J. (2014) *Ireland and the European Convention on Human Rights: 60 Years and Beyond.* Bloomsbury: Dublin.

Erdman, J. (2011) 'Access to information on safe abortion: a harm reduction and human rights approach', *Harvard Journal of Law and Gender* 34: 413.

European Committee of Social Rights (2014) *Decision on the Merits: International Planned Parenthood Federation – European Network (IPPF EN)* v. *Italy*, Complaint No. 87/2012. Strasbourg.

European Parliamentary Assembly (2010) *Resolution 1763.* Strasbourg.

Fiala, C. and Arthur, J. (2014) '"Dishonourable disobedience" – why refusal to treat in reproductive healthcare is not conscientious objection', *Woman – Psychosomatic Gynaecology and Obstetrics*, 1: 12

Fletcher, R. (1998) '"Pro-life" absolutes, feminist challenges: the fundamentalist narrative of Irish abortion law 1986–92', *Osgoode Hall Law Journal*, 36: 1.

Fletcher, R. (2008) 'Reproductive justice and Article 40 3 3', in J. Schweppe (ed.), *The Unborn Child, Article 40 3 3 and Abortion in Ireland: 25 Years of Protection?* Dublin: Liffey Press, pp. 319–48.

Fletcher, R. (2013a) 'Peripheral governance: administering transnational healthcare flows', *International Journal of Law in Context*, 9: 161.

Fletcher, R. (2013b) 'Submission to the Health Committee on the General Scheme of the Protection of Life During Pregnancy Bill, 2013', in Houses of the Oireachtas Joint Committee on Health and Children, *Report on Protection of Life During Pregnancy Bill 2013 (Heads of)* (Volume 1) May: 402–412. Dublin.

Fletcher, R. (2014) 'Conscientious objection and harm reduction in Europe', in *T-388/2009 Conscientious Objection and Abortion: A Global Perspective on the Colombian Experience*. Washington and Bogota: O'Neill Institute for National and Global Health Law and Women's Link Worldwide.

Gallagher, C.T., Holton, A., McDonald, L.J. and Gallagher, P.J. (2013) 'The fox and the grapes: an Anglo-Irish perspective on conscientious objection to the supply of emergency hormonal contraception without prescription', *Journal of Medical Ethics*, 39: 638.

GMC (General Medical Council) (2013a) *Good Medical Practice*. London.

GMC (General Medical Council) (2013b) *Personal Beliefs and Medical Practice*. London.

Holland, K. (2013) 'Mater Hospital to comply with legislation', *Irish Times*, 25 September.

Joffe, C. (1996) *Doctors of Conscience*. Boston, Beacon Press.

Kantymir, L. and McLeod, C. (2014) 'Justification for conscience exemptions in health care', *Bioethics*, 28(1): 16.

Kelleher, Paul, J. (2010) 'Emergency contraception and conscientious objection', *Journal of Applied Philosophy*, 27(3): 290.

Lamacková, A. (2008) 'Conscientious objection in reproductive health care: analysis of *Pichon and Sajous* v. *France*', *European Journal of Health Law*, 15(1): 7.

Medical Council (2009) *Guide to Professional Conduct and Ethics*, 7th edn. Dublin.

Melling, L. and Lee, J. (2014) 'Lessons from Colombia to the United States', in *T-388/2009 Conscientious Objection and Abortion: A Global Perspective on the Colombian Experience*. Washington and Bogota: O'Neill Institute for National and Global Health and Women's Link Worldwide.

Montgomery, J. (2015) 'Conscientious objection: personal and professional ethics in the public square' *Medical Law Review*, 23(2): 200–20

Murphy, M. (2014) 'Abortion law strangled at birth by medical guidelines', *Irish Independent*, 9 August.

Murray, C. (2013) 'The narrative of the hysterical woman: the discourse on the inclusion of suicide in the Irish legislation on abortion', Reforming Abortion Law: Comparative Perspectives Conference, University College Cork, 22 March.

Neal, M. (2014) 'Commentary: the scope of the conscience-based exemption in section 4(1) of the Abortion Act 1967: *Doogan and Wood* v. *NHS Greater Glasgow and Clyde Health Board* [2013] CSIH 36', *Medical Law Review*, 22(3): 409.

O'Brien, B. (2013) 'Mater Hospital nuns must stand up to bullying', *The Irish Times*, 5 October.

O'Carroll, S. (2013a) 'Emotional plea for change: wrap your arms around us, don't kick us out', *The Journal*, 13 November.

O'Carroll, S. (2013b) 'Mater hospital says it will comply with new abortion laws', *The Journal*, 15 September.

Raz, J. (2009) *The Authority of Law*. Oxford: Oxford University Press.

Raz, J. (2013) 'Death in our life', *Journal of Applied Philosophy*, 30(1): 1.

Royal College of Nursing (2013) *Termination of Pregnancy: A Nursing Framework*. London.

Savulescu, J. (2006) 'Conscientious objection in medicine', *British Medical Journal*, 332: 294.

Schweppe, J. and Spain, E. (2013) 'When is a foetus not an unborn? Fatal foetal abnormalities and Article 40 3 3', *Irish Journal of Legal Studies*, 3(3): 92.

Sepper, E. (2012) 'Taking conscience seriously', *Virginia Law Review*, 98: 101.

Sepper, E. (2013) 'Contraception and the birth of corporate conscience', *Washington University in St Louis Legal Studies Research Paper*. Available at: http://papers.ssrn.com/sol3/papers.cfm?abstract_id=2289383.

Sepper, E. (2014) 'Doctoring discrimination in the same sex marriage debates', *Indiana Law Journal*, 89: 703.

Thomson, M. (2013) 'Abortion law and professional boundaries', *Social and Legal Studies*, 22(2): 191.

Westeson, J. (2013) 'Reproductive health information and abortion services: standards developed by the European Court of Human Rights', *International Journal of Gynecology and Obstetrics*, 122: 173.

Whyte, G. (2013) 'Five issues could prompt referral of abortion legislation to Supreme Court', *The Irish Times*, 17 July.

Wicclair, M. (2011) *Conscientious Objection in Healthcare: An Ethical Analysis*. Cambridge: Cambridge University Press.

Women's Link Worldwide (2012) *Maternal Mortality, Unsafe Abortion and the Harm Reduction Model: The Legal Platform*. Available at: www.womenslink-worldwide.org/wlw/new.php?modo=detalle_proyectos&dc=66.

3

Why care about carers?

Claire Murray

Introduction

Rights are increasingly important in health law, both from a theoretical and a practical perspective. Respecting the autonomy and dignity rights of individuals should ultimately lead to more positive outcomes for people who engage with the health services because recognising them as rights subjects requires that they are treated with respect and their voices are listened to. Many of the chapters in this book are concerned with rights: identifying areas where rights have not been respected; teasing out how rights could best be protected; considering how to balance competing rights. The understanding of rights we are most familiar with is based on a traditional liberal approach which is very individualistic (Rawls, 1999; 2005). It conceives of the rights holder as an individual existing in isolation and fails to acknowledge the reality that individuals exist in contexts – they are situated within communities and in relationships with others. Very often those relationships are caring in nature. However, a rights-based framework grounded in traditional liberalism cannot accommodate a dependent rights subject. The result is that the position of carers and those who depend on care is not adequately recognised or supported within the legal framework.

This chapter argues that we should care about carers, and this should be recognised in the law, because this more accurately reflects the reality of people's lives and because carers and cared for persons have highlighted the practical difficulties that arise when the legal framework fails to acknowledge this reality. As Kittay has observed, 'when care is not adequately supported, either the cost of care is borne by the caregiver alone or the charge fails to receive adequate care – or both suffer' (2001: 575). If we accept that we should care about carers then it is very important that we think about how we conceptualise the caring relationship. This is because how we think about the caring relationship will impact on what a reformed legal framework which recognises carers looks like and how it operates. As Nedelsky notes, 'a relational self requires relational conceptions of values, which then require appropriate forms of law and rights built around those conceptions' (2011: 5). In considering a contextual approach to rights, which is what a recognition of carers requires, it is possible to consider the carer and the cared for person as one unit or it is possible to see them as two separate individuals who are interconnected through the relationship of care. Each of these approaches gives rise to very different outcomes for the people involved and both will be interrogated in this chapter.

This chapter first considers why we should care about carers and engages with different theoretical approaches to recognising the caring relationship and the implications of this for those involved in such relationships. In particular the chapter considers an approach grounded in the ethic of care and one based on relational autonomy. The chapter then moves on to examine an area of Irish health law where carers are clearly excluded from the legal framework – the mental health system. The mental health system is a useful case study as it illustrates the complexities around this issue. Ultimately this chapter concludes that it is important to care about carers, but doing so must be in a manner which continues to respect the distinct individual rights of each of the parties to the caring relationship.

The situated subject, relational autonomy and rights

There are theoretical, legal and practical reasons why it makes sense to acknowledge within the legal framework that individuals exist in relationships with others. Arguably the strongest reason to do this is because it is in fact the reality of the situation. Feminist theorists and others arguing from a critical perspective have repeatedly highlighted the shortcomings of the traditional liberal rights-based model which is developed around the fictional abstract individual (Gilligan, 1982; Minow, 1990; Sandel, 1998; Mullally, 2006). Engagement with a more nuanced theoretical foundation for the legal framework, based around a situated subject, allows for the development of laws which more accurately reflect the lived realities of those directly affected by them. This ensures that the laws are more likely to effectively meet the needs of those they are designed to protect. At present there is a strong sense among carers that the work that they do is not recognised or appreciated by the state,[1] and this impacts on both carers and those cared for.

Traditional liberal rights discourse is developed around the construct of the abstract, rational, autonomous individual. This rights subject is devoid of characteristics and is not connected to others. The individualist model of law is underpinned by this conception of the subject of rights. Critiques of traditional liberal rights discourse highlight the fictional nature of this subject and urge us to look beyond this traditionally accepted rights subject and instead to look to the realities of peoples' lives (Sandel, 1998: 179). The process of critically engaging with this liberal construction of the subject of rights has led to the development within feminist theories of the concept of the situated subject. This involves recognising that people exist within relationships: with family, with carers and in communities. Feminist theorists believe that such a subject – clothed in characteristics and interconnected to others – provides a more realistic foundation on which to base a theory of morality.

Ethic of care

One theoretical framework which centres on interconnection is based on an 'ethic of care'. The meaning of 'ethic of care' is not fixed and unmoving but Herring sets out a number of principles which underpin this theoretical approach (Herring, 2013: 49–64). The first is that care is part of being human and as such it should be valued. The second is that emotions are ethically significant. Third, people are relational and their interests are interconnected. Fourth, responsibilities are important. Finally, an ethic of care requires a rejection of abstract moral rules. In discussing the concept of interconnection, Herring states that 'emphasising interdependence and mutuality means that the division between carer and cared for dissolves' (2013: 166). This suggests that within this understanding of the ethic of care it is appropriate to view those in a caring relationship as one unit. Herring refers to 'give and take' in the carer and cared for relationship and highlights the importance of seeing decisions in the context of the relationship between the two people. According to Herring, this will avoid carers being treated as 'objects to be manipulated as part of patient care' (2013: 167). In what he acknowledges to be a controversial claim, Herring goes on to state that 'even an interference in the wishes of a person with capacity can be justified when the relational context is taken into account' (2013: 173).

This version of the situated subject, and this conception of the ethic of care, raises concerns that it defines an individual too much in relation to others and it is in fact paternalism operating under another name. The risk is that the particular needs and rights of the individual subject become engulfed within the needs of the group or community or become overshadowed by the needs of the other party to the relationship. By stating that the ultimate consideration is the relational self, without the backdrop of a rights framework, we lose a valuable means of supporting weaker groups in society. This has the potential to cause particular difficulties for individuals who already tend to be recognised in relation to another, such as women, children and people with disabilities. Another group that could come within this category are carers as they too are very often defined in relation to the person they are caring for.

Situated subject/relational autonomy

There is therefore a need to balance an awareness of the situated subject with an acknowledgment of individual rights that inhere in *each* person. This is at the core of relational autonomy theory (MacKenzie and Stoljar, 2000). The concept of relational autonomy is subject to varied definitions (MacKenzie and Stoljar, 2000; Herring, 2013; Sclater et al., 2009). However, it often draws on critical feminist theories and as Nedelsky notes, 'one of the contributions of feminism to relational theory is that it is particularly unlikely to make the mistake of romanticising community or relationship' (2011: 32). For the purpose of this chapter what is significant is that theories of relational autonomy emphasise the individual in context while also retaining the importance of autonomy. Nedelsky sees the aim of relational autonomy as 'transforming a traditionally individual conception of the self into a relational one without subsuming the individual into the collective' (2011: 13).

This insistence on retaining the distinct rights of the parties while acknowledging their interdependence is particularly important in areas where individual rights have so recently been recognised, for example for people with disabilities. The challenge then is to develop a legal framework which balances the rights and interests of the parties to a relationship and which supports those involved in the relationship to ensure that it is a positive and functioning relationship to the greatest extent possible.

The conception of autonomy within a relational approach is different from that set out in the traditional liberal understanding. According to Nedelsky, under a relational approach autonomy is not equated with independence but rather 'autonomy is made possible by constructive relationships' (2011: 118). Therefore it is through the existence of positive relationships and supports, including relationships of care, that individuals are in a position to exercise autonomy. As noted previously, relational autonomy is a useful approach as it does not assume that all relationships are beneficial and it does not seek to maintain them in all circumstances (Donnelly and Murray, 2013: 399). A functioning relational approach to law therefore should operate to balance the rights and needs of both parties and allow individuals to extricate themselves from bad relationships and enhance positive relationships which support the exercise of autonomy. An approach that views the parties to a relationship as one unit, as discussed above, would make this much more difficult. Failing to have any regard for the needs and rights of either party to a relationship of care will not contribute to developing a constructive relationship between the parties involved. It does not permit the carer or the cared for person to flourish or to exercise his or her right to autonomy and both are essential to the development and maintenance of positive relationships. Kittay argues from a relational perspective that those who advocate on behalf of people with disabilities (she is primarily concerned with people with profound intellectual disabilities) must look beyond liberalism, while still respecting the core values of autonomy and liberty, to 'seek conditions that are just to the caregiver as well as conducive to good care and justice for the charge' (Kittay, 2001: 562).

Human rights context

Article 8 of the European Convention on Human Rights (ECHR) protects the right to private and family life. This has been recognised as giving rise to rights for carers on their own behalf in England and Wales in the case of *R (A and B, X and Y)* v. *East Sussex County Council and the Disability Rights Commission* [2003] EWHC 167 (Admin) and by the European Court of Human Rights in *Dordevic* v. *Croatia* [2012] ECHR 1640. One of the key concerns for carers is an absence of information (REFOCUS, 2013; Wilson et al., 2014). As noted by the REFOCUS group, carers 'wish to support the patient and the clinician in the process of recovery and, in this context, the provision of appropriate and agreed information is crucial' (REFOCUS, 2013: 8). Article 8 could possibly be used to ground a right to information for carers within the legal framework. Herring states that if a decision is being taken by or in relation to an individual that would seriously impact on the carer then the carer's Article 8 rights will also be engaged (2013: 166). However, it is important to note that the privacy rights of individuals are very important and must be respected and taken into consideration, they cannot be disregarded because the person is in a caring relationship. As Nedelsky states, 'to insist on the centrality of relationships in human lives is not to deny the value of privacy or solitude' (2011: 33).

While the ECHR has been interpreted as recognising some rights for carers, the position in relation to carers is not quite as strong in the Convention on the Rights of Persons with Disabilities (CRPD). The family is mentioned in the CRPD in the Preamble which states, as an underlying premise, that:

> [T]he family is the natural and fundamental group unit of society and is entitled to protection by society and the State, and that persons with disabilities and their family members should receive the necessary protection and assistance to enable families to contribute towards the full and equal enjoyment of the rights of persons with disabilities.

The Preamble, however, does not contain binding obligations and the CRPD itself does not include any distinct and independent rights for family members or carers (Kayess and French, 2008: 25). In fact the CRPD elevates the rights of the individual with a disability above those of the family members. Kayess and French state that the CRPD challenges the accepted construction of people with disabilities as burdens on family members and of always being in a dependant role within the family (2008: 5). Within the rights-based framework of the CRPD, people with disabilities are cast in an instrumental rather than a passive role. While this can be welcomed as a move away from a more controlling or paternalistic approach to people with disabilities, it is argued that it does serve to further perpetuate the individualistic model of rights. Yes, it is important that people with disabilities are seen as having an independent, autonomous existence and are not *always* viewed in association with family members/carers. However, the other extreme is also unsatisfactory, where people with disabilities are viewed out of context, without acknowledging the very important familial and caring relationships which do exist. This chapter is based on the understanding that the reality is that all human beings exist within relationships and require care at some point and failing to recognise that within the legal framework results in laws which are not fit for purpose because they do not reflect the lived reality of those affected by them (Fineman, 2008; 2012).

That said there are also provisions within the CRPD which could be said to support a contextual approach and greater recognition of carers. Article 19 requires States Parties to recognise the right of persons with disabilities to live independently and to be included in the community, and this includes access to in-home, residential and other community support services necessary to achieve this (Article 19(b)). Article 12 of the CRPD concerns legal capacity and recognises the importance of support and assistance to facilitate persons with disabilities to make and communicate decisions and in this respect adopts a relational understanding of autonomy. The CRPD also places an obligation on States Parties to provide support to families and carers so they can fulfil the necessary support role for persons with disabilities (Article 12).

Having set out the theoretical and human rights justifications for why we should care about carers and argued in favour of conceptualising the caring relationship from a relational autonomy perspective, this chapter now turns to examine the current Irish provisions in relation to carers in the context of the mental health system.

The current position of carers in the mental health system in Ireland

Government policy and medical practice is beginning to acknowledge the importance of carers of those with mental illness in Ireland but the legislation, the Mental Health Act 2001 (MHA 2001), is completely silent on the issue. This gives rise to a situation where the key stakeholders are moving towards a more relational approach but the underlying legal framework cannot support this. There are historical reasons for this situation; until very recently the individual rights of mental health service users were not recognised and very significant powers were placed in the hands of others, including family members and carers. As a result the MHA 2001 adopted a strictly individualistic approach to rights. Mental health law and the mental health system in Ireland therefore provides a useful case study for considering the question of recognising carers as it illustrates the difficulties that arise when the law does not engage with carers but it also stands as a warning about the risks associated with neglecting the individual rights of vulnerable people. This section of the chapter will outline government policy in relation to carers and highlight the difficulties identified by carers who engage with the system before setting out the current legal position. This will demonstrate the dissonance between the law and the broader operation of the system.

Government policy on carers

The National Carers' Strategy, *Recognised, Supported, Empowered*, was published in 2012 (Department of Health, 2012). This developed from a commitment in the Programme for Government (2011) to support carers. The strategy sets out a vision statement that 'carers will be recognised and respected as key care partners. They will be supported to maintain their own health and wellbeing and to care with confidence' (Department of Health, 2012: 2). While this is commendable, the strategy almost immediately goes on to note the difficult financial circumstances in which the recognition of carers is being introduced and the proposals to reform the health system in Ireland and therefore commits to '[a]ctions for the short to medium term, which can, to the greatest extent possible, be achieved on a cost neutral basis' (Department of Health, 2012: 4). Nevertheless it is significant that government policy explicitly recognises that caring about carers is important and that the strategy recognises the need to support carers to provide good care but also to ensure that they maintain their own health and do not become socially isolated (Department of Health, 2012: 9).

While carers are not explicitly recognised in the MHA 2001, they do feature in the government policy on mental health set out in the *A Vision for Change* document (Expert Group on Mental Health Policy, 2006). Chapter 3 is entitled 'Partnership in care: service users and carers' and it notes that 'there is a need to formally recognise and support through practical means the crucial role of family care in mental health service provision' (Expert Group on Mental Health Policy, 2006: 28). The Expert Group which drew up *A Vision for Change* recommended the provision of practical supports to carers such as access to information and education, planned respite care and inclusion in the care planning process (with the agreement of the service user) (Expert Group on Mental Health Policy, 2006: 29). However, delivering on these recommendations has proved almost impossible in circumstances where there is no statutory obligation to recognise the role and position of carers in supporting the provision of mental health services and where limited resources have seen an increasing move towards what Carney characterises as the 'hollowed-out State' (Carney, 2008: 102).

Concerns of carers

In spite of these policy commitments, carers of people with mental illness continue to face challenges when engaging with the law and the mental health system. The REFOCUS forum of the College of Psychiatrists of Ireland published a paper on the needs of carers in 2013. The forum consists of service users and carers and the paper identifies ten themes, some interlinking and overlapping, identified by carers and it is worth setting those out. The themes are: the need for explicit recognition of the crucial role of carers; the need to acknowledge the unique impact of mental health difficulties of a family member on carers; the need for provision of information, knowledge and prognoses to carers; the recognition of the possible enduring nature of mental health problems; the use/abuse of patient confidentiality to justify lack of communication; the importance of continuity of care; the issues of aftercare and follow-up; the role and importance of support groups and self-help organisations; the need for a formal, robust complaints mechanism and information in relation to same; formal and structured recognition of carers as important contributors in the training of psychiatrists (REFOCUS, 2013). Many of these themes are also identifiable in the government policy and strategy documents discussed above. This illustrates the disconnect between the aspirations of the service providers and the experience of those engaging with the service. In the conclusion to this document the REFOCUS forum states that:

> [T]he perspective of carers needs to be incorporated, and structured in a formal manner, into the curricula of trainee psychiatrists and ongoing CPD programmes. It is only in this way that the perspective of carers will have a transformative and enduring impact on the provision of mental health services in the country. (REFOCUS, 2013: 12)

This is significant as it is important to ensure that any recognition of carers within the mental health system is taken on board by those charged with delivering the service at the front line. Experience with the implementation of the MHA 2001 has illustrated that changing the law alone is insufficient to ensure a change in practice (Murray, 2013). However, this chapter argues that a change in policy and practice alone is also insufficient. The changes in policy and practice outlined here are welcome developments but there needs to be a formal recognition of carers in the legal framework as well, as without this the contribution of carers and their rights and interests will remain invisible within the normative framework. The consequence is that the individualistic model of rights will remain, with the result that the rights and interests of one party in the caring relationship will continue to be prioritised over the other. This is not a just outcome for the carer or the cared for person.

Mental health law

The MHA 2001 was heralded as a rights-based model of mental health law when introduced and, given that it incorporated automatic periodic review of detention (section 17 and section 18) and enshrined the principle that people admitted under the terms of the Act could consent to treatment (section 56) for the first time in Ireland, this claim had a certain legitimacy.[2] However, the interpretation of the MHA 2001 by the courts and those implementing the statutory provisions has resulted in a reduction in the effectiveness of the rights-based model (Murray, 2013; Whelan, Chapter 14). The exclusive focus on individual rights in the MHA 2001 was in part a response to the very central role accorded to family members in the preceding legislation, the Mental Treatment Act 1945 (the 1945 Act). Under the 1945 Act there were many instances of family members committing people into institutional care with very little oversight and, in the absence of adequate (or any) review mechanisms, people could spend a considerable period incarcerated in inappropriate conditions (Boland and Laing, [1999] 2000; Boland, 2001; Barry, 2009; Prior, 2012).[3] Given this historical background, it is perhaps unsurprising that the MHA 2001 provides a very minimal and peripheral role for relatives/carers. However, the consequence is that carers are almost invisible within Irish mental health law.

To the extent that carers have a role within the framework of the MHA 2001, it is in relation to involuntary admission – relatives and spouses (who very often fulfil a caring role) are included in the list of people who can apply to a medical practitioner for a recommendation for involuntary admission. The MHA 2001 states that a person may be admitted to an 'approved centre' on the basis that he or she suffers from a 'mental disorder'. The application for admission may be made by a spouse or (same sex) civil partner; by a relative; by an authorised officer (generally, a social worker); a member of the Garda Síochána; and, finally, by any other person (which may include carers who are not related to the individual). As noted elsewhere, a 'relative' is extremely broadly defined and there is no statutory hierarchy of relatives, with all having an equal right to apply for admission (Donnelly and Murray, 2012; 2013: 386). The reality in Ireland is that the majority of involuntary admissions are commenced by the spouse or relative of the person admitted. This can have a detrimental impact on the relationship between the family members involved. In many instances it would be more appropriate for such an application to be commenced by an independent outsider. Unfortunately, there are very few authorised officers in Ireland and so this alternative route to admission is very often not available.

Once the application for a recommendation has been made, the role of the relative/carer disappears. Family members have no legal entitlement either to apply for discharge of the patient or to be informed in respect of the decision to discharge or of the discharge itself. There is no statutory requirement that the relatives/carers be given information relating to the rights of the individual who is involuntarily admitted even where the person admitted lacks capacity. Section 4(2) of the MHA 2001 requires that patients should be provided with notification of proposed recommendations or treatment and that they must be entitled to make representations in relation to the proposals. However, where the person lacks capacity, there is no legislative requirement to notify family members or carers and they have no statutory entitlement to make representations on behalf of the patient. The proposed capacity legislation is likely to address this shortcoming as there will be an obligation on medical professionals treating an individual to engage with carers where the carer is fulfilling a role under the terms of the capacity legislation. However, this will not apply to all people admitted under the terms of the MHA 2001.

Finally, in any discussion of the absence of carers within the MHA 2001 it is important to note that the current legislative framework locates very considerable power with the medical profession. The lack of a role for carers could therefore also be a consequence of a heavily medicalised model of care and treatment which does not allow for any perspectives other than those of the consultant psychiatrist.

Conclusion

This chapter argues that the current individualistic framework for rights in healthcare fails to reflect the reality that individuals exist in relationships with others and argues that what is required instead is a contextual approach to rights. It is for this reason that we should care about carers and this should be reflected in the legal framework – at present the law is out of line with government policy on this issue. However, it is important to take time to consider how we conceptualise the caring relationship as this will shape how carers are recognised in law and this will have consequences for both carers and those cared for. The chapter rejects an approach based on the ethic of care which sees the parties to a caring relationship as one unit because of concerns that the individual becomes subsumed within the bigger unit. This is particularly damaging for those who have traditionally not been recognised as rights holders. Instead the chapter argues in favour of adopting a relational autonomy approach which recognises the individual in context while continuing to respect the individual autonomy rights of the parties involved. Such an approach would ensure that the rights and interests of both parties are taken into consideration and this would be more likely to give rise to positive relationships of care which allow both parties to flourish.

Notes

1 See O'Sullivan (2008). See also submissions by the Carers' Association at www.carersireland.com.

2 During the Dáil debates on the introduction of the Mental Health Bill there was a concern that the existing statutory framework, the Mental Treatment Act 1945, was not compliant with the provisions of the European Convention on Human Rights. For further discussion see Keys (2002: para. 25-04). For discussion on the difficulties with the MHA 2001 from a rights-based perspective see Murray (2013).

3 There were a number of cases on this issue, two examples are: first, *O'Reilly* v. *Moroney* [1992] 2 IR 145 (High Court); unreported Supreme Court 16 November 1993, where a woman who was experiencing marital difficulties had, at the instigation of her husband and father, been admitted on the basis of a certificate by a general practitioner who had not spoken to her and had merely observed her reaction to her husband's arrival from a position in the front garden; second, *Bailey* v. *Gallagher* [1996] 2 ILRM 433, where the appellant was admitted by his wife in the midst of considerable marital and business difficulties and was detained notwithstanding the absence of any evidence of mental disorder.

References

Barry, S. (2009) *The Secret Scripture.* London: Faber.

Boland, F. (2001) 'Compulsory detention and the general practitioner in Irish mental health law: armour or weapon in wrongful committals?', *Northern Ireland Law Quarterly*, 52: 205.

Boland, F. and Laing, J. ([1999] 2000) 'Out of sight and out of mind? A feminist perspective on civil commitment in Britain and Ireland', *Contemporary Issues in Law*, 257.

Carney, T. (2008) 'The mental health service crisis of neoliberalism: an antipodean perspective', *International Journal of Law and Psychiatry*, 31: 101.

Department of Health (2012) *National Carers' Strategy.* Dublin: Brunswick Press Ltd.

Donnelly, M. and Murray, C. (2012) 'Unpaid carers: an invisible presence in Irish health and care law', *Medico-Legal Journal of Ireland*, 18(1): 6.

Donnelly, M. and Murray, C. (2013) 'The role of family in mental health law: a framework for transformation', *Child and Family Law Quarterly*, 25(4): 380

Expert Group on Mental Health Policy (2006) *A Vision for Change: Report of the Expert Group on Mental Health Policy.* Dublin: The Stationery Office.

Fineman, M. (2008) 'The vulnerable subject: anchoring equality in the human condition', *Yale Journal of Law and Feminism*, 20: 1.

Fineman, M. (2012) '"Elderly" as vulnerable: rethinking the nature of individual and social responsibility', *The Elder Law Journal*, 20: 101.

Gilligan, C. (1982) *In a Different Voice: Psychological Theory and Women's Development.* Cambridge, MA and London: Harvard University Press.

Herring, J. (2013) *Caring and the Law.* Oxford: Hart Publishing.

Kayess, R. and French, P. (2008) 'Out of the darkness and into light? Introducing the Convention on the Rights of Persons with Disabilities', *Human Rights Law Review*, 8(1): 1.

Keys, M. (2002) *Mental Health Act 2001, Irish Current Law Statutes Annotated.* Dublin: Round Hall.

Kittay, E.F. (2001) 'When caring is just and justice is caring: justice and mental retardation', *Public Culture*, 13(3): 557.

MacKenzie, C. and Stoljar, N. (eds) (2000) *Relational Autonomy: Feminist*

Perspectives on Autonomy, Agency and the Social Self. Oxford: Oxford University Press.

Minow, M. (1990) *Making All the Difference, Inclusion and American Law.* Ithaca and London: Cornell University Press.

Mullally, S. (2006) *Gender, Culture and Human Rights: Reclaiming Universalism.* Oxford and Portland, OR: Hart Publishing.

Murray, C. (2013) 'Moving towards rights-based mental health law: the limits of legislative reform', *Irish Jurist*, 49: 161.

Nedelsky, J. (2011) *Law's Relations: A Relational Theory of Self, Autonomy and Law.* Oxford: Oxford University Press.

O'Sullivan, L. (2008) *Health and Wellbeing of Family Carers in Ireland: Results of a Survey of the Recipients of the Carers' Allowance.* Dublin: Combat Poverty Agency.

Prior, P. (ed.) (2012) *Asylums, Mental Health Care, and the Irish: Historical Studies 1800–2010.* Dublin: Irish Academic Press.

Programme for Government (2011) *Government for National Recovery 2011–2016.* Dublin.

Rawls, J. (1999) *A Theory of Justice*, revised edn. Cambridge, MA: Harvard University Press.

Rawls, J. (2005) *Political Liberalism*, expanded edn. New York: Columbia University Press.

REFOCUS (Recovery Experience Forum of Carers and Users of Services) (2013) *Who Cares? Listening to the Needs and Experiences of Carers of People with Mental Illness.* Dublin: College of Psychiatrists of Ireland.

Sandel, M. (1998) *Liberalism and the Limits of Justice*, 2nd edn. London: Cambridge University Press.

Sclater, S.D., Ebtehaj, F., Jackson, E. and Richards, M. (eds) (2009) *Regulating Autonomy: Sex, Reproduction and Family.* Oxford: Hart Publishing.

Wilson, L., Pillay, D., Kelly, B.D. and Casey, P. (2014) 'Mental health professionals and information sharing: carer perspectives', *Irish Journal of Medical Science Irish Journal of Medical Science.* Available at: www.springer.com/medicine/internal/journal/11845 (accessed 11 June 2015).

II

RIGHTS AND RESPONSIBILITIES

4

The limits of autonomy: an exploration of the role of autonomy in the debate about assisted suicide

Louise Campbell

Introduction

Several important issues must be considered in any discussion of the permissibility of assisted death,[1] including the obligation to relieve suffering, the need to protect vulnerable persons, the effectiveness of safeguards against coercion and abuse, the quality of end-of-life care and the values of medicine as a profession. Arguments which rely on the concept of autonomy also play a prominent role in this debate, but what is meant by the term *autonomy* in the context of requesting a hastened death is rarely examined in any depth. While autonomy is more commonly associated with arguments which defend the permissibility of assistance in dying, there are in fact 'autonomy interests on both sides of the assisted suicide debate' (Gorsuch, 2006: 82). Those who defend the permissibility of assisted death argue that a person suffering from a terminal illness or enduring intractable pain should have a right to determine the point at which his or her life should end. Opponents of assisted death argue variously that such claims distort the 'true' meaning of autonomy, that decriminalising assistance in dying will violate the autonomy of vulnerable persons, and that autonomy should not take priority when its exercise threatens the rights or interests of healthcare professionals, family members or others. The purpose of the present discussion is to examine the role played by the concept of autonomy in the discussion of assisted suicide, using as a point of reference the case of Marie Fleming, the first challenge to the prohibition on assistance in dying to be heard by the Irish courts.

In what follows I will examine briefly the role played by the concept of autonomy in *Fleming* v. *Ireland and Others* [2013] IEHC 2; [2013] IESC 19, followed by an analysis of the salient autonomy-based arguments used on both sides of the assisted suicide debate. I will conclude by contrasting philosophical theories of autonomy with the more pared-down account of autonomy generally found in the bioethics literature.

The role of autonomy in *Fleming* v. *Ireland and Ors*

Fleming *v.* Ireland and Ors: *background*

Assisted suicide and euthanasia are prohibited in all jurisdictions with the exception of Belgium, the Netherlands, Luxembourg, Switzerland, Colombia and the US states of Oregon, Montana, Vermont and Washington. While suicide itself was decriminalised in Ireland by the Criminal Law (Suicide) Act 1993 (the 1993 Act), the act of 'aiding, abetting, counselling or procuring' the suicide of another person remains a criminal offence under section 2(2) of the same law and carries a maximum penalty of 14 years in prison. Prior to late 2012, the question of the right to assistance in dying had received little attention from the Irish public and had never been heard in the Irish courts. During a landmark six-day hearing in October 2012, Marie Fleming, a mentally competent but severely disabled woman in the final stages of multiple sclerosis, challenged the constitutionality of the prohibition on assisted suicide and sought a declaration that section 2(2) of the 1993 Act was incompatible with the obligations of the Irish state under the European Convention on Human Rights (ECHR).[2] Ms Fleming's claims were dismissed by a three-person High Court in January 2013, in a judgment which described her courage as 'humbling and inspiring', but indicated that a relaxation of the ban on assisted suicide even in exceptional cases would be 'inimical to the public interest in protecting the most vulnerable members of society'. An appeal brought before the Supreme Court was dismissed in April 2013. Marie Fleming died on 22 December 2013.

Autonomy is a value which is central to the liberal tradition in the UK, the US, Canada, Australia and Ireland – all jurisdictions in which challenges to the ban on assisted suicide have recently come before the courts – yet it coexists with other values which also deserve promotion, such as justice, social cohesion and the welfare of citizens. A central theme in *Fleming* v. *Ireland and Ors*, and common to all recent challenges to the prohibition on assisted suicide,[3] is the question of how the autonomy of the individual seeking assistance in dying is to be balanced against the right of vulnerable persons to the protection of the state (see also *R (on the application of Purdy)* v. *Director of Public Prosecutions* [2009] UKHL 45, 65). The concept of autonomy played a role in all recent rulings on assisted suicide, yet it is not clear what weight it carries or how it is balanced against countervailing concerns, and the courts generally have not been persuaded by it. Those who request assistance to end their lives at a time of their own choosing do so for a variety of reasons. Some people wish to avoid the painful terminal phase of an illness; some wish to avoid an 'undignified' death; some simply wish to regain some measure of control in a context of radical unpredictability. Others, however, request a hastened death because they see no benefit in continuing to live with severe impairments or because they fear being a burden on their families or on the state (Dworkin, 1993: 190). These people are considered vulnerable in the sense that they are less aware of, or less able to advocate for, their rights: they may be living in poverty, unable to access appropriate supports or subject to intractable pain or depression. Although there is a legitimate concern that the decriminalisation of assisted suicide would place people in these kinds of situations at risk, there is at present no conclusive evidence to support this claim (Battin et al., 2007: 597). What is clear is that, if the concept of autonomy is to be used to support the permissibility of assisted death, it cannot be construed as a right which trumps all other rights, but must be considered in relation to the vulnerabilities of the person making the request for assistance in dying.

Autonomy as a 'core constitutional value'

The High Court judgment in *Fleming* v. *Ireland and Ors* makes the claim that the protection of 'personal autonomy' in 'decisions concerning … personal welfare, including medical treatment' is a core constitutional value (2013: para. 49). Although it is not explicitly mentioned in the Constitution of Ireland, autonomy is generally treated as one of the 'unenumerated' rights protected by Article 40.3.1.[4] The Supreme Court judgment in *Fleming* v. *Ireland and Ors* states that both the Irish Constitution and the Convention on the Rights of Persons with Disabilities (CRPD) 'confer autonomy upon individuals in respect of their core life choices' (2013: para. 24). Kearns J in the High Court describes Ms Fleming's decision to seek assistance in ending her life 'in the face of a terminal illness which has ravaged her body and rendered her life one of almost complete misery' as a decision which is engaged by, and 'a facet of … the right to personal autonomy which lies at the core of the protection of the person by Article 40.3.2' (2013: para. 52). No guidance in relation to how to interpret the meaning of autonomy or how much weight to give it in this or any other context is provided in either the High Court or the Supreme Court decisions. This is significant insofar as autonomy is said to be a *right* protected by the Constitution and was given weight in the adjudication of Ms Fleming's specific claim that the ban on assisted suicide violated her constitutional rights. Autonomy appears almost parenthetically in Irish jurisprudence, loosely interpreted as a general capacity for self-rule or self-determination: the ability to govern oneself and make one's own choices without undue interference. It is often mentioned in conjunction with liberty, but not explicitly distinguished from it. Irish jurisprudence, however, is not unique in ascribing importance to the concept of autonomy while failing to describe the implications of so doing.

The autonomy continuum and assisted suicide

During the course of the past four decades, the concept of autonomy has evolved from a subject of philosophical analysis to a prerequisite of ethical and legal decision-making in the healthcare setting. Operationalised in law by the informed consent process, patient autonomy now plays a prominent role in healthcare practice and the promotion of autonomy has influenced health legislation and policy development in many jurisdictions, including Ireland. In contemporary Western medicine, it has become commonplace that a patient who is informed and capable of decision-making should not be subjected to an intervention which he or she does not want. While the concept of autonomy initially assumed prominence in discussions about a patient's right to authorise or refuse medical treatment, more recently it has become central to discussions about the permissibility of discontinuing life-prolonging treatments which may prove non-beneficial to the patient. For proponents of assistance in dying, the debate about assisted suicide is played out against a backdrop of the 'unfolding of a commitment to rights of autonomy' (Beauchamp, 2000: 111); demands for the right to assistance in dying, on this view, represent another successive stage in the 'extraordinary transformation' of the role of patient autonomy (Beauchamp, 2000: 113). Predictably, the idea that refusal of non-beneficial treatment and requests for a hastened death exist along the same continuum of autonomy has been rejected by opponents of assistance in dying, on the grounds that assisted death in all of its forms represents a betrayal of the ideals of medicine (Callahan, 2000: 102). Other opponents of assistance in dying argue that, because assisted suicide 'requires the connivance of others, it cannot be seen as an act that solely expresses the ideal of individual autonomy' (Salem, 1999: 32). Those who reject the validity of autonomy-based arguments in favour of permitting assisted death maintain that the crucial difference between sanctioning a person's autonomous refusal of treatment and acceding to an autonomous request to assist a person to die is that the latter implicates a third party, who performs an action deliberately intended to end that person's life.

Autonomy and the right to assistance in dying

Often used in conjunction with arguments based on the duty to relieve suffering, assertions about the value of autonomy play a prominent role in arguments in favour of assisted death. Proponents of assistance in dying argue that an individual who is terminally – or in some cases, chronically – ill, capable of decision-making and physically impaired should have a right to choose the timing of his or her death and to seek the assistance necessary to do so. Whether it is motivated by the avoidance of pain, or fear of future indignity, or by a desire to regain control in the face of illness (Pearlman and Starks, 2004:

94), this is one of the most profoundly personal and intimate decisions a person can make. Those who defend the importance of autonomous choice in requests for assistance in dying maintain that decisions of this kind are irreducibly private in nature and that state incursion into this private sphere is illegitimate. In *R (on the application of Purdy)* v. *Director of Public Prosecutions* [2009] UKHL 45, Baroness Hale acknowledges the need for safeguards to protect those who are vulnerable, but makes the claim that '[i]f we are serious about protecting autonomy, we have to accept that autonomous individuals have different views about what makes their life worth living' (2009: para. 65). In an influential *amicus curiae* brief filed by six philosophers in two Supreme Court cases heard in the US in 1997 (*Washington* v. *Glucksberg* 521 U.S. 702 (1997) and *Vacco* v. *Quill* 521 U.S. 793 (1997)), Ronald Dworkin and colleagues defended the 'moral and constitutional' principle that 'every competent person has the right to make momentous personal decisions which invoke fundamental religious or philosophical *convictions about life's value* for himself' (Dworkin et al., 1997: 41, emphasis added). This claim is defended alongside the acknowledgement that some persons may, out of desperation, make decisions which do not 'reflect their enduring convictions'. Dworkin and colleagues urged the court to affirm that citizens have a constitutional right to seek physician assistance in dying in a limited class of cases. Their argument drew on the Supreme Court decision in *Planned Parenthood* v. *Casey*, 505 U.S. 833, 851 (1992), which recognised a person's right to make decisions about matters 'involving the most intimate and personal choices a person may make in a lifetime, choices central to personal dignity and autonomy'.

What these claims have in common is the idea that no 'objective' values may be appealed to in making or adjudicating a request for assistance in dying: 'there is no objective standard, but only the competent patient's judgement [that] … continued life is no longer a benefit' (Brock, 1992: 11). Individuals have different ideas, not only about what constitutes a good life, but also about what constitutes an 'appropriate' death: recognising a person's autonomy in this context means understanding the importance they place on dying in a manner which 'keeps faith with the way … [they] want to have lived' (Dworkin, 1993: 199). In all of these arguments, however, the liberty to make autonomous decisions is asserted as a right, without further justification; as such, this position is vulnerable to John Keown's criticism that advocates of autonomy fail to agree 'on what constitutes an "autonomous" choice or to offer any convincing account for why respect for someone else's choice should be regarded as a moral principle, let alone a core or dominant moral principle' (Jackson and Keown, 2012: 87). If Keown's objection is to be refuted, more work is needed on the foundation of autonomy as a right. The question of the permissibility of assisted suicide on the basis of autonomous choice rests on the more basic question of whether 'preserving our liberty of action is … worth the costs of exercising choice' – whether, under certain conditions, there is a realm of choice which can be described as 'sacrosanct' (Conly, 2013: 17). Ultimately, the meaning and value of autonomy in human affairs is contested; for some, autonomy has intrinsic value, but for others, autonomy is just one value among others and it may or may not be accorded prominence in any given debate.

The role of autonomy in arguments opposing the permissibility of assisted dying

Opponents of assisted dying who invoke the concept of autonomy tend to deploy one of two strategies: the first is to diminish the value of autonomy by reducing it to a need for control or to what Onora O'Neill refers to as 'mere, sheer choice'. In her testimony to the Commission on Assisted Dying, O'Neill distinguished various forms of 'rational' autonomy – broadly construed as self-determination which is reflective or authentic – from an 'existentialist' conception of autonomy, construed in terms of the idea that 'any choice counts, however good, however bad, however self-destructive, however informed, however uninformed; mere sheer choice is what we're out to protect' (Commission on Assisted Dying, 2012: 72). Cautioning against the latter, O'Neill professes scepticism about the possibility of drafting adequate safeguards to protect those at risk 'without invoking misleading and unrealisable fantasies about individual autonomy' (Commission on Assisted Dying, 2012: 72). Similarly, John Keown asserts that contemporary discussions of autonomy 'consist of little more than the naked assertion that a person's choice merits respect *simply because it is his choice, whatever that choice may be*' (Keown, 2002: 54). These views reflect a legitimate worry that community values and social cohesion have been undermined by the recent development of a 'culture of autonomy', namely, a society defined by an emphasis on autonomy at the expense of other values, such as social justice or the 'common good' (Gaylin and Jennings, 2003: 67).

In *The Troubled Dream of Life*, Dan Callahan argues that 'nothing seems so feared' as the loss of self-determination, and speaks of a 'preoccupation with control [which] has become both subtly demeaning and socially troubling' (Callahan, 2000: 16–17). Elsewhere he argues that permitting assisted death 'would sanction a view of autonomy holding that individuals may, in the name of their own *private, idiosyncratic view of the good life*, call upon others, including such institutions as medicine, to help them pursue that life, even at the risk of harm to the common good' (Callahan, 1992: 52, emphasis added). Callahan's point would seem to be that the desire for choice or control has become an end in itself, with little regard for the societal consequences which follow from this privileging of self-determination. Asking in the *New York Times* about who really benefits from the decriminalisation of assisted suicide, Ezekiel Emanuel concludes that it is '[w]ell-off, well-educated people, typically suffering from cancer, who are used to controlling everything in their lives – the top 0.2 percent. And who are the people most likely to be abused if assisted suicide is legalized? The poor, poorly educated, dying patients who pose a burden to their relatives' (Emanuel, 2012). These arguments, however, fail to show that a preoccupation with control is the inevitable result of the capacity to exercise autonomy (Preston et al., 2004: 44). Further, both arguments fail to contextualise requests for assisted death by neglecting to consider the rationale a person might have for valuing control or choice in a situation defined by severe impairment or intolerable suffering.

The second strategy deployed by opponents of assisted death involves restricting the legitimate application of the term *autonomy* to actions based on certain types of values. Repudiating the idea of what he terms 'absolute respect for autonomy', Keown argues that autonomy 'merits respect only when it is exercised in accordance with a framework of sound moral values' (Keown, 2002: 53). The 'mere fact' that someone has chosen to act in a certain way does not entitle him or her to respect: for Keown, 'the character of the choice must satisfy certain criteria in order to warrant our respect' (Jackson and Keown, 2012: 88). In a similar vein, Luke Gormally limits the range of autonomous choice, claiming that 'true' autonomy consists in exercising the capacity for self-determination in a manner which leads to 'human flourishing and well-being' (Gormally, 1995: 119). According to this view of autonomy, some of our choices 'undermine rather than make for human well-being'; thus, if an action undermines the intrinsic value or dignity of human life, for example, it cannot be described as autonomous. Although Gormally maintains that the development of autonomy must allow some scope for 'erroneous' choices, he follows Keown in asserting that there is nothing 'in the character of self-destructive choices which commands our respect' (Gormally, 1995: 119).

Analysing autonomy in the assisted suicide debate

The term *autonomy* has become so ubiquitous in the literature on biomedical ethics that further attempts to delineate its meaning may appear superfluous. However, the frequency with which a term appears in a given discussion is not necessarily an indicator of appropriate use. Autonomy is a protean concept; even limiting the discussion of autonomy to the context of healthcare ethics, 'we have one concept and many conceptions of autonomy' (Dworkin, 1988: 9). Given the reiteration of appeals to autonomy in the debate about assisted dying, it is remarkable that so little attention has been paid to what it might *mean* to respect a person's 'autonomous' choice in this context. Contemporary philosophical discussions of the concept of autonomy yield a richer understanding of autonomy than does the bioethics literature, and this more nuanced analysis appears more promising as a basis for arguments supporting the practice of assisted death. In the remainder of this chapter, I will examine briefly a selection of these theories and attempt to specify preconditions of autonomous choice in the context of requests for assistance in dying.

Most contemporary discussions of autonomy view it as a form of independence (O'Neill, 2002: 28) derived from the liberal ideal of non-interference. In the most general sense, autonomy stands for the human capacity for self-determination: life lived according to a self-chosen plan, without external manipulation or undue interference. Autonomy, understood as self-government, is 'the ability of a person to guide her life from her own perspective rather than being manipulated by others or forced into a particular path by irresistible or surreptitious forces ... which disallow one's own independent judgement and choice' (Christman, 2007: 3). In their canonical text, *Principles of Biomedical Ethics*, Beauchamp and Childress define autonomy as self-rule which is substantially free from the controlling influence of others and from internal limitations which prevent 'meaningful' choice (Beauchamp and Childress, 2001: 58–9). An action which is autonomous according to this minimal definition is intended by its agent, carried out with an understanding of its implications and free from external interference. An autonomous agent is someone who is 'capable of deliberation about personal goals and of acting under the direction of such deliberation' (The National Commission for the Protection of Human Subjects of Biomedical and Behavioural Research, 1979), and respecting a person's autonomy involves recognising that person's right 'to hold views, to make choices and to take actions based on personal values and beliefs' (Beauchamp and Childress, 2001: 63).

Beauchamp and Childress explicitly distinguish their conception of autonomy from the idea that autonomy presupposes a higher-order reflection on, or authentication of, one's first-order desires and preferences. For Gerald Dworkin, it is precisely this ability to reflect on and endorse or alter one's first-order preferences, intentions and reasons for acting which constitutes autonomy (Dworkin, 1988: 17). Liberty – freedom from internal constraints and external compulsion – on this view, is an insufficient condition of autonomy.[5] Dworkin's theory owes much to Harry Frankfurt's influential 'hierarchical' account of freedom of the will, according to which the person who is free is not only free to do what they desire, but free to *want to have* the desires they have and free to be motivated by the desires they want to have (Frankfurt, 2009: 14–17).[6] As such, the capacity for autonomy is not merely a capacity to reflect on and evaluate one's desires or preferences, but also an ability 'to alter one's preferences and to make them effective in one's actions, and indeed, *to make them effective because* one has reflected upon them and adopted them as one's own' (Dworkin, 1988: 17, emphasis added). Autonomy, construed more robustly in terms of the authenticity of one's preferences, 'is essentially a matter of whether we are active rather than passive in our motives and choices

– whether, however we acquire them, they are the motives and choices that we really want and are therefore in no way alien to us' (Frankfurt, 2004: 20).

According to hierarchical theories, then, the exercise of autonomy requires identifying, evaluating and ultimately endorsing the values underpinning one's proposed action, values which 'have developed in an uncoerced and conscious fashion' (Oshana, 1998: 82). Beauchamp and Childress view this emphasis on higher-order reflection as an aspirational ideal which is 'beyond the reach of normal choosers', and in a later version of the *Principles* they insist that 'ordinary persons' who have not reflected on their higher-order preferences must also be 'deserving of respect for their autonomous choices' (Beauchamp and Childress, 2001: 59). Anticipating this criticism, Dworkin argues that, even in the absence of extensive education, it is possible for someone to 'shape and mould' their life – to form opinions, to change – in accordance with 'reflective procedures' (Dworkin, 1988: 17). The crux of this disagreement resides in the question of whether or not the exercise of autonomy requires a 'threshold of … evaluative competence' (O'Shea, 2011); whether or not reflection and endorsement are necessary prerequisites of autonomous choice. In a later essay, Beauchamp returns to the idea that 'ordinary choices' must also count as autonomous, 'even when persons have not reflected on their preferences at a higher level and even when they are hesitant to identify with one type of desire rather than another' (Beauchamp, 2005: 319). Beauchamp's concern is that agents who fail to reflect on their preferences at a higher level will not be seen to deserve respect for actions which issue from their 'most deep-seated commitments, desires and preferences' (Beauchamp. 2005: 320). The corollary of this is that decisions which would ordinarily – under a less demanding set of conditions for autonomy – be understood as autonomous will have to be classified as non-autonomous, including decisions routinely made by patients about their healthcare (Beauchamp, 2005: 322).

Procedural and substantive theories of autonomy

The 'content-less' conceptions of autonomy discussed above may be described as *procedural* accounts of autonomy: they specify certain conditions of autonomous choice or action – such as the processes by which an agent's motives and decisions are formed – but they remain neutral in relation to the content of what can be autonomously willed. Procedural accounts of autonomy are distinguished from *substantive* theories of autonomy, which impose 'normative restrictions' on the content of the values which autonomous agents can form or act upon (Benson, 2005: 125). According to substantive accounts of autonomy, whether or not an action can be called autonomous depends on the kinds of values or preferences motivating it.[7] What is problematic about substantive accounts of autonomy (exemplified by the positions put forward by Gormally (1995) and Jackson and Keown (2012)) is that they rest on a particular interpretation of the good, usually defined in opposition to the values of liberal individualism and resting on some conception of the intrinsic value of human life. Interestingly, however, it is this criticism which John Safranek levels against *procedural* theories of autonomy, claiming that their neutrality is undermined because they implicitly presuppose a criterion for distinguishing permissible from injurious autonomous acts (Safranek, 1998: 33). As Preston and colleagues point out, however, this criticism is true only of theories which defend an absolute right to autonomy (Preston et al., 2004: 48) – a right which does not in fact exist, because it is constrained by a set of social structures and norms which limit the kinds of preferences a citizen can act upon. While substantive theories of autonomy redefine autonomy to make it compatible with a particular worldview, procedural accounts set limits on 'absolute' autonomy by requiring that all agents mutually recognise one another's autonomy. Whatever its flaws, liberalism as a political ideology can be said to endorse a procedural conception of autonomy, insofar as it 'rejects a privileged perspective which might be imposed' and places constraints on what May refers to as the 'social application of personal [or partial] versions of the good' (May, 2005: 301–2).

Conditions of autonomous choice

If the concept of autonomy is to carry any weight in the argument for permitting assisted suicide in limited circumstances, it must be understood as involving some reflective component and some awareness of the role played by the agent's deeply held values in decisions which have significance for him or her. Autonomy in this more robust sense can be said to play a role in competent requests for assistance in dying. Minimally, autonomous choice presupposes both the absence of coercion or external interference and the absence of internal limitations which prevent meaningful choice, in addition to full understanding of the implications of the proposed decision. The decision in question must engage the agent's 'critical interests' (Dworkin, 1993: 201); the agent must have a significant stake in the outcome of the decision; and the interests they act upon, if satisfied, must be understood by them as genuinely improving their situation. At the same time, the agent must have the capacity to identify and evaluate their values and to see those values as motivating their decision.

Beauchamp claims that the key moral issue in the debate about assisted suicide is 'the liberty to choose the means to one's death and the justification, if any, for limiting that liberty' (Beauchamp, 2000: 111). This misses the point: the key issue is whether a reflectively endorsed, competent request for a hastened death, based upon a set of 'relatively stable values or a conception of the good life' (Buchanan and Brock, 1989: 84), counts as a sufficient justification for legitimising a practice in which 'the social stakes ... are extraordinarily high' (Callahan, 2000: 105). If autonomy is to play a role in the justification of assisted death, the conditions of autonomous choice *must* be demanding. Because he reduces autonomy to liberty or 'freedom of choice', Beauchamp fails to explain how a putatively autonomous decision can be based on a person's deep-seated commitments *in the absence* of the agent's explicit awareness of the values which motivate their decision. It is difficult to understand how someone can be motivated to act in accordance with their values if they haven't reached an understanding of how those values came to be their own. As Marina Oshana points out, freedom involves the power to decide or to act – to realise one's will – whereas autonomy additionally requires 'authority over and ownership of the affective and cognitive states as well as the social roles and relationships which provoke action' (Oshana, 2005: 195). Beauchamp's conflation of autonomy and liberty overstates the significance of the majority of the quotidian decisions we make, and trivialises the decisions which should properly be described as autonomous. My point here is that not all decisions – in fact, very few decisions – present us with an opportunity to reflect on and evaluate the values on which we propose to base our actions. For the most part, we don't have cause to reflect on what motivates us in our daily choices, unless we have a deeper interest in the outcome of those decisions. Even routine healthcare decisions which meet the criteria for informed consent do not, for the most part, present us with this opportunity (Sumner, 2011: 88). The implications of this argument are obvious: very few of our everyday choices are autonomous in the strong sense outlined above. But the decisions which do merit being classified as autonomous should be taken seriously.

The question of harm

Several persuasive arguments have been put forward in opposition to permitting or decriminalising assisted suicide, the most compelling of which focuses on the dangers posed to people living with depression, disability or chronic pain or illness, and to persons with compromised decision-making capacity or 'diminished life prospects' (Marquis, 1998: 274). The concern here is that it may not be possible to devise adequate safeguards to protect vulnerable persons from requesting an end to their own lives or having their lives ended by unscrupulous carers or health professionals (O'Neill, 2011). Other significant dangers include the possibility that, if assisted death is decriminalised, persons with disabilities may, over time, come to view their lives as less valuable than the lives of the able-bodied and may as a result request a hastened death. Underlying all of these concerns is the suggestion that acceding to genuinely autonomous requests for assistance in dying may, as social mores change and the practice becomes more widely accepted, compromise the autonomy of those who, for a variety of reasons, are less capable of asserting their rights. These are vital questions which are beyond the scope of the present discussion. It may be possible, however, that a more robust account of autonomy will provide the conceptual resources needed to distinguish requests for assistance in dying which are ill-considered or based on transient desires from competent decisions based on values which are transparent, cherished and consistently held.

Conclusion

What needs to be borne in mind is that the concept of autonomy, although it may be defined in different ways, represents a single ideal: the ascription to agents of a capacity to form values, and to commit to and express these values in the choices they make about matters which are important to them. This concept loses meaning if it is stretched so far that routine, everyday choices can in principle be described as autonomous, and similarly if constraints are placed on the content of what can count as autonomous choice or action. As a *capacity*, autonomy should be attributed to agents, whether or not they actually exercise it; it is in virtue of this attribution of autonomy as capacity that we are prohibited from overriding the will of others through coercion or manipulation. Ultimately autonomy stands for a rejection of the idea that people can be treated in such a manner 'that they can't share the purposes of those who are so treating them (Dworkin, 1988: 31).

On 5 December 2012, Marie Fleming asked the justices of the High Court to allow her to die peacefully and with dignity in her own home, surrounded by her partner and family (*Irish Times*, 5 December 2012). A former university lecturer, Ms Fleming described to the court the extent of her debilitation, the severity of her pain, the onerous medical regime she followed, her fear of losing her ability to speak and of choking to death, and her plans for her own funeral. She argued that accepting the level of medication required to relieve her pain would render her unresponsive and do 'an injustice' to the person she was. She wanted to die with the assurance that her partner would not be prosecuted for providing her with assistance. When her application to the High Court was unsuccessful, Ms Fleming appealed the decision. These are the actions of a competent, rational individual with a clear and settled desire to end a life which she found incompatible with her sense of what that life should be. It is difficult to see how the interests of the vulnerable can be served by condemning someone in Ms Fleming's situation to live a life so entirely at odds with her own purposes. This complex, tragic case and others similar to it highlight the value of autonomy and underscore the point that 'to respect autonomy only when it is cost-free or not socially disruptive is to fail to take it seriously' (Gaylin and Jennings, 2003: 45).

Notes

1 The terms 'assisted death' and 'assistance in dying' refer to the action of helping to bring about the death of a seriously ill person for compassionate reasons and encompass assisted

suicide, assisted dying (hastening the death of a person who is actively dying) and euthanasia. In the case of assisted suicide, the patient him- or herself performs the action that will result in death, assisted by a willing third party (either a doctor or a trusted relative or friend). In the case of euthanasia, a doctor or trained healthcare professional performs the action that results in the patient's death. Euthanasia may be categorised as voluntary, involuntary or non-voluntary. Although the starting point for this discussion is the issue of assisted suicide, the terms 'assisted death' and 'assistance in dying' will be used where appropriate – namely, where it is immaterial to the argument whether the patient or doctor 'acts last'.

2 Under section 2(4) of the 1993 Act, a prosecution for the offence can only be brought with the consent of the Director of Public Prosecutions, but the DPP may exercise discretion when determining whether or not to prosecute someone for assisting in the suicide of another. The DPP has published general guidelines for prosecutors but these do not specifically address the issue of assisted suicide. Ms Fleming requested the publication of guidelines stating the factors which would be taken into consideration by the DPP when determining whether to prosecute any individual who assisted her in ending her own life.

3 A range of challenges to the ban on assisted suicide have been brought in several jurisdictions, in which plaintiffs have variously claimed infringements of their right to equality under the UN Convention on Human Rights, and of their constitutional right to privacy and family life, liberty and security of the person: see e.g. *Rodriguez* v. *British Columbia*, [1993] 3 SCR 519; *Carter* v. *Canada*, 2012 BCSC 886; [2015] SCC 5 (Canada); *Vacco* v. *Quill*, 521 U.S. 793 (1997); *Washington* v. *Glucksberg*, 521 U.S. 702 (1997) (United States); *Pretty* v. *United Kingdom* [2002] ECHR 427.

4 Article 40.3.1 of the Constitution guarantees the fundamental 'personal rights' of Irish citizens, among them, the rights to personal liberty, freedom of expression and equality before the law.

5 In a famous essay from 1958, 'Two concepts of liberty', Isaiah Berlin distinguishes positive from negative liberty. Negative liberty is the freedom to enact one's desires without external interference, whereas positive liberty is associated with self-mastery: the ability to select and pursue goals and the identification with 'higher' part of the self.

6 According to Frankfurt, '[i]t is in securing the conformity of his will to his second-order volitions that a person exercises freedom of the will' (2009: 20). Critics of this account of different 'orders' or levels of desire object that the hierarchical account does not yet have an account of the '*agential authority* of certain higher-order attitudes'; what is needed is not an appeal to higher-order volitions, but 'evaluative judgements about "what is most worth pursuing"'. See Bratman (2005: 37–8).

7 Procedural accounts of autonomy, by contrast, define autonomy in terms of the processes by which an agent's motives and decisions are formed, independently of the specific content of the preferences or desires which lead a person to act (Benson, 2005: 126).

References

Battin M.P., van der Heide, A., Ganzini, L., van der Wal, G. and Onwuteaka-Philipsen, B.D. (2007) 'Legal physician-assisted dying in Oregon and the Netherlands: evidence concerning the impact on patients in "vulnerable" groups', *Journal of Medical Ethics*, 33: 591.

Beauchamp, T. (2000) 'The autonomy turn in physician-assisted suicide', *Annals of the New York Academy of Sciences*, 913: 111.

Beauchamp, T. (2005) 'Who deserves autonomy, and whose autonomy deserves respect?', in J.S. Taylor (ed.), *Personal Autonomy: New Essays on Personal Autonomy and its Role in Contemporary Moral Philosophy*. New York: Cambridge University Press, pp. 310–29.

Beauchamp, T. and Childress, J. (2001) *Principles of Biomedical Ethics*, 5th edn. New York: Oxford University Press.

Benson, P. (2005) 'Feminist intuitions and the normative substance of autonomy', in J.S. Taylor (ed.), *Personal Autonomy: New Essays on Personal Autonomy and its Role in Contemporary Moral Philosophy*. New York: Cambridge University Press, pp. 124–42.

Bratman, M.E. (2005) 'Planning agency, autonomous agency', in J.S. Taylor (ed.), *Personal Autonomy: New Essays on Personal Autonomy and its Role in Contemporary Moral Philosophy*. New York: Cambridge University Press, pp. 33–57.

Brock, D.W. (1992) 'Voluntary active euthanasia', *Hastings Center Report*, 22(2): 10.

Buchanan, A.E. and Brock, D.W. (1989) *Deciding for Others: The Ethics of Surrogate Decision-Making*. Cambridge: Cambridge University Press.

Callahan, D. (1992) 'When self-determination runs amok', *The Hastings Center Report*, 22(2): 52.

Callahan, D. (2000) *The Troubled Dream of Life: In Search of a Peaceful Death*. Washington DC: Georgetown University Press.

Christman, J. (2007) 'Autonomy, history and the subject of justice', *Social Theory and Practice*, 33(1): 1.

Commission on Assisted Dying (2012) *Final Report of the Commission on Assisted Dying*. London: Demos.

Conly, S. (2013) *Against Autonomy: Justifying Coercive Paternalism*. Cambridge and New York: Cambridge University Press.

Dworkin, G. (1988) *The Theory and Practice of Autonomy*. Cambridge and New York: Cambridge University Press.

Dworkin, R. (1993) *Life's Dominion: An Argument About Abortion, Euthanasia and Individual Freedom*. New York: Alfred A. Knopff.

Dworkin, R., Nagel. T., Nozick, R., Rawls, J. and Jarvis Thomson, J. (1997) 'Assisted suicide: the philosophers' brief', *New York Review of Books*, March.

Emanuel, E.J. (2012) 'Four myths about doctor-assisted suicide', *New York Times*, October 27.

Frankfurt, H.G. (2004) *The Reasons of Love*. Princeton: Princeton University Press.

Frankfurt, H.G. (2009) 'Freedom of the Will and the Concept of a Person (1971)', in H.G. Frankfurt, *The Importance of What We Care About*. Cambridge and New York: Cambridge University Press, pp. 11–25.

Gaylin, W. and Jennings, B. (2003) *The Perversion of Autonomy: Coercion and Constraints in a Liberal Society.* Washington DC: Georgetown University Press.

Gormally, L. (1995) 'Walton, Davies, Boyd and the legalization of euthanasia, in J. Keown, (ed.), *Euthanasia Examined: Ethical, Clinical and Legal Perspectives.* Cambridge: Cambridge University Press, pp. 113–39.

Gorsuch, N.M. (2006) *The Future of Assisted Suicide and Euthanasia.* Princeton and Oxford: Princeton University Press.

Jackson, E. and Keown, J. (2012) *Debating Euthanasia.* Oxford: Hart Publishing.

Keown, J. (2002) *Euthanasia, Ethics and Public Policy: An Argument Against Legalisation* Cambridge and New York: Cambridge University Press.

Marquis, D. (1998) 'The weakness of the case for legalizing physician-assisted suicide', in M. Battin, R. Rhodes and A. Silvers (eds), *Physician Assisted Suicide: Expanding the Debate.* New York and London: Routledge, pp. 267–78.

May, T. (2005) 'The concept of autonomy in bioethics', in J.S. Taylor (ed.), *Personal Autonomy: New Essays on Personal Autonomy and its Role in Contemporary Moral Philosophy.* New York: Cambridge University Press, pp. 299–309.

The National Commission for the Protection of Human Subjects of Biomedical and Behavioural Research (1979) *The Belmont Report.* Washington: United States Government Printing Office.

O'Neill, O. (2011) *Transcript of Evidence from Baroness Onora O'Neill to the Commission on Assisted Dying.* London: Demos.

Oshana, M. (1998) 'Personal autonomy and society', *Journal of Social Philosophy,* 29(1): 81.

Oshana, M. (2005) 'Personal autonomy and free agency', in J.S. Taylor (ed.), *Personal Autonomy: New Essays on Personal Autonomy and its Role in Contemporary Moral Philosophy.* New York: Cambridge University Press.

O'Shea, T. (2011) 'Autonomy and value'. Essex Autonomy Project Green Paper Report. University of Essex: Essex Autonomy Project.

Pearlman, R.A. and Starks, H. (2004) 'Why do people seek physician-assisted death?', in T.E. Quill and M.P. Battin (eds), *Physician-Assisted Dying: The Case for Palliative Care and Patient Choice.* Baltimore and London: The Johns Hopkins University Press, pp. 91–101.

Preston, T., Gunderson, M. and Mayo, D.J. (2004) 'The role of autonomy in choosing physician aid in dying', in I. Quill, T.E. and Battin, M.P (eds), *Physician-Assisted Dying: The Case for Palliative Care and Patient Choice.* Baltimore and London: The Johns Hopkins University Press. pp. 102–17.

Safranek, J.P. (1998) 'Autonomy and assisted suicide: the execution of freedom', *The Hastings Center Report,* 28(4): 32.

Salem, T. (1999) 'Physician assisted suicide – promoting autonomy or medicalising suicide?' *Hastings Center Report*, 29(3): 30.
Sumner, W. (2011) *Assisted Death: A Study in Ethics and Law.* Oxford and New York: Oxford University Press.

5

If they can consent, why can't they refuse?

Tom Walker

Introduction

Medical ethics and medical law both hold that where the patient is a competent adult (in Ireland that is a competent person over 18) it would always be wrong to give them medical treatment that they have refused. In contrast while section 23 of the Non-Fatal Offences Against the Person Act 1997 stipulates that young people in Ireland who are 16 or over can consent to medical treatment, it does not specifically include an entitlement to refuse treatment. As such, it would appear that in Ireland 16 and 17 year olds can consent to medical treatment but it is not clear that they can effectively refuse it (Law Reform Commission, 2011: 50–6; *HSE* v. *JM and Another* [2013] IEHC 12; *XY and McEvoy* v. *HSE* [2013] IEHC 490). This is not, of course, to deny that they can say they do not want treatment; it is to say that it is not clear that their refusal is sufficient to prevent them from being given the treatment. This situation is not unique to Ireland. Something similar is the case in relation to children's consent to, and refusal of, treatment in other jurisdictions, including that of Northern Ireland. In these jurisdictions while a child of whatever age can give consent provided they have sufficient understanding and intelligence to enable them to fully understand what is proposed, the courts have allowed this refusal of treatment to be overridden where this is judged to be in the best interests of the child (see Archard (2007); Gilmore and Herring (2011); Law Reform Commission (2011: 56–89); Cave and Wallbank (2012) for a discussion of these cases).

The idea that a person could consent to medical treatment but not effectively refuse it, however, seems problematic. This is because there appears to be a necessary connection between consenting and refusing. In consenting what the patient does is, in David Owens' phrase, shape the normative landscape (Owens, 2012) – they bring it about that it would not be wrong to do something that it would otherwise be wrong to do in the absence of that consent. As a result, if 16 and 17 year olds (who I will refer to as young people) can consent to medical treatment then it must be the case that it would be wrong to give them that treatment without their consent. Because of this close connection between consent and refusal the Law Reform Commission in its 2011 *Report on Children and the Law: Medical Treatment* recommended that 'legislation should clearly provide that, in general, a person who is 16 or 17 years of age is presumed to have the capacity to consent to, and refuse, health care treatment' (Law Reform Commission, 2011: 92), and that as a result in general terms 'a 16 and 17 year old would not be subject to any countervailing test, such as whether the specific treatment is in their "best interests"' (Law Reform Commission, 2011: 93). The Report recommends an exception to this in some cases where the treatment refused would be life sustaining (Law Reform Commission, 2011: 94–5).

In this chapter I want to argue against this proposal and argue that it is not required by the close connection between consent and refusal. There are in fact two ways in which we might set out this connection, each of which locates the source of the problem in a different place. The first focuses on the claim that it would be morally wrong to give a patient medical treatment without their *voluntary* consent, and argues that for it to be possible to voluntarily consent to something we must believe that it will not happen if we do not agree to it being done. The second focuses on the reasons it would be morally wrong to give a patient medical treatment they have refused, and the role played by consent in ensuring that giving such treatment would not be morally wrong. I will consider these in turn. As we will see, at least for the majority of cases, there is a fairly straightforward response to the first way of setting out the problem. In contrast, whether the second way of setting out the link between consent and refusal creates a problem will turn out to depend on whether young people are autonomous. If, as I will argue, they are, then there is a relatively straightforward argument to support the idea that they can consent to, but not effectively refuse, medical treatment. What will turn out to require further explanation, at least on standard ways of approaching medical ethics, is the idea that it is always morally wrong to give an adult treatment that they refuse.

The meaning of consent

Before starting, however, I need to say a bit more about consent. In practice a patient consents to medical treatment by communicating to the relevant healthcare provider their agreement to being given that treatment. However, as is well known merely agreeing to something being done does not always shape the normative landscape in the required way. As Stephen Wilkinson has pointed out, if a person issues a 'your money or your life' threat and you agree to give them your money, while you have consented (that is, agreed) to them taking the money it is nevertheless still wrong for them to take it (Wilkinson, 2003: 75). For this reason for a patient's consent to change the normative situation from one in which it would be wrong for their doctor to give them treatment to one where doing this would not be wrong, their consent has to meet certain conditions. These are standardly taken to be that: they are competent, their consent is given voluntarily, and they are sufficiently informed about what is being proposed (Gillon, 1986: 113; Wilkinson, 2003: 76–8). Where a patient's agreement to have medical treatment meets these three conditions they are said to have given valid consent. It is for reasons such as this that most work in bioethics refers to valid consent rather than simply to consent.

If we take the word 'consent' as used in the previous paragraph to refer to an agreement, then there will turn out to be no problem in holding that a person can consent to something but cannot effectively refuse it. As we have seen with Wilkinson's example there is no problem with being able to agree to something that you believe will happen anyway. To consent, however, also has a second meaning in English – to grant permission or to make permissible. When used in this way 'consent' refers to something that, as I put it above, shapes the normative landscape in a particular way. If a person consents to your doing something in this sense they make it the case that it is not wrong for you to do that thing (Feinberg, 1986: 177; Raz, 1986: 81; Manson, 2007: 297–8). On this way of using the word, in contrast to what was said above, you have not consented to the robber taking your money (though you have agreed to him doing so). It is consent in this sense, something that makes permissible an act that would otherwise be wrong, that creates the problem I am concerned with in this chapter. As such, when I refer to a patient giving consent for medical treatment in what follows I mean to refer to the patient making it the case that the doctor would not be acting wrongly were they to give that patient that treatment.

Can you *voluntarily* agree if you cannot effectively refuse?

The first way of setting up the link between consent and refusal rests on the idea that for a patient's agreement to make a difference to whether or not it is morally wrong to give them treatment, their agreement must (along with meeting certain other requirements) be given voluntarily. This is because a patient's voluntary agreement to have a certain treatment indicates that they have decided of their own free will to have that treatment rather than some other treatment or no treatment at all. In contrast, their saying they agree to the treatment in a situation where they believe it will be given to them even if they refuse indicates no such thing. In this case the choice they face is not between having this treatment and not having it (or having some other treatment), it is between going along with something that is going to happen anyway or resisting it. Their saying they agree to have the treatment in this case does not mean they have voluntarily agreed to have the treatment but rather that they have acquiesced to being given it. And acquiescing to something we take to be inevitable does not constitute giving permission (and hence does not constitute giving consent) for it to be done. It is for this reason that Neil Manson and Onora O'Neill argue that for a person to be able to consent to medical treatment they must know that they have a real choice about whether or not to have it (Manson and O'Neill, 2007: 93). If this is right then in order to be able to consent to medical treatment a person must believe that they have a real choice about whether or not to have it. But if it would be given to them even if they do not agree, then they do not have a real choice in this way. Hence, in that situation the fact that they cannot effectively refuse means that they cannot really consent.[1]

There is certainly something in this, but it may not be as big a problem as it at first appears. This is because the key point being made here is that a patient cannot effectively consent to treatment if they believe that they would be given it anyway. While there may be cases of this type when it comes to young people (those cases where treatment would be given to them if they refuse) there are many other cases that are not like this. That is, even if it were permissible to give a young person treatment they refuse, it does not follow that they will be given that treatment if they refuse it. It is in practice difficult to give medical treatment to a young person who does not want it, particularly where the treatment requires the young person's co-operation (as is the case where it requires them to take medication at regular intervals or to comply with restrictions on their lifestyle). In these cases for all practical purposes the young person has an effective veto over whether or not they receive the treatment, something they may well be aware of. In cases of this type it is not true that medical treatment will be given to the young person irrespective of what they want.

Because as we have seen in many cases a young person's refusal of treatment will not in practice be overridden (something that they may well be aware of) in these cases it seems that there is nothing in what has been said so far to show that they cannot consent to those treatments. Things may be different in those limited number of cases where their refusal would be overridden were they to refuse. Even here, however, whether the patient can voluntarily agree to the treatment will depend on whether or not they believe it is up to them whether it is given or not. If they believe it is then there is nothing to say that their agreement could not be given voluntarily, even if it turns out that were they to refuse that refusal would be overridden.

As such, while it is true that a person cannot consent to something that they believe will happen anyway, and so need to believe that if they refuse treatment this will not be overridden if they are to be able to consent to that treatment, this does not create the blanket problem for the idea that young people can consent that it appeared to. The points made here about the connection between consent and refusal show they are linked, but this link is very specifically tied to the details of the particular case. There is no problem, for all that has been said so far, in it being the case that young people can consent to some treatments (and in these cases if they refuse they will not be given the treatment) but cannot consent to others (those cases in which if they refuse they will be given the treatment anyway). That is, this way of setting up the objection does not show that there is a real problem with the combination of normative positions we started with (young people can consent to treatment but it is permissible to give them medical treatment even if they refuse). The problem dissolves once we see that the things they can consent to and the things that they cannot refuse are not one and the same.

Consent and respect for autonomy

The argument we have just been considering focuses on what the patient believes would happen if they refuse treatment. However, we could also set out the link between consent and refusal in a way that is not affected by the practicalities of giving patients treatment they do not want. Recall that consenting in the sense that is important here is a making permissible – in particular where a patient consents to medical treatment they make it the case that something that would otherwise be morally wrong, giving them the treatment, would not be morally wrong. This creates a necessary link between consent and effective refusal. If it would not be wrong to give a patient treatment they refuse then they cannot make it permissible for you to give them that treatment (and hence cannot effectively consent to that treatment) because it is already permissible for you to do so. On the other hand, if they can consent it must be the case that it would be wrong to give them the treatment without their consent, and hence wrong to give them treatment they have refused.

In the case of competent adults it is standardly held that the reason it would be wrong to give them treatment without their consent is that to do so would fail to respect their autonomy, and doctors have an obligation to respect their patients' autonomy. A patient's consent changes the normative status of providing treatment because it brings it about that in providing that treatment their doctor is not acting in a way that fails to respect their autonomy – something the doctor would be doing were they to give their patient treatment they have refused. As such, if the young people who are our concern in this chapter are autonomous it would be the case, just as it is with adults, both that they can consent to medical treatment and that it would be wrong to give them treatment they refuse. On the other hand, if they are not autonomous then it would not be a failure to respect their autonomy to give them treatment they have refused – and so would not be wrong on those grounds. In addition in that case they would not be able to consent – that is, they would not be able by agreeing to treatment to change the normative situation to bring it about that it is not wrong on the grounds of failing to respect their autonomy to give them the treatment. The reason for this is that you cannot change the situation to bring it about that something would not be wrong if it is already the case that it is not wrong. In the next section I will argue that there is at least one sense in which competent young people are autonomous and it is this that explains why they can consent to treatment. Then, in the final section, I will argue that despite this there will be cases where it is not wrong to give them treatment they have refused.

Are young people autonomous?

To be autonomous is to be self-governing. But what it means to be self-governing, and hence to be autonomous, can be conceptualised in a variety of different ways (Dworkin, 1988: 3–6; Arpaly, 2003: 117–48). Not all of these are relevant to discussions in medical ethics but even within this field different writers use the term in different ways (Wilson, 2007; Walker, 2013). In this section I want to argue that there is a sense of autonomy that both supports the idea that giving a competent patient medical treatment they refuse is wrong on the grounds that it does not respect their autonomy, and according to which the young people that are our concern in this chapter are autonomous.[2]

In order to be self-governing an individual needs to be able to do certain things. What they need to be able to do has been spelt out in different ways. Raanan Gillon for example takes autonomy to be 'the ability and tendency to think for oneself, to make decisions for oneself about the way one wishes to lead one's life based on that thinking, and then to enact those decisions …' (Gillon, 2003: 310). Gerald Dworkin, on the other hand, takes it that autonomy is the capacity to think about what one wants or prefers, and either to identify with those preferences (where this simply means that if one were to reflect on whether one really wanted these things one would judge that one did, or would be content to be a person with these wants) or to change them (Dworkin, 1988: 108). At its heart, then, this type of account says that autonomy is the capacity to think about what you want, to make decisions about what you want taking into account your aims and values, and then to act on those decisions.

That someone has a particular ability does not necessarily pose any obligations on others. For example, that I have in some sense the ability to learn Russian does not mean that anyone else has any obligation to teach me Russian. But the capacity for autonomy is not like this. We not only have this capacity, it is also important to us that we exercise it. There are both instrumental and intrinsic reasons for this (Dworkin, 1988: 112). When I exercise my capacity for autonomy to decide what to do, or what will be done to me, I make that decision taking into account my aims and the things that are important to me. Others, even where they care about me, will tend to make decisions about what is to be done to me on the basis of what they think is important. Because what I judge to be important and what others judge to be important may well vary, if

I make the decision about what is to be done then it is more likely that this will achieve my aims. As such, it seems that my life will go better if I am the one to choose what happens to me (Mill, 1859; Dworkin, 1988: 111–12; Owens, 2012: 166–7).

However, being the one to make decisions for myself is not valuable to me just because it promotes my well-being. It is also valuable to me because, as Dworkin puts it, '[t]he exercise of the capacity of autonomy is what makes my life *mine*' (Dworkin, 1988: 111). Because of this it is important to us as individuals that we be recognised and treated as individuals who have this capacity. As David Owens has put it, '[i]f I live in a society in which most people are allowed the choice of whether to wear a crash helmet whilst cycling, the fact that I (and people like me) are deprived of this choice will be demeaning. It carries the message that they are competent to decide this matter but I am not' (Owens, 2011: 409). That is, given the value that we place on being treated as if we have the capacity for autonomy, to fail to treat someone as having that capacity would constitute a failure to respect them as a person, and doing so can be very hurtful to the person concerned (for a similar view in relation to respect for persons see Raz, 2001: 169–75). The basic idea here is that failure to respect autonomy in this sense is morally problematic given the importance we attach to making our own decisions about how our life might go.

We can now see why giving an autonomous patient medical treatment that they have refused is morally wrong. To treat them in this way would be to fail to take adequate account of their interest in deciding for themselves the way their life should go and also fail to take account of their interest in being allowed to make this decision for themselves. If a doctor were to act in this way, they would be failing to recognise both the importance to the patient of making this type of decision for themselves, and the importance to the patient of being treated as someone who can make this type of decision. Instead of treating their patient as an agent capable of making up their own mind, the doctor would be treating them as someone incapable of doing so, or as someone who would do it so badly that they need someone else to make decisions for them. This would be a failure to respect their patient's autonomy in the sense we are concerned with here. On the other hand if a patient has voluntarily agreed to have a particular treatment then in making that decision they exercise their capacity for autonomy. In then giving them the treatment their doctor respects their autonomy (in the relevant sense). The doctor does not in any way set back their patient's interest in being treated as a person who can make, and be trusted to make, their own decisions. And nor do they set back their patient's interest in making their life their own and controlling what happens to them.

Having set out this account of autonomy and its relation to consent we now need to consider whether young people are autonomous in this sense. It seems that they are. Anyone who meets the criteria by which an adult would be judged as being competent to make a certain decision will also be autonomous (Dworkin, 1988: 111). This is because the criteria for being a competent person and those for being an autonomous person 'are strikingly similar' (Beauchamp and Childress, 2009: 113) to the extent that as Tom Beauchamp and James Childress point out, '[l]aw, medicine, and, to some extent, philosophy, presume a context in which the characteristics of a competent person are also the properties possessed by the autonomous person' (Beauchamp and Childress, 2009: 113). It is widely accepted that at least some young people meet these criteria. Furthermore, it would seem that 16 and 17 year olds have an interest in being recognised as able to make decisions for themselves, and take it that being treated as able to do so is important to them. The importance of shaping our own lives and making our own decisions, and of being treated as an equal in this respect, is not something that comes on overnight. It develops over time and as it does so our interest in being treated like an adult develops with it. Given this, if all those who are 18 have this set of interests, it must be the case that at least some of those under 18 also have them.

What we can conclude from this is that young people who meet the standard for an adult to be competent are autonomous – that is they have the capacities needed to be judged as being autonomous – at least in this context. We can also conclude that it would be wrong to give a competent young person medical treatment they refuse because to do so would fail to respect their interests in making, and being treated as competent to make, their own decisions about what is to happen to them. In this the wrong that would be done to a competent young person by giving them treatment they refuse is just the same type of wrong that would be done by giving a competent adult medical treatment they refuse. Similarly, just as an adult's voluntarily given, informed, agreement to have treatment means that in giving them the treatment the doctor would be respecting their autonomy, the same would be the case for the voluntarily given, informed, agreement of a competent young person. Because of this the young person's consent is needed in order to respect their autonomy (just as for an adult), and it would be wrong to give them treatment without that consent – to do so would be to fail to respect their autonomy (and hence wrong on the same grounds that giving a competent adult treatment without their consent would be wrong). Furthermore, because the interest that is being protected by the requirement for consent is an interest in a young person making their own decisions there are no grounds for holding that a different standard should be used to determine the capacity to refuse from that used to determine the capacity to consent. To do so would be to hold that whether or not a young person is autonomous, that is whether or not they have the capacity to decide which course of action to take, depends on what they actually decide.

Is it always wrong to give a young person treatment they have refused?

If what has been said so far is correct then young people who pass the (adult) threshold for competence can consent to medical treatment in exactly the same way and for exactly the same reasons as adults. It might appear that this means that it would always be morally wrong to give such a young person medical treatment that they refuse. In this section I want to look at a possible response to this point – one that would allow us to hold that, despite all that has been said so far, it is not always wrong to give a competent young person medical treatment they refuse. As we will see on a widely held position in medical ethics this turns out to be what we should expect.

The position we have arrived at is that it would always be wrong, because it would be a failure to respect their autonomy, to give a competent young person medical treatment that they refuse. However, doctors do not only have an obligation to respect autonomy. Standardly they are also thought to have obligations to act on the duties of beneficence, non-maleficence and justice (Gillon, 1986; Beauchamp and Childress, 2009). In practice these different obligations sometimes require conflicting things of us. A standard example to illustrate this would be a case in which a competent adult refuses treatment (and so ought not to be given treatment because to do so would fail to respect their autonomy) that is best for them (and so giving them the treatment is required in order to fulfil the duty of beneficence). In such situations one way of determining what we should do is to weigh the conflicting obligations against one another to see which is most important in the given circumstances (Beauchamp and Childress, 2009: 19–24). What this means is that something could be *prima facie* wrong on the grounds that it fails to respect a person's autonomy, but not wrong all things considered. This would be the case where some other obligation, such as the obligation to do what is best for the patient, outweighs the obligation to respect their autonomy. The problem, it might be thought, with the argument so far is that it fails to be clear about this distinction.

This general line of argument – which takes account of different obligations that doctors have – might seem to explain well the situation that we find with young people. They can consent to treatment. This is because it would be a failure to respect their autonomy were we to treat them without their voluntary informed agreement, but not a failure to respect their autonomy were we to treat them with that agreement. As such, their voluntary informed agreement to medical treatment changes the normative status of the act of giving them the treatment from one which is wrong on the grounds that it fails to respect their autonomy to one that is not wrong on those grounds. But because the obligation to respect their autonomy is only a *prima facie* obligation it can be overridden in some cases. Where the treatment is required to provide some considerable benefit to a young person the doctor's obligation to do what is best for their patient can override the obligation to respect the patient's autonomy. In such situations it is not, all things considered, wrong to give medical treatment to a young person who has refused it. In this way it seems that the practice by which the courts have overridden refusals of treatment by competent young people on the grounds that this is in their best interests is what is in fact called for if they are to support the moral obligations healthcare professionals have towards patients.

If there is a problem here it is that everything I have said about respect for autonomy and what it requires would apply equally to the case where an adult is the patient. If this is right then there would be cases where the obligation to respect their autonomy is outweighed by other moral obligations (Dawson and Garrard, 2006). However, it might well be thought that there is an important difference between the obligations that we have to adults and those we have to young people (even where they are competent) that explains the difference in the way that we treat refusals. This is that the obligation to benefit someone, or to act in ways that prevent some harm befalling them, is stronger when that individual is not yet an adult than it is when they are an adult. We have, it might also be thought, obligations to protect those who are not adults from harm (including harm that they might impose on themselves) that we do not have (or at least do not have to the same extent) when it comes to adults. Conversely, it might also be thought that we have a stronger obligation to respect the autonomy of adults than of autonomous young people. This is because our interest in being recognised as someone who is capable of making our own decisions, and for whom it is important that we make our own decisions, develops over time and is thus stronger when we are adults than it is when we are 16 or 17. As such, it is worse, so this line of argument goes, to treat an adult as if they were incompetent (or more colloquially to treat them as a child) than it would be to treat a 16 year old in this way. If all this is right then when we come to balance the obligation to benefit the patient against the obligation to respect their autonomy (which we will need to do in all cases where a competent patient refuses treatment that is best for them) this is more likely to tip in favour of giving the treatment (and so doing what is best for the patient) over not doing so (and so doing what will respect their autonomy) when the patient is a young person than when the patient is an adult. This will be the case even where the benefits of treatment are comparable in the two cases.

Conclusion

The starting point of this chapter was that there is an apparent anomaly in Irish law in that when it comes to consenting to medical treatment young people are treated in the same way as adults (their consent is needed and is morally significant) whereas when it comes to refusals of treatment they are treated in the same way as younger children (their refusal can legitimately be overridden in order to benefit them). The problem with this is that consent and refusal seem to be necessarily connected such that if one can consent then one can refuse, and if one cannot refuse then one cannot consent. The existing legal position therefore looks to be problematic, and has led to recommendations that the law be changed to make explicit that young people can both consent to and refuse medical treatment (Law Reform Commission, 2011: 92–3).

I have argued that appearances are deceptive here and that we should resist this move. It is important that we keep in mind two distinctions that are easy to overlook. The first is between cases in which young people can consent and those in which they are unable to refuse. The second is between things that are *prima facie* morally wrong and those things that are wrong all things considered. My argument has been that the young people we are concerned with in this chapter are autonomous in the sense standardly used in medical ethics – they have an interest in making decisions for themselves, an interest that their doctor should respect. Because of this it would be *prima facie* morally wrong to give them medical treatment without their consent, just as would be the case if they were a competent adult. But doctors also have another obligation – to do what is best for the patient – that can come into conflict with the obligation to obtain consent before giving treatment. Where the obligation to benefit is the stronger, then this will outweigh the obligation to obtain consent (that is, the obligation to respect the patient's autonomy). In such cases it would not be wrong, all things considered, to give the patient the treatment even if they refuse it. That is, the widely held account in medical ethics, that doctors have a number of potentially conflicting *prima facie* obligations, would support the current way in which young people's consent and refusal are treated.

The problem from the perspective of medical ethics is not with how young people are treated but with how adults are treated. In particular, it is unlikely that the position outlined here can support the idea that it is always morally wrong, all things considered, to give a competent adult medical treatment they refuse. It is important to note, however, that this does not in itself show that there is anything wrong with the law in Ireland as it stands. This will depend on the justification for the requirement that the patient's consent be obtained in all cases before treatment is given to a competent adult. For example, it may be justifiable to impose a blanket ban on giving treatment to competent adults where they have refused it if there is a risk that doctors might impose treatment on the basis that this is what is best for the patient – where this judgement reflects the doctor's own value system, and views about how other people should live – on patients with very different views about what is best for them. This is not the place to enter this debate. My aim has rather been to argue that the current situation in which young people can consent to treatment, but where it is sometimes treated as justifiable, all things considered, to give them treatment they refuse is both coherent and what would be supported by considerations of doctors' moral obligations to their patients.

Notes

1 This is not, of course, to deny that they can agree to being given the treatment. It may in practice be important to gain that agreement even in cases like this. It is much easier to give treatment to a co-operative patient than it is to give it to a patient who resists. But such agreement would not constitute consent – that is, it would not change the normative status of the act of providing the treatment.

2 In setting out this account I will be taking autonomy to be a feature of persons rather than a feature of choices – where an autonomous choice is an intentional choice made without controlling influences by a person who has understanding of relevant information – as occurs in some parts of the medical ethics literature (see, for example, Beauchamp and Childress, 2009: 100–1). The reason for this is that such accounts struggle to explain why it would be wrong to give a competent patient treatment they have refused where that refusal does not count as autonomous – for example because the patient lacks understanding of what is proposed (see Walker, 2013).

References

Archard, D.W. (2007) 'Children's consent to medical treatment', in R.E. Ashcroft, A. Dawson, H. Draper and J.R. McMillan (eds), *Principles of Health Care Ethics*, 2nd edn. Chichester: John Wiley and Sons Ltd.

Arpaly, N. (2003) *Unprincipled Virtue: An Inquiry into Moral Agency*. Oxford: Oxford University Press.

Beauchamp, T.L. and Childress, J.F. (2009) *Principles of Biomedical Ethics*, 6th edn. Oxford: Oxford University Press.

Cave, E. and Wallbank, J. (2012) 'Minor's capacity to refuse treatment: a reply to Gilmore and Herring', *Medical Law Review*, 20: 423.

Dawson, A. and Garrard, E. (2006) 'In defence of moral imperialism: four equal and universal *prima facie* principles', *Journal of Medical Ethics*, 32: 200.

Dworkin, G. (1988) *The Theory and Practice of Autonomy*. Cambridge: Cambridge University Press.

Feinberg, J. (1986) *The Moral Limits of the Criminal Law: Harm to Self*. New York: Oxford University Press.

Gillon, R. (1986) *Philosophical Medical Ethics*. Chichester: Wiley.

Gillon, R. (2003) 'Ethics needs principles: four can encompass the rest and respect for autonomy should be "first among equals"', *Journal of Medical Ethics*, 29: 307.

Gilmore, S. and Herring, J. (2011) '"No" is the hardest word: consent and children's autonomy', *Child and Family Law Quarterly*, 21: 3.

Law Reform Commission (2011) *Report on Children and the Law: Medical Treatment*. Dublin: Law Reform Commission.

Manson, N. (2007) 'Consent and informed consent' in R.E. Ashcroft, A. Dawson, H. Draper and J.R. McMillan (eds), *Principles of Health Care Ethics* 2nd edn. Chichester: John Wiley and Sons Ltd.

Manson, N. and O'Neill, O. (2007) *Rethinking Informed Consent in Bioethics*. Cambridge: Cambridge University Press.

Mill, J.S. (1859) *On Liberty*. London: John W. Parker and Sons.

Owens, D. (2011) 'The possibility of consent', *Ratio*, 24: 402.

Owens, D. (2012) *Shaping the Normative Landscape*. Oxford: Oxford University Press.

Raz, J. (1986) *The Morality of Freedom*. Oxford: Clarendon Press.

Raz, J. (2001) *Value, Respect, and Attachment*. Cambridge: Cambridge University Press.

Walker, T. (2013) 'Respecting autonomy without disclosing information', *Bioethics*, 27(7): 388.

Wilkinson, S. (2003) *Bodies for Sale*. London: Routledge.

Wilson, J. (2007) 'Is respect for autonomy defensible?' *Journal of Medical Ethics*, 33: 353.

6

Patient autonomy and responsibilities within the patient–doctor partnership: two sides of the same unequal coin?

Asim A. Sheikh

Introduction

The autonomous patient has the ability to engage with a healthcare provider in relation to his or her health on a wide range of issues. This ability and control are central to a patient's autonomy and self-determination. This chapter will consider whether this ability confers both rights and responsibilities upon patients. It asks whether the language and idea of the healthcare provider and healthcare receiver ('doctor–patient') *partnership*, which embraces the notion of patient autonomy, is one which also places responsibilities on patients as well as on healthcare providers.

In turn, what precisely does this mean, and more importantly for the purposes of the law, what precisely does this entail? A failure to fulfil the responsibilities on the part of the doctor has legal consequences, for example, a finding of negligence against a doctor. If the patient is also held to bear responsibilities, does it therefore follow that a failure to fulfil these, whatever they may be, might result in the imposition of liability upon a plaintiff/patient? Can a medical practitioner in a negligence action against him or her, make a plea of contributory negligence against the plaintiff/patient, for example, in a situation where an adverse outcome occurs or is contributed to due to a decision made by the patient? This chapter begins by outlining the duties and responsibilities of doctors and the development of the understanding of the doctor–patient relationship as one of partnership. It then analyses the implications of this, looking at the legal responsibilities of the autonomous patient in the context of an action for medical negligence.

Duties and responsibilities of doctors

It is axiomatic that a healthcare professional has duties, obligations and responsibilities towards a patient. Of this there can be no doubt ethically, professionally or legally. When one looks, in a very general way, at some core medico-legal issues which most commonly affect the doctor–patient relationship, for example diagnosis and treatment, consent and confidentiality, to name but some, the basic responsibilities are long-standing and generally understood. Irish law reports and texts are now replete with examples of obligations and responsibilities placed on medical practitioners by the courts directly or through implication of the facts, through the process of litigation. Therefore, where an accident and emergency department opens its doors to patients, medical services must be provided and patients must be seen (*Barnett* v. *Chelsea and Kensington Hospital Management Committee* [1968] 2 W.L.R. 422). Where a sentinel event occurs in any operative or medical procedure, the medical practitioner should record a note in relation to it.[1] Medical practitioners must monitor the medication of patients and also ensure consultation and communication.[2] In relation to assessing the standard of care in relation to medical treatment and diagnosis, in examining a practitioner's behaviour towards his or her patient in any given scenario where an accusation of negligence is made by a patient, the court will examine, *inter alia*, whether the practitioner was, 'guilty of such failure as no other practitioner of equal specialist or general status and skill would be guilty of if acting with ordinary care' (*Dunne* v. *National Maternity Hospital* [1989] IR 91, at 109, Finlay CJ).

In relation to doctor–patient confidentiality, the *Declaration of Geneva* (WMA, 1948–2006) states the basic premise of the doctor's pledge that: 'I will respect the secrets which are confided in me, even after the patient has died'. That basic premise is also stated in the current Irish Medical Council guidelines (2009: 14) as well as being a responsibility endorsed by the common law courts (*Hunter* v. *Mann* [1974] QB 767, at 772, Boreham J). Likewise in relation to the obtaining of consent, every medical lawyer will know Cardozo J's now over 100-year-old observation from the case of *Schloendorff* v. *Society of New York Hospital*, 105 NE 92 (1914), that, '[e]very human being of adult years and sound mind has a right to determine what shall be done with his own body; and a surgeon who performs an operation without his patient's consent, commits an assault for which he is liable in damages'. This is the basic commandment which every medical practitioner and healthcare professional is aware of: that he or she is responsible for obtaining consent from a patient prior to medical treatment. It is a commandment without doubt in principle, and has been endorsed by the Supreme Court in Ireland (*In Re a Ward of Court* (No. 2) [1996] 2 IR 79, at 156, Denham J).

Reflecting this rationale, the Health Service Executive (HSE) National Consent Policy (HSE Guidelines), outlines in general, the purpose and nature of consent in a healthcare context, emphasising respect for self-determination/autonomy, control, privacy and non-interference, while also maximising health and minimising harm (HSE, 2013: 21). A patient with full and undoubted capacity is entitled to indulge in a very wide range of behaviour from the most mundane everyday task such as driving a car or riding a bicycle, to engaging in lawful but risky personal, work or sports activities. Arising from this, and as is stated by Kennedy (1988: 53), 'a doctor has a duty to respect the integrity and individuality of the person before him. A more specific duty derived from this is the duty to respect the person's autonomy'.

In the spectrum of the wide range of behaviour that an individual is generally entitled to indulge in therefore, and in line with this respect for autonomy, the ultimate expression an individual can make in relation to their self-determination, is a refusal of medical treatment, especially if this were to lead to the individual's death. As noted by O'Flaherty J, 'consent to medical treatment is required in the case of a competent person … and, as a corollary, there is an absolute right in a competent person to refuse medical treatment even if it leads to death' (*In Re a Ward of Court* [1996] 2 IR 79, at 129).

The HSE Guidelines state that, '[t]he person who has capacity can make their own choices, however foolish, irrational or idiosyncratic others may consider those choices' (HSE, 2013: 30). These guidelines use the term 'responsibility' on 12 occasions in relation to the professional or the service provider. Similarly, professional guidelines which bind registered medical practitioners also discuss issues of the 'responsibility' of the practitioner vis-à-vis the patient. The Irish Medical Council makes it clear that, '[y]our paramount professional responsibility is to act in the best interests of your patients' (Irish Medical Council, 2009: 26). Other healthcare professionals such as nurses, social workers and radiographers also have ideals of responsibility placed upon them (Social Workers Registration Board, 2011; Radiographers Registration Board, 2013; Nursing and Midwifery Board of Ireland, 2014: 16). Again, the guidelines emphasise the responsibility which is placed on the professional.

The move towards a partnership approach

In observing the various professional guidelines above, there is a large degree of emphasis on the doctor being the 'responsible party' and it is this party that carries the burden of duty towards the patient. While it has been noted that a number of professional guidelines in various jurisdictions operate on the basis whereby, '[a]utonomy is seen primarily as a matter of non-interference' (Donnelly, 2010: 16), some professional guidelines have begun using the terminology of 'partnership' (GMC, 2013: 13–17). It appears that clinical professional guidelines have been undergoing a process of evolution. Traditionally these primarily discussed the responsibilities of the doctor. Then, they began to embrace notions of partnership, which entail patient responsibilities. Thereafter, they have gone further by encouraging the active engagement of patients in relation to professional responsibilities. In this respect, the HSE Guidelines also state that '[t]he relationship between those who provide health and social care and the service user should be *a partnership* based on openness, trust and good communication' (HSE, 2013: 21). The Irish Medical Council's *Guide to Professional Conduct and Ethics* (2009) also states that the relationship between doctors and patients is 'a relationship based on *partnership* and underpinned by *shared responsibilities*' (2009: 7). It goes on to state that '[m]edical professionalism is a core element of being a good doctor. Good medical practice ... *involves a partnership between patient and doctor* that is based on mutual respect, confidentiality, honesty, responsibility and accountability' (2009: 10, emphasis added).[3]

If this relationship is a 'partnership', it might be useful to first inquire as to the obvious: what is a 'partnership'? The classic dictionary definition of 'partner' is quite simply, 'a person who *shares* or *takes part with another* or others (esp. in a business firm with shared risks and profits)' (*Concise Oxford Dictionary*, 1990). However, an example of a business partnership as a comparator does not recognise the unique nature of the doctor–patient relationship in terms of the inequality of status between the doctor and patient.

Consequences of a doctor–patient 'partnership'

In considering the consequences of the move towards an approach based on a doctor–patient partnership, the question arises of whether the autonomous patient has responsibilities towards his or her healthcare.

Patient responsibilities

It has been stated that patients do have duties, certainly moral ones, in certain contexts. It is a developing area of consideration, and the issues of 'the reasonable duties and responsibilities of the patient are among the moody adolescents of the growing family of bioethics matters' (Evans, 2007: 689). It has also been argued that 'not allowing patients to carry moral responsibility for their own avoidable errors compromises their social role and personhood in the context of the systems they inhabit, and so may increase risks to patients' (Buetow and Elwyn, 2006: 262).

The American Medical Association (AMA) in its guidance documentation entitled *Patient Responsibilities* (1994–2001) is of the opinion that:

> Like patients' rights, patients' responsibilities are derived from the principle of autonomy ... This principle also recognizes the human capacity to self-govern and choose a course of action from among different alternative options. Autonomous, competent patients assert some control over the decisions which direct their health care. With that exercise of self-governance and free choice comes a number of responsibilities.

Other professional guidelines have also emphasised the viewpoint that patients have responsibilities in relation to their own healthcare. The Royal College of Surgeons of England (2005: 2) states that healthcare is 'a two-way process between you, the patient, and the staff who care for you'. The guidance states that a patient has the responsibility, *inter alia*, to attend appointments on time, to consider consequences of refusing treatment or not following medical advice and accepting responsibility for his or her own actions, to inform staff of allergies/sensitivities to medication, to give staff full information about his or her condition and medication, to inform staff of any change in health, to take medication as instructed, and to attend follow-up appointments as requested (2005: 3). The National Health Service Scotland (Scottish Government, 2012: 12) also tells patients to take some personal responsibility for their health, to take an active part in discussions and decisions about healthcare and treatment, to inform staff about changes in health condition, to follow advice in relation to medication and treatment, and to tell staff of any allergies or side-effects.

If we apply the idea of partnership to the doctor–patient relationship, it is undoubtedly the case that there is a sharing which takes place between the two parties. For example, a general practitioner (GP) receives an unwell patient and asks the question, 'What is the problem?' or, the patient may ask, 'What is wrong with me Doctor?' or words to that effect. The patient may then relay information regarding medical history, symptoms, duration of malady, etc., which may then be followed by an examination of the patient by the GP, a consideration of all of the issues, concluding with a diagnosis, or that further tests may be needed, or that onward referral is required. In this scenario, the 'sharing' or 'taking part' by the patient is in relation to the delivery of information to the medical practitioner about his or her medical history and symptoms, on foot of which an attempt can be made to come to a diagnosis by the practitioner. In this respect, in the 8th edition of Kumar and Clark's *Clinical Medicine*, it is stated that:

> Patient-centred care depends on a consulting style that fosters trust and communication skills, with the attributes of flexibility, openness, partnership, and collaboration with the patient … Patient-centred communication involves reaching the common ground about the illness, its treatment, and the rules that the clinician and the patient will assume. It means discovering and connecting both the biomedical facts of the patient's illness in detail and the patient's ideas, concerns, expectations and feelings. This information is essential for diagnosis and appropriate management and also to gain the patient's confidence, trust and involvement. (Bowman and Cushing, 2012: 8)

The authors go on to state the good balance, which they consider of relevance in patient-centred communication, and then explore the transaction of history taking in more detail in what they describe as 'the medical interview'. They examine the seven essential steps in the medical interview: building a relationship, opening the discussion, gathering information, understanding the patient, sharing information, reaching agreement on management and providing closure. They list listening skills and questioning styles as elements of gathering information stating that '[t]he way a clinician asks questions determines whether the patient speaks freely or just gives one word or brief answers. Start with the open questions ("what problems have brought you in today?") and move to screening ("is there anything else?"), focused ("can you tell me more about the pain?") and closed questions ("where is the pain?")' (Bowman and Cushing, 2012: 10; see also Judson et al., 2013).

Therefore, if this exchange goes according to plan, the patient will give the doctor all of the relevant information he or she requires, to enable a diagnosis and a treatment plan. The partners will both have played and shared their respective roles, which would confirm the ideal that '[p]hysician and patient are bound in a partnership that requires both individuals to take an active role in the healing process' (AMA, 1994–2001). It is to be noted that Bowman and Cushing (2012) place the burden of elucidating the information from the patient on the doctor, which would suggest that the doctor–patient relationship is not one which can be presumed to be of equality, as otherwise why would one partner have to go to all the effort of obtaining information from the other? The parties do not enter the relationship on an equal footing or necessarily with familiarity of context.

However, what if the partner suffering from the ailment, that is the patient, does not play his or her respective part, for example by not providing relevant or enough information to the doctor and which therefore has the effect that the doctor misdiagnoses the problem, which results in an unfavourable outcome for the patient. Is the patient, in the circumstances, to be held responsible for not fulfilling his or her role in the doctor–patient partnership?

The issue of communication arose in the case of *Collins* v. *Mid-Western Health Board and Anor* [2000] 2 IR 154; [1999] IESC 73. In this case, Mr Collins (patient) went to see a GP having been taken ill suddenly while at work (he experienced the sudden onset of a headache) (Sheikh and Cusack, 2000). He was seen on three occasions by a GP without an improvement in his condition. He was eventually referred by another GP to the hospital, examined and then discharged. After two days the plaintiff suffered a subarachnoid haemorrhage and was admitted to the emergency department but died five days later. One of the issues at trial and on appeal was in relation to manner and nature of the GP's history taking and in this respect the Supreme Court concluded that the GP had been negligent. Barron J found that:

> The second defendant was not expected to make the correct diagnosis. But he was expected to be in a position to know when his patient should be referred to a specialist ... In the present case, a question arises as to whether the second defendant was entitled to rely upon what he was told by the deceased. Obviously yes, but that did not absolve him from asking questions to establish that his patient had left nothing out that he as a doctor would have considered material to a proper diagnosis. Here, the information was given in reply to 'tell me all about it'. While

> that must be a good starting point, it should not be the finishing point also. He has to be satisfied that the patient has left out nothing which might be of significance to the doctor. Simple questions would probably be all that was necessary to satisfy the doctor that what he has been told does not mask anything else. ([2000] 2 IR 154, at 161)

In this case, there was an acknowledgement by the Supreme Court that it is not for patients 'to volunteer everything they can think of' ([1999] IESC 73, para. 21). Rather, the duties rest on the practitioner to elucidate details of symptoms and illicit appropriate responses.

While this might seem as if the bar is set high for GPs (Binchy, 2004: 45; McMahon and Binchy, 2013: 534), it seems to accord with the ingredients of a 'medical interview' as discussed by Bowman and Cushing (2012: 10–12). Therefore, in this particular relationship as seen in the *Collins* case, notwithstanding the fact that the patient did not volunteer the important information in relation to the sudden onset of headache, that failure did not result in any legal consequences for him, nor did this seem to be raised as an issue in the defence of the action, by way of a plea of contributory negligence. It should be noted that in the *Collins* case, there was no suggestion that the deceased was lacking capacity.

In the Canadian case of *Leadbetter* v. *Brand* (1980) 107 D.L.R. (3d) 252 (NS, Can) (Healy, 2009: 337), Mrs Leadbetter suffered severe brain damage following a cardiac arrest while under general anaesthetic during a dental procedure to extract teeth. It was claimed that there was a failure to take a proper history, which, if taken, would have disclosed a predisposition to cardiac collapse due to a history of high blood pressure, which was not fully disclosed. Therefore, the court was satisfied that an anaesthetist was 'entitled to rely on the answers given to him by his patient when there is nothing about the patient's physical condition to alert the anesthetist … The fact of the matter is that Mrs. Leadbetter failed to give correct information to Dr Brand. Had she told Dr Brand that she was being treated for high blood pressure, he may not have proceeded' (1980: paras. 49–57). In the circumstances, the plaintiff's case was dismissed. On a factual basis, the *Leadbetter* case can be distinguished from the *Collins* decision as in this case it was found that there was nothing in the patient's condition to place the practitioners on suspicion of any risk, whereas, in *Collins* the patient's continuing illness, and third-party information from family, should have put the practitioner on notice to enquire further.

From an examination of the cases above, it seems that where there are enough indicators and indices of suspicion to alert the doctor to a potential problem, he or she must probe further to discover what the problem may be, even where the patient has not volunteered all of the relevant medical information. However, where no such indicator or index of suspicion exists, then, if a patient fails to forward relevant clinical information which leads to an adverse outcome, a practitioner will not be held responsible for such outcome.

Therefore, the law does not expect that a patient is a font of existing medical wisdom with abilities to elucidate relevant history in its fullest to a doctor. This may be reflective of the understanding that there exist barriers to open exchange and interaction between doctor and patient in medicine even today. In this respect, it has been observed by Judson et al. (2013: 2325–6) that:

> The traditional paternalistic dynamic between patient and physician, though diminishing over time, looms as another barrier to patients asking questions. An asymmetry of power is inherent to the patient–physician relationship, not just because of differences in knowledge and experience but also because patients perceive that physicians can easily alter the level of service they provide.

Therefore, if there is a partnership in the doctor–patient relationship, it is unlikely to be a partnership/relationship of actual equality. The 'asymmetry of power' indicates the reality that '[s]uch a partnership does not imply that both partners have identical responsibilities or equal power' (AMA, 1994–2001). It seems that the two sides of the same coin may in fact be unequal, although it cannot be said with any certainty that there exists wide-ranging agreement on this point (Goodwin and Richardson, 2009: 249).

Contributory negligence

Notwithstanding any inequality between the parties, certain actions, or lack thereof, can have legal consequences where a patient subsequently brings a negligence action against the practitioner. The failure of the patient to attend to his or her responsibilities may allow the defendant/doctor to argue and plead that the plaintiff/patient is guilty of contributory negligence. If this plea is successful, it will have the effect of reducing any damages that may be allowed, and which are then apportioned in accordance with the fault of both parties.

Contributory negligence arises '[w]here, in any action brought by one person in respect of a wrong committed by any other person, it is proved that the damage suffered by the plaintiff was caused partly by the negligence or want of care of the plaintiff or of one for whose acts he is responsible' (section 34(1) of the Civil Liability Act 1961). The concept has been explained as follows: '[g]enerally, when the patient's negligence or the negligence of those acting for him proximately causes or contributes to the injury incurred, the patient's contemplated recovery is either barred or damages are reduced by the amount of negligence attributable to the patient' (Fraley, 1994: 109).

The stages at which contributory negligence may occur would seem to be, 'contemporaneous with or after the negligent conduct of the physician' (Hoyt, 1967: 149). In relation to the behaviour or the lifestyle choices of a patient prior to their interaction with the doctor, McMahon and Binchy (2013: 569–70) state that:

> Broadly speaking, it is not open to a doctor to argue that, because the patient who came to see him or her was, for example, a person who had abused alcohol, that some reduction in compensation should on that account alone be made … If the same patient insisted on drinking excessively *after* the operation, contrary to clear medical advice, the court would rightly reduce compensation to take account of that contributory negligence (as well as factoring this conduct into the issues of causation and quantum of damages).

The authors state that the defence of contributory negligence may arise in four circumstances: failure by the patient to disclose pertinent information, failure to comply with medical instructions, failure to undergo necessary medical treatment, and dangerous lifestyle choices (if such choices are made contrary to medical advice after treatment/advice is given).

Cases from other jurisdictions reveal that contributory negligence can be found if a patient fails in his or her duty to follow all reasonable advice and to procure any assistance that a doctor may require in treating the patient. Thus, in the Canadian case of *Dumais* v. *Hamilton* [1998] ABCA 218, the Court of Appeal reversed the finding of the trial judge that a patient was not guilty of contributory negligence on the basis that the patient was not told why it was dangerous to smoke. In this case, the patient had undergone a tummy tuck operation and had been told not to smoke. This instruction was also recorded in the records. The patient nevertheless did smoke and this led to tissue necrosis and loss of skin. At first instance, it was held that the loss was actually caused by the defendant's failure to advise adequately of the risk of skin loss. However, the Court of Appeal reversed and held that '[t]he proper question to ask is whether she took reasonable care of herself in the circumstances: … In this case, she persisted in smoking after the operation, despite clear and repeated advice from Dr Hamilton that she should not do so. In our view, that behaviour was not reasonable' (1998, para. 16).

The rationale of the decision has been questioned by McMahon and Binchy (2013: 567) on the basis that it seems to suggest that '[p]atients should defer unquestioningly to the wisdom of their doctor's judgement and act in accordance with it simply because the doctor has advised a particular course of action'. A similar approach to that in *Dumais* was adopted in the Canadian case of *Brushett* v. *Cowan*, (1987) 40 DLR (4th) 488; affirmed 69 DLR (4th) 743 (Newfoundland CA), where, although the doctor ordered the patient to use crutches, he did not advise her as to the dangers of not using the crutches. The court found that the plaintiff on her next visit to the doctor made no enquiries regarding the use of crutches. In this respect, the court stated that the plaintiff was required to do what was reasonable for her own safety and that in the circumstances, 'the reasonable course of action would have been to make enquiries of Dr Cowan to clarify what the proper use of crutches was … The plaintiff failed to do so' (1987: 495). As a result, she was found to have been contributorily negligent.

While a patient has a duty to mitigate his or her damage, generally it seems, a patient is entitled to refuse to undergo treatment which has been advised, if it poses any risk to the patient (*Morris* v. *Despain*, 104 Ill. App. 452 (2d Dist. 1902)). Further, the courts have found that a failure to disclose complete and accurate medical history can attract a charge of contributory negligence. However, and in line with the rationale of the *Collins* case, the 'patient is not required to volunteer information which the physician does not solicit from him. This qualification is based on the theory that the patient is not obliged to diagnose his own condition. The physician is responsible for making necessary inquiries' (Fraley, 1994: 111–12).

The doctor's duty to follow up, or failure to do so, has also featured in a number of cases and, perhaps in contrast with the Canadian cases discussed above, suggests the primacy of the professional responsibility over that of the patient. In the South Australian case of *Kite* v. *Malycha* [1998] 71 SASR 321, the plaintiff consulted the defendant, a general surgeon specialising in breast surgery on 2 December 1994. A biopsy was performed. The defendant had no record of receiving results of the biopsy from the pathologists. The defendant did not have any system to ensure results were received and brought to his attention. The defendant did not follow up on whether the reports were received, and did not follow up when the plaintiff failed to attend at a subsequent appointment. The pathology report from the biopsy indicated an underlying carcinoma. The plaintiff was later diagnosed with breast cancer and surgery was performed, but prognosis and life expectancy were worse than had the cancer been diagnosed in December 1994. It was alleged that the plaintiff should be liable in contributory negligence for failing to contact the defendant's rooms to obtain results of the biopsy and failing to consult with the defendant at a subsequent appointment. The court found in favour of the plaintiff and rejected the plea of contributory negligence. Perry J stated that he did not think that 'the courts should be quick to find contributory negligence on the part of patients who have put themselves in the hands of competent medical practitioners for advice and treatment. In general terms, Mrs Kite owed a duty to exercise reasonable care for her own safety and well-being. But her conduct must be judged in the light of the circumstances as a whole' (paras. 336–337).

In the New South Wales case of *Tai* v. *Hatzistavrou* [1999] NSWCA 306, the plaintiff was the defendant gynaecologist's patient for 12 years. She had regular check-ups for cancer. The defendant advised the plaintiff to have a precautionary operation and asked the plaintiff to arrange a time for the operation with the hospital. The plaintiff lodged the request for an admission form. In the ordinary course, the hospital would have fixed a date for the operation within about two months and notified the plaintiff. However, the hospital did not notify the plaintiff of any operation date. The operation was eventually done and cancer was discovered about five or six months later than it would have been if done when originally intended.

It was found that the defendant had not made any enquiry about the plaintiff not being scheduled for operation in accordance with his advice. The defendant had no follow up system for such eventualities and the cancer would have been discovered by the earlier operation had it been done. The plaintiff suffered damage by the delay and the court found the defendant liable. This was upheld on appeal. Priestly JA, found that:

> [W]hen a doctor is treating a patient for what may be a serious health problem, and the doctor thinks it necessary, even if only for prudential reasons, that the patient should submit to a particular surgical procedure, then the doctor has a continuing duty to advise the patient to submit to the surgical procedure, so long as the doctor/patient relationship is on foot. This does not mean that the doctor should seek to impose the doctor's view upon the patient against the patient's will, but it does mean that the doctor has a duty to keep the doctor's opinion and advice before the attention of the patient so that the patient can decide upon the patient's course in light of up to date knowledge of the doctor's opinion. (para. 75)

Powell JA, went on to state that:

> It seems to me that, in a case such as this was, in which a patient consults a doctor concerning what appears to be a persisting health problem, the doctor is, as a consequence of his being consulted, and with a view to restoring the patient's health, called upon to examine the patient; to carry out, or have carried out, such tests or procedures as might be thought necessary, or desirable, to be carried out to enable or to assist in, diagnosis; to diagnose the cause of the patient's problem; to determine what treatment is called for; to prescribe that treatment, or to set in train steps for that treatment to be given; and to advise the patient in relation to the condition diagnosed and the treatment prescribed or proposed. (para. 101)

In *Pidgeon* v. *Doncaster Health Authority* [2002] Lloyd's Rep Med 130, which appears to be the only reported UK clinical negligence case in which there was a successful plea of contributory negligence (Herring and Foster, 2009), the patient was held two-thirds responsible for her injury (cervical carcinoma) as she did not have smear tests even though she was told to have them done on seven occasions, and their importance was emphasised to her. The court, in reducing damages, found the claimant/plaintiff two thirds responsible on the basis that:

> It seems to me to be that in 1991 and 1994 it must have been brought home to her in particular that there was a need for testing that a failure to participate carried certain risks. To fail to attend once in 1991 was blameworthy and showed some unreasonable care for her own health and welfare; to fail to respond again in 1994 was doubly so, against a background of increasingly strong warnings from her GP. (2002: 136, Bullimore J)

In Ireland, the matter of contributory negligence and follow-up in a clinical negligence scenario came to be considered in *Philp* v. *Ryan and Bon Secours*

[2004] IEHC 77, Unrep. HC 11/3/04.[4] In this case, the plaintiff was suffering from prostate cancer. The crux of the matter was the communication to the plaintiff of a test (which showed increased level of PSA indicating cancer), which would have resulted in earlier treatment. Peart J found as a fact that the doctor had asked the patient to communicate with him and the patient had failed to do so. However, he also found that the doctor could not then 'sit back safe in the knowledge that he has now shifted to the plaintiff the responsibility for his future state of health and treatment, even to some extent' (at 9671). In examining the doctor's duty of care Peart J recognised the 'particularly dependent nature of the relationship between the specialist and his patient' and stated that 'in the doctor/patient relationship there is a total reliance placed by the patient upon the doctor' (at 9659–9660). In relation to contributory negligence, the court found that '[t]he plaintiff ought to have made contact with Mr Ryan, but was not guilty of contributory negligence by not doing so, since Mr Ryan never informed the plaintiff of what a PSA test was, and what consequences hung on the results' (at 9673).

In the circumstances and in looking at all of the cases discussed above, there is no doubt that patients have responsibilities. These responsibilities, or a failure towards them, can have both factual, moral and some legal consequences. While none of the cases are exactly the same in circumstance or legal outcome, they do highlight a number of important principles outlined below:

(i) It is unreasonable for a doctor to rely on the patient in relation to a follow-up appointment;
(ii) A doctor's lack of procedure to track and follow-up a patient, especially where the patient may not have received notice of an appointment, will be criticised and does not meet the required standard of care;
(iii) Patients owe a duty to exercise reasonable care for their own safety and well-being;
(iv) The whole of the circumstances will be taken into account. A plea of contributory negligence may succeed where the patient:
  - was fully informed and fully aware and knew what the procedure/test was, and the ramifications of not having the procedure/test done, and
  - having knowledge, was told to have the relevant procedure carried out or attend a follow-up appointment, but failed to do so;
(v) Even where a patient knows that he/she must re-contact a doctor and does not do so, the doctor must take steps to follow-up the patient. The doctor's responsibility in that regard does not shift to the patient;
(vi) As a result of the total reliance placed on the doctor by the patient, the issue of contributory negligence may differ in the doctor–patient relationship compared to other relationships.

Clearly, the courts take cognisance of the fact that patients do bear responsibility for their own safety, with the Canadian courts, perhaps, taking a 'more robust attitude' in this respect (Kryworuk et al., 2007)). However, the inequality of the relationship is clearly recognised by the courts, resulting in a reluctance to allow the medical practitioner to abdicate any degree of responsibility to the patient, that may be permissible in other types of legal relationships. Perhaps this does harken back to a paternalistic approach by the law, as seen in the *Philp* case, and as expressed by the Supreme Court in the *Dunne* case when it stated that '[t]he *complete dependence of patients on the skill and care of their medical attendants* and the gravity from their point of view of a failure in such care, makes it undesirable and unjustifiable to accept as a matter of law a lax or permissive standard of care for the purpose of assessing what is and is not medical negligence' (1989: 110, emphasis added). The words of the Supreme Court in *Dunne* in 1989 and of the High Court in *Philp* in 2004 indicate that in Ireland, from a judicial perspective, there still exists an inequality of power in the doctor–patient partnership and therefore, a hesitation in easily visiting a finding of contributory negligence on a patient/plaintiff. This attitude, as Herring and Foster comment, is reflective of a traditional paternalistic model where:

> The patients' role is essentially a passive one. They are taken to have no medical knowledge, and any expertise lies with the doctor. The job of the patient is to answer the questions asked and to do what the doctor told them. In short, there was little the patient can do that would be regarded as negligent, save outright lying to the doctor … There is little room for contributory negligence in such a model. (2009: 83)

Perhaps today's patient is not *so* passive, but perhaps neither is the doctor–patient relationship so equal? Can it be said that this imbalance of power or status within the doctor–patient relationship has, in fact and reality, lessened or disappeared in the last ten years since the *Philp* case, despite what guidelines might be perceived to suggest as being a relationship of equality?

Conclusion

Having briefly looked at the traditional placing of responsibility on the healthcare professional, it was then observed that clinical guidelines have emphasised that the doctor–patient relationship was a 'partnership'. In examining the potential nature of this partnership, it can be seen that it involves an exchange of information, which is clearly required for the purposes of diagnosis, treatment and ongoing care. Within this notion of partnership, it is increasingly emphasised that apart from healthcare professionals having responsibilities, responsibilities also reside with patients. However, the courts, while accepting that patients must take responsibility for their own health, safety and welfare,

are, generally, reluctant to allow an abdication of responsibility, which primarily resides with the practitioner. Nevertheless, the evolution to further involve the patient has continued to the extent that patients are increasingly being asked to get involved in matters traditionally reserved within the domain of professional responsibility. This has raised some concern. Is this attempt at 'patient empowerment' actually an attempt to gradually shift responsibility onto a patient, in relation to everyday matters of the patient's clinical health, such as pain administration, or areas pertaining to patient safety?

In this respect, caution has been advised in relation to programmes and guidelines which encourage patients to get involved in areas of patient safety such as asking healthcare professionals whether they have washed their hands, to having detailed knowledge of how medication is dispensed. Such 'advisories' seem to have been drafted in a manner whereby 'the emphasis is generally on actions patients should take to directly help ensure their own safety' (Entwistle et al., 2005: 492). Concern has been expressed that '[t]he advisories render policymakers and healthcare providers vulnerable to the suspicion that they are inappropriately shifting responsibility for the safety of professionally delivered healthcare on to patients' (Entwistle et al., 2005: 492). It has also been emphasised that '[e]ngaging patients in the safety of the care delivered to them, however, should not be taken to mean that the patients should carry the ultimate responsibility for the safety of the care that they receive. Patients can only function as a safety buffer (often, the very last one) in addition to those in the healthcare system that are already in place' (Davis et al., 2007: 260; see also Davis et al., 2011).

Therefore, while in theory, healthcare practice is slowly moving away from the paternalistic model of dealing with patients, there is a clear need to ensure that the provision of information to enable a patient to have a greater degree of control and understanding in relation to their healthcare, and which will ultimately lead to a better quality of healthcare, is led and driven by healthcare professionals and organisations, with a view, not to shift responsibility to patients but, to properly empower patients and to facilitate a patient to be 'in a state of being empowered' (Holmström and Röing, 2010: 171), and to take responsibility. This can only be done if the proper treatment information and contextual information is appropriately communicated to the patient in relation to their condition, diagnosis, prognosis and follow-up and future care.

While the mechanism of the plea of contributory negligence, utilised once litigation has commenced, may be a useful way of emphasising patient responsibility in certain circumstances, such findings of patient negligence will be carefully considered by the courts to ensure that there is no unreasonable attempt to abdicate responsibility from the party to the relationship who is still considered to be the more dominant (the doctor). Essentially, it appears that many responsibilities which patients may possess arise from being informed and knowledge being enhanced by that dominant party, if a patient's failure to meet those responsibilities is to have legal consequence in the form of a finding of contributory negligence.

It seems that the 'doctor who knows best' may still be a very useful individual in modern medicine – but as an ally, partner and carer to a less equal but fully autonomous patient and individual, in a context where both medicine and the law recognise the inequality between the two parties, while striving to lessen it. While the doctor–patient partnership may still lack equality, ultimately, as has been stated, '[e]ncouraging patients to ask questions is a start but needs to be part of a more fundamental re-engineering of health care toward a patient-centred experience in which white coats provoke more open dialogue and less apprehensive silence' (Judson et al., 2013: 2326).

Of course, when and if the balance of power changes, the courts in Ireland may be more inclined to take a more 'robust' approach towards autonomous and empowered patients who are regarded as being fully engrained with responsibilities, a breach of which would result in legal liabilities. At that stage, the two sides of the doctor–patient coin might be equal, or more equal than they are at the current time.

Notes

1 See *O'Sullivan* v. *Bon Secours*, Unrep., 2 April, 2004, O'Neill J. In this case, during labour a shoulder dystocia was encountered. To deal with this problem, the first defendant (obstetrician) in his defence stated that the plaintiff had been placed in a particular position. However, there was no note recorded that this had been done. The court commented that this should have been recorded.

2 See *Myles* v. *McQuillan and Anor* [2007] IEHC 333. In this case, the patient successfully took proceedings against the hospital on the basis of the mismanagement of her ulcerative colitis leading to extremely serious symptoms and consequences stretching permanently into the future. Quirke J found the defendant to be negligent on a number of grounds in relation to a failure to properly consult and communicate with the patient and her family and also in relation to the monitoring of her medication, of which the court was extremely critical.

3 However, the guide does not elaborate in any specific detail on the actual and precise nature of this partnership.

4 The matter was appealed to the Supreme Court but only on the basis of costs: [2004] 4 IR 241. Peart J also elucidated the principles of contributory negligence in *Hussey* v. *Twomey* [2005] IEHC 17.

References

American Medical Association (1994–2001) *Patient Responsibilities*. Opinion 10.2.

Binchy, W. (2004) 'Recent developments in the law of torts', *Judicial Studies Institute Journal*, 4(1): 8.

Bowman, D. and Cushing A. (2012) 'Ethics, law and communication', in P. Kumar and M. Clark, *Clinical Medicine*, 8th edn. Edinburgh and New York: Saunders Elsevier Ltd, pp. 1–16.

Buetow, S. and Elwyn, G. (2006) 'Are patients morally responsible for their errors?', *Journal of Medical Ethics*, 32: 260.

The Concise Oxford Dictionary, 8th edn (1990) Oxford: Oxford University Press.

Davis, R.E., Jacklin, R., Sevdalis, N. and Vincent, C.A. (2007) 'Patient involvement in patient safety: what factors influence patient participation and engagement?', *Health Expectations*, 10: 259.

Davis, R.E., Sevdalis, N. and Vincent, C.A. (2011) 'Patient involvement in patient safety: how willing are patients to participate?', *BMJ Quality & Safety*, 20: 108.

Donnelly, M. (2010) *Healthcare Decision-Making and the Law: Autonomy, Capacity and the Limits of Liberalism*. Cambridge: Cambridge University Press.

Entwistle, V.A., Mello, M.M. and Brennan, T.A. (2005) 'Advising patients about patient safety: current initiatives risk shifting responsibility', *Joint Commission Journal on Quality and Patient Safety*, 31(9): 483.

Evans, H.M. (2007) 'Do patients have duties?' *Journal of Medical Ethics*, 33: 689.

Fraley, L. (1994) 'The evolution and status of the contributory negligence defence to medical malpractice actions in North Carolina – *McGill* v. *French*', *Campbell Law Review*, 16: 103.

GMC (General Medical Council) (2013) *Good Medical Practice*. London.

Goodwin, M. and Richardson, L.S. (2009) 'Patient negligence', *Law and Contemporary Problems*, 72: 223.

Healy, J. (2009) *Medical Malpractice Law*. Round Hall Press: Dublin.

Herring, J. and Foster C. (2009) 'Blaming the patient: contributory negligence in medical malpractice litigation', *Professional Negligence*, 25(2): 76.

Holmström, I. and Röing, M. (2010) 'The relation between patient-centeredness and patient empowerment: a discussion on concepts', *Patient Education and Counselling*, 79: 167.

Hoyt, M.C. (1967) 'Contributory negligence as a defense in malpractice litigation', *Chicago-Kent Law Review*, 44(2): 148.

HSE (Health Service Executive) (2013) *National Consent Policy*. Dublin.

Irish Medical Council (2009) *Guide to Professional Conduct and Ethics for Registered Medical Practitioners*, 7th edn. Dublin.

Judson, T.J., Detsky, A.S. and Press, M.L. (2013) 'Encouraging patients to ask questions: how to overcome "white-coat silence"', *JAMA*, 309(22): 2325.

Kennedy, I. (1988) *Treat Me Right: Essays in Medical Law and Ethics*. Oxford: Clarendon Press.

Kryworuk, P.W., Ventresca, Y.S. and Chambers, S.D. (2007) 'With patient rights come patient responsibilities: contributory negligence in medical negligence actions', *The Advocates Quarterly*, 33: 207.

McMahon, B. and Binchy, W. (2013) *Law of Torts*. 4th edn. Dublin: Bloomsbury.

Nursing and Midwifery Board of Ireland (2014) *Code of Professional Conduct and Ethics for Registered Nurses and Registered Midwives*. Dublin.

Radiographers Registration Board (2013) *Code of Professional Conduct and Ethics*, October. Dublin.

Royal College of Surgeons of England Patient Liaison Group (2005) *Patient Rights and Responsibilities*. London.

Scottish Government (2012) *The Charter of Patient Rights and Responsibilities*. Edinburgh.

Sheikh A.A. and Cusack D. (2000) '*Collins* v. *Mid-Western Health Board & O'Connor* – GPs, hospital doctors, hospitals and their duty of care', *Medico-Legal Journal of Ireland*, 6: 1.

Social Workers Registration Board (2011) *Code of Professional Conduct and Ethics for Social Workers*. Dublin.

WMA (World Medical Association) (1948–2006) *Declaration of Geneva*. Geneva: World Medical Association.

7

Older people, human rights, law and policy

Mary Keys

Introduction

There is general recognition that the population of the world is ageing faster than at any other time in history and those over 60 are the fastest growing population worldwide. Almost 700 million people are now over 60. In 2050, that figure will be over 2 billion and for the first time in human history, there will be more people over 60 than children in the world – more than one in five of the world's population will be aged 60 or older (UN DESA, 2012). Gender is an issue in the midst of these figures, as there are twice as many women among those aged 80 and over.

This gender difference is also reflected in Ireland where women outnumber men in the over 60s by approximately 50,000. The number of people aged 65 and over will rise from the figure of 532,000 in 2011 to almost 1.4 million by 2046 (CSO, 2011). It is estimated that there are about 41,740 people with dementia in Ireland, with approximately 26,000 living at home. Approximately 4,000 new cases of dementia arise in the Irish population every year. The numbers are expected to rise threefold so that by 2046 there will be between 141,000 and 147,000 people living with dementia indicating a higher incidence than cancer or heart disease (Cahill et al., 2012).

One of the first challenges in articulating the rights of older people is to attempt to define them as a distinct group. Mégret refers to the fact 'that "old age" is a quite relative concept … making the exact boundaries of older persons as a group somewhat hard to ascertain' (Mégret, 2011: 42). They are distinguished from the rest of the population mainly by their age, which is difficult to defend since it is not age itself that creates a specific focus but the diminishing physical and mental capacities associated with ageing. The World Health Organisation defines ageing as the 'process of progressive change in the biological, psychological and social structures of individuals' (WHO, 1999: 4). It needs to be understood that not all older people have disabilities although the majority of people with disabilities are over 65 years. The Office for the High

Commissioner for Human Rights (OHCHR) states that from a human rights perspective:

> [A]ge is not merely a numerical designation, but a social construct based on custom, practice and the perception of the role a person plays in his or her community. The specific vulnerabilities of older persons can be the result of physical and mental conditions, but can also result from the obstacles encountered due to societal perception and the interaction of an individual with his or her environment. (UN OHCHR, 2012: para. 8)

This statement recognises not just the reality of impairment but also the barriers in society that may impact on vulnerability. Older people are not a homogenous group and should not be treated as such. Different experiences of old age apply to men and woman as well as between ages, e.g. people in their 60s compared with people in their 80s. The common experiences of older people are of stereotyping, discrimination, disempowerment and other social disadvantages, which accompany ageing (LRC, 2003). In Ireland, an Equality Authority Report confirmed that 'negative and ill-informed assumptions as to the relationship between a person's age and capacity all too often shape decision-making' (Equality Authority, 2001: 1).

The rights applicable to older people are currently scattered throughout international and regional human rights instruments making it more difficult to avoid fragmentation in government responses (Mégret, 2011: 51). There is a growing belief that 'strengthening older people's human rights is the best single response to the recognised difficulties' (Help Age International, 2009). Mégret argues for a human rights framework for older people 'focusing on justice and dignity rather than the frame of health and welfare, to avoid the problematising of old age needing a variety of solutions' (Mégret, 2011: 38). Governments would then have an explicit legal framework and guidance towards the realisation of the rights of older people.

This chapter identifies the area of decision-making as central to the protection of the rights older people. It addresses the recognition of legal capacity as a central issue to avoid choices being ignored and not respected. This chapter discusses some of the law and policy reforms necessary to meet these standards. Lessons from research in other jurisdictions are highlighted to avoid the pitfalls identified from similar law reform elsewhere.

Difficulties encountered by older people

The particular difficulties of older people being treated equally need to be recognised. In recognition of this, the UN developed the *Principles for Older Persons* (1991). The statement of the UN Special Rapporteur on the Right to Health, Anand Grover, is apt in this regard when he said in 2011, '[a]s you reach old age, you are more likely to be ignored, patronized, denied access to social security or healthcare, abused, forcefully medicated without your consent or denied medical treatment at all due to your age' (Grover, 2011: 4). Despite advances leading to longevity, large numbers of older people are subject to prejudice, stigma and discrimination. The Global Alliance for the rights of older people recognises that discrimination and ageism are tolerated across the world, and will increase due to unprecedented demographic ageing (Global Alliance, 2014). Ageism can be defined as the view that 'people cease to be people, cease to be the same people, or become people of a distinct and inferior kind, by virtue of having lived a specified number of years' (Johnson and Slater, 1993: 200). A right that may have been respected when the person is younger may not be well respected in older age, e.g. the right to make decisions for oneself. Describing ageism as 'pervasive for older people' in the research on the interface between disability, ageing and quality of life in Ireland, Murphy et al. found that:

> Ageism exacerbates the potential for exclusion that disability presents. There is evidence of rationing by age for participants through delaying care and provision rather than through overt denial of services ... one of the key features of being old with a disability in Ireland is waiting. People wait for services and appointments that sometimes never come. (2007: 29)

Specific difficulties arise in relation to medication and medical treatment of older people. The Health Information and Quality Authority (HIQA) monitors the use of medication in healthcare settings, where previously little information was offered, as to why particular drugs are used, or the possibility of adverse side-effects. Research confirms older people were more likely than other patients to suffer from over-prescription, being prescribed incorrect medication, and poor monitoring of side-effects (Royal College of Physicians, 1997; Oborne and Hooper, 2002). Treatment given without consent which results in severe side-effects should be used only where no less intrusive means is available (Council of Europe, 2010). These views are supported at UN level in the recognition of the 'intimate link between forced medical interventions based on discrimination and the deprivation of legal capacity' (Mendez, 2013: para. 30). As will be discussed, older people are at greater risk of being found to lack legal capacity and to be subject to discrimination on this basis. In light of the foregoing, it is more important than ever to focus on the identification of mechanisms by which the rights of older people are protected.

Human rights frameworks for older people

The UN carried out an analysis of the standards in international human rights law for older people in 2011. The report identified inadequate protection for older people arising from normative gaps, as well as fragmentation and a lack of coherence and specificity of standards as they relate to the experience of older people. While highly relevant human rights provisions such as recognition of legal capacity and equality before the law, and freedom from inhuman and degrading treatment, are contained in various international human rights agreements, few apply specifically to older people (UN OHCHR, 2011).

UN Convention on the Rights of Persons with Disabilities

While ageing and disability intersect, clearly not all older people have disabilities. The standards of the UN Convention on the Rights of Persons with Disabilities (CRPD) are nonetheless relevant to older people even though they are not designed with the older person as the key focus. The purpose of the CRPD is 'to promote, protect and ensure the full and equal enjoyment of all human rights by all people with disabilities, and to promote respect for their inherent dignity' (CRPD: Article 1). Equality and non-discrimination are the dominant values underpinning the CRPD. The CRPD does not include a definition of disability; instead an inclusive description states that 'persons with disabilities include those who have long-term physical, mental, intellectual or sensory impairments which in interaction with various barriers may hinder their full and effective participation in society on an equal basis with others' (CRPD: Article 1).

Disability is regarded as an evolving concept resulting from the interaction between people with impairments and the barriers that prevent their full participation in society on an equal basis with others. A person with dementia might be considered to have a 'long term mental impairment'. The focus, therefore, is not on a person's inability to participate in aspects of life, but on the difficulties created by the various barriers in society to participation. The focus is on the accommodations society makes to ensure that people are supported to maintain their capabilities and to lead a life of their choosing as far as possible. This is a fundamental shift away from the narrower medical model towards a social and human rights model of disability.

The social model differentiates 'impairment from dependency … [i]t refers to the possibility that dependency is created through social forces and social structures impacting on the ability of older people to take control of their own lives' (Murphy et al., 2007). As well as decision-making barriers, experiences shared by older people and people with disabilities include the barriers to living independently and being excluded from society (Council of Europe, 2013).

In a study on the quality of life of older people with a disability in Ireland one observation was that the disability movement has been more successful than the ageing sector in identifying and overcoming social obstacles to independence (Murphy et al., 2007). In contrast, the ageing sector tends to be excluded from participation in decision-making and rarely consulted regarding service provision or decision-making concerning living arrangements. The CRPD can benefit older persons, particularly Article 12 and the recognition of legal capacity, but also Article 3, participation in decision-making and Article 19 on inclusive and independent living.

The focus of the guiding principles of the CRPD in Article 3 is the inherent dignity and autonomy of the person and the freedom to make one's own choices. Article 3 refers to the 'full and effective participation and inclusion in society' as a general principle not restricted by any age limit. The UN Special Rapporteur on the Right to the Highest Standard of Physical and Mental Health endorsed 'the right of persons with mental disabilities to participate in decision making processes that affect their health and development' (Hunt, 2005: para. 59).

Article 12 of the CRPD states that 'persons with disabilities have the right to recognition everywhere as persons before the law ... [and] enjoy legal capacity on an equal basis with others in all aspects of life'. Quinn says that Article 12 'lies at the very heart of the revolution in disability – treating people as "subjects" and not as "objects"' (Quinn, 2009: 45). Access to support to exercise legal capacity must be provided and decisions must respect the 'rights, will and preferences' of the person and any measures must ensure appropriate and effective safeguards against abuse.

Legal capacity is the law's recognition of a person's ability to hold rights and duties, in other words to have legal standing and to exercise those rights, e.g. entering contracts to buy property, making a will, voting or marrying. It is the key to accessing legally recognised participation in society. Mental capacity on the other hand focuses on the person's decision-making skills or abilities, which may vary from time to time, from one decision to another and will vary between persons. Mental capacity is influenced by a wide variety of factors including social, emotional and environmental factors. There is a tendency to conflate mental and legal capacity in most jurisdictions so when a person is found to lack the decision-making capacity for a particular purpose, he or she is then deemed to lack legal capacity.

In contrast, Article 12(3) of the CRPD requires that the person retains their legal capacity and is provided with support to make a particular decision in order that his or her 'will and preferences' are respected. The requirement under Article 12 is to transition from a substituted decision-making regime, where someone else makes a decision for the person deemed legally incapable, to one based on supported decision-making. Bach and Kerzner refer to decision-making supports as including: life planning, independent advocacy, communicational, interpretive, and representational assistance and relationship building (Bach and Kerzner, 2010: 74).

Generally there are three approaches to assessing decision-making capacity: the status, the outcome and the functional approach with the latter recognised as the more recent development. Where the mere fact of, for example, being an older person with dementia results in that person being deemed incapable, this is known as the status approach, and is no longer acceptable. The outcome approach arises where the person is found to lack capacity because they do not agree with what is being proposed, for example healthcare staff believe the older person needs residential care but the person wants to go home (Williams et al., 2012; Emmett et al., 2013). Neither approach takes account of what the person wants. The law then facilitates substituted decision-making by delegating power to others to make decisions for a person informally or by making the person deemed to lack decision-making capacity subject to wardship legislation.

The functional approach uses a series of cognitive tests based on information and communication to test understanding and appreciation and is issue and time specific, allowing for fluctuating capacity. Although it is at the forefront of current reforms, there are a variety of concerns about the limitations of the functional approach (Donnelly, 2010). There is limited scope for the views of the person, their emotions or personal identity and connections. Herring suggests '[a]n assessment of capacity should be of an individual located within their network of family, friends, and care-givers' and not in isolation (Herring, 2009: 92). Dhanda believes that capacity determinations are discriminatory because they disproportionately affect persons with disabilities and are based on a non-disabled standard that denies legal capacity to those who cannot meet it (Dhanda, 2012: 181).

The denial of legal capacity affects a disproportionate number of older people, who are excluded from making decisions, resulting in a cycle of disempowerment and invisibility (Hammarberg, 2011; Lewis, 2012). In the important intersection between ageing and disability, reform of capacity law and policy presents one of the most important and urgent challenges facing policy-makers and legislators in Ireland. This right of legal capacity affects all other rights. Recent reports indicate that 40% of people in general hospitals in the UK have dementia (Department of Health, 2010). There is strong evidence that hospital admission 'hastens the transition from home into residential care' (Emmett et al., 2013). Although many older people express the wish to return home, others, like relatives and healthcare professionals, may view such a move as no longer appropriate. This disagreement may trigger an assessment of mental capacity and often the diagnosis of dementia is enough to have capacity called into question. Emmett et al. (2013) carried out research that addressed how assessments of capacity regarding choice of residence are actually performed on general hospital wards and how they compare with broad legal standards for assessing capacity set out in the Mental Capacity Act 2005 (England and Wales) (MCA). The research concluded that assessments of capacity, particularly when deciding questions of residence, 'should now receive closer scrutiny than ever before' (Emmett et al., 2013: 74).

Closely related to legal capacity is the right to independent living in Article 19 of the CRPD which involves inclusion and participation in the community, the choice of where and with whom to live, as well as access to a range of community support services. There is ample evidence that older people may experience pressure to move into particular residential settings in the absence of alternative supports (Murphy et al., 2007; Emmett et al., 2013). Some are institutional in ethos, in isolated places and offer little choice about any aspect of life. It is worth including the European Coalition for Community Living definition of an institution as:

> [A]ny place in which people who have been labelled as having a disability are isolated, segregated and/or compelled to live together. An institution is also any place in which people do not have, or are not allowed to exercise control over their lives and their day to day decisions. An institution is not defined merely by its size. (European Coalition for Community Living, 2012: 1)

The typically rigid routines that apply in both small and large institutions often result in disempowerment and loss of identity (European Agency for Fundamental Rights, 2013). Service providers assume authority in decision-making and in the efficient management of the lives of older people receiving services. Justification often centres on risk to the older person if they are not sent to a care facility. Parker and Clements argue that the real cause of risk is the absence of appropriate community services and supports (Parker and Clements, 2008). Less attention is paid to the threat to quality of life impacted by the paucity of community supports. The focus of financial support and monitoring is on residential provision with patchy attention paid to community support in spite of policy commitments (Ahern et al., 2007). Articles 3, 12 and 19 of the CRPD point to the challenges ahead which will require persistence and new strategies to move towards their implementation. The obligations and legal duties arising under these Articles provide clarification and direction for future development of the rights of persons with disabilities.

European frameworks

The Council of Europe acknowledges the discrimination and denial of human rights resulting from the interaction of ageing with social attitudes and other barriers and has focused on capacity and advance planning in anticipation of diminished capacity (Council of Europe, 1999; 2009; Parliamentary Assembly of the Council of Europe, 2012a; 2012b). While the European Convention on Human Rights (ECHR) applies to everyone in the Council of Europe region, specific references to rights for older people are limited. Despite this, many of the decisions of the European Court of Human Rights (ECtHR) are directly or indirectly applicable. Respect for human dignity and human freedom is at the core of the ECHR regardless of legal capacity status. The potential application of Articles 3, 5 and 8 of the ECHR, which are closely linked, are addressed here to explore their application to older people who have diminished decision-making capacity.

Article 3

Specific state obligations arise in relation to preventing torture, inhuman and degrading treatment in Article 3 and could apply where an older person is subject to various coercive measures including forced treatment, or to poor conditions in residential care (*Stanev* v. *Bulgaria* (2012) 36760/06 ECHR 46). In *Bures* v. *The Czech Republic* Application No. 37679/08, 18 January 2013, which involved the use of mechanical restraints in a healthcare setting, the ECtHR said Article 3 prohibits in absolute terms torture or inhuman or degrading treatment or punishment, irrespective of the circumstances or the victim's behaviour. It stated that 'physical restraints can be used only exceptionally, as a matter of last resort and when their application is the only means available to prevent immediate or imminent harm to the person or others' (para. 9). The UN Special Rapporteur on Torture addressed restraint in healthcare settings saying that even for a short time any restraint on people with mental disabilities may constitute torture and ill-treatment (Mendez, 2013).

Article 5

The purpose of Article 5 is to protect the right not to be deprived of liberty by having procedural safeguards in place. Apart from the Mental Health Act 2001 or where the person is a ward of court, there are no legal procedures addressing the admission and detention of older people who have diminished capacity in nursing home facilities (see O'Keeffe, Chapter 8). In these circumstances, Article 5 requires procedural safeguards establishing reasons for the detention and regular and independent oversight of the need for continuing detention (*HL* v. *United Kingdom* (2005) 40 EHRR 32; *Winterwerp* v. *The Netherlands* (1980) 2 EHRR 387). The placement must be a proportionate response to the circumstances of the person (*Litwa* v. *Poland*, No. 26629/95, ECHR 2000).

The question of impaired capacity and the deprivation of liberty arose in *HL* v. *United Kingdom* (2005) 40 EHRR 32. This case concerned a man with autism who was admitted to a psychiatric unit and despite his informal status he was sedated, not permitted to leave the hospital or to see his foster family for four months. The ECtHR set out the test for a deprivation of liberty under Article 5(1). The actual situation of HL was that the healthcare professionals exercised complete control over his movements and care from the outset including his assessment, treatment, contacts and his residence (2005, para. 121). The impact for him was that he was under continuous supervision and control and was not free to leave. The court concluded that he was deprived of his liberty in breach of Article 5 and without access to any safeguards. Deprivation of liberty is not always easy to identify due to being case sensitive but in *Storck* v. *Germany* (2006) 43 EHRR, the ECtHR focused on three elements: an objective element – a person's confinement in a certain limited space for a not negligible time; a subjective element – that the person has not validly consented to the confinement; and, whether the deprivation of liberty is one for which the state is responsible. Other decisions of the ECtHR indicate that the person should be consulted and their wishes should be reflected as far as possible in any protective measures applied (*Stanev* v. *Bulgaria* (2012) 36760/06 ECHR 46; *Mihailovs* v. *Latvia* (2013) No. 35939/10 ECHR 65).

Deprivation of liberty safeguards were introduced in England and Wales by the MCA to address the so-called 'Bournewood gap' exposed in *HL*. In a subsequent review these legal provisions were found to be unfit for purpose due to the large numbers of people being deprived of liberty without the intended safeguards (House of Lords, 2014). The Report recommended adopting a new approach based on the empowering principles in the MCA.

The link between a denial of legal capacity and the loss of liberty in a social care setting was established in *Stanev* v. *Bulgaria* (2012) 36760/06 ECHR 46 where a deprivation of liberty and a breach of Article 5 were established. Placed in partial guardianship without consultation and forced to live 'voluntarily' in an institution for eight years, Mr Stanev had been arbitrarily deprived of his liberty under Article 5(1). He had frequently asked to leave and have his legal capacity restored and to be released from guardianship but he was unable to access a court. The *Stanev* case highlights obligations on the state to examine life in community facilities where the subtleties of control and lack of personal choice require a rigorous approach to the recognition of legal capacity and to ensuring a truly supportive environment for older people (Tedstone-Doherty et al., 2007).

Article 8

Article 8 is highly significant for older people as it contains rights to respect for private life, family life and home and requires that any interferences with these rights must be justifiable and proportionate. In *Pretty* v. *United Kingdom* (2002) 35 EHRR 1, the ECtHR stated that personal autonomy is an important principle underlying the interpretation of its guarantees. Communication of information is essential to the success of personal autonomy and is particularly important for older people who may require support to understand the issues. Evidence from research indicates that information for older people is deficient and does not take account of vulnerable older people, particularly those with limited formal education (Sugarman et al., 1998). Often this is due to a lack of staff but also other resource constraints which impact negatively on the time available for discussion. Arguably, this affects frail older people more than others, particularly in the context of the need for more frequent review of treatment and medication. Informed consent policies are increasingly important in the context of the ageing population, pointing to the need to have sustainable systems of support in making decisions (HSE, 2013). It may be impossible to have advocates available when needed but Anand Grover suggests that countries should establish 'peer groups who would provide older persons with information before their visit to a doctor or other care provider for treatment' (Grover, 2011: para. 68) .

The right to respect for family life in Article 8 is relevant in the context of placement of an older person in residential care. This may be at a distance from family, or where one spouse has to enter residential care and the other spouse is placed in a different institution, effectively being forced apart. In an English decision, *London Borough of Hillingdon* v. *Neary and others* [2011] EWHC 1377, the court said that the principles in Article 8 apply directly to cases where the legitimacy of removal of a person from a family is in question. It referred to 'the primary question' of where a person should be living rather than solely focusing on the lawfulness of the deprivation of liberty. This indicates that what is required is a more proactive approach to the appropriateness of the living arrangements, taking account of what the person wishes, prior to any issue arising regarding a deprivation of liberty. Parker argues that Article 8 has the potential 'to extend to situations of passive institutionalisation – essentially where the care regime is constructed in such a way as to make institutionalisation the default option', where there are few services for people to remain in their own homes (Parker and Clements, 2008: 516).

Article 10

The rights of older people in residential care arose indirectly in *Heinisch* v. *Germany* 28274/08 21 July 2011, which primarily concerned a whistle-blower's right to freedom of expression under Article 10 of the ECHR. Heinisch, a nurse at a high support residential centre for older people, made several complaints to her employer concerning her work conditions, including a criminal complaint that the poor care exposed the residents to risk. She was dismissed without notice following the publication of a leaflet outlining her complaint. Placing the public interest at the heart of the judgment, the ECtHR recognised the vulnerability of older people and stated:

> In societies with an ever growing part of their elderly population being subject to institutional care, and taking into account the particular vulnerability of the patients concerned, who often may not be in a position to draw attention to shortcomings in the care rendered on their own initiative, the dissemination of information about the quality or deficiencies of such care is of vital importance with a view to preventing abuse. (2011, para. 71)

Law reform in Ireland

Law reform is underway in Ireland to replace the wardship legislation contained in the Lunacy Regulation (Ireland) Act 1871, which clearly does not meet international and European human rights standards. The proposed legislation is set out in the Assisted Decision Making (Capacity) Bill 2013 (ADM Bill). This legislation will also reform the law on enduring powers of attorney and will introduce advance healthcare directives.

Reform began in earnest with the Law Reform Commission (LRC) Consultation Paper in 2003, the *Law and the Elderly*, and the Report on *Vulnerable Adults and the Law* in 2006 (LRC, 2003; 2006). This Report included a draft scheme of a Mental Capacity and Guardianship Bill that in turn formed the basis of the government *Scheme of a Mental Capacity Bill*, 2008 (Department of Justice, 2008). This Scheme developed, with some amendments, including the title, into the ADM Bill. The title reflects the intention of the legislators to introduce a law aimed at supporting people to exercise their legal capacity.

Among the notable aspects of the ADM Bill is the removal of best interests as a basis for making decisions and the replacement of this with guiding principles which include the requirement to respect the 'the past and present will and preferences of the person' as far as practicable in any intervention. The ADM Bill includes a hierarchy of formal mechanisms with which people can be assisted to make decisions as well as provision for the appointment of a decision-making representative.

The perspective of older people must be central in developing capacity legislation and implementing this in practice. One issue of particular relevance to older people, which will give rise to challenges, is the decision about where to live (see also O'Keeffe, Chapter 8). The final part of this chapter identifies some of the issues which will arise in this context, drawing on the experience under the Mental Capacity Act 2005 (MCA) in England and Wales.

Capacity in the context of decisions about where to live

Research on the MCA indicates that, despite training, assessors of mental capacity are not adept at disentangling unwise decisions from an assessment that the person lacks capacity. In cases involving older people, the triggers for assessment frequently involve care and protection (Williams et al., 2012: para. 3; Emmett et al., 2013: 74). Many of the care decisions concerning people with dementia related to a change of accommodation. Outcomes for these people 'were often limited by resources, the availability of home care and the need to consider relatives' (Williams et al., 2012: para. 10) (see Murray, Chapter 3; O'Keeffe, Chapter 8).

Research indicates in relation to patients with dementia that 'professionals routinely made assessments that were outcome driven rather than based on an assessment of mental function … [w]here assessors did not agree with patients' decisions they were prone to interpret the decision as lacking insight and thus the decision maker as lacking capacity' (Emmett et al., 2013: 77). Understandably, concerns arise where the person wants to return home in a context of fluctuating capacity where the potential risks are unpredictable and the ever-present welfare, risk and autonomy tensions are heightened. Hospital staff are faced with responsibility to ensure the person is not unreasonably exposed to dangers, while at the same time balancing the need to support the person's will and preferences. The avoidance of physical risk tends to take precedence over the person's wish to be at home. One of the issues exposed in research is that the healthcare team is not always 'explicit' when examining the potential of long-term institutional care and instead use euphemisms like, 'somewhere where you can get a bit more help', which means the person is not making a decision on clear information. One of the conclusions of Emmett et al.'s research is that the MCA is not robust enough to assess the person's capacity to return home and that 'more specific legal standards, greater interventions and safeguards are required' (2013: 80).

Capacity to decide on residence arose in the English case of *Re KK; CC* v. *KK* (2012) EWHC 2136 (COP). KK was an 82-year-old woman with significant needs who had been placed in a nursing home and wished to return home. The court had to decide whether KK had capacity to make decisions about her residence and care, and whether she had been, or was being, deprived of her liberty. The court held that she had capacity to decide on her residence and was not being deprived of her liberty. The court stated that both professionals and the court must not be overly influenced by the 'protection imperative' and be drawn to an outcome that is unduly protective of the adult so much so that the capacity assessment is not detached and objective.

Referring to the outcome approach, the court pointed to 'the cardinal rule, enshrined in statute, that a person is not to be treated as unable to make a decision merely because she makes what is perceived as being an unwise one' (2012, para. 67):

> I consider her frank observation that 'if I fall over and die on the floor, then I die on the floor' demonstrates to me that she is aware of, and has weighed up, the greater risk of physical harm if she goes home. I venture to think that many and probably most people in her position would take a similar view. It is not an unreasonable view to hold. It does not show … a lack of capacity to weigh up information. Rather it is an example of how different individuals may give different weight to different factors. (2012, para. 73)

The court went on to emphasise the importance of the principle of the presumption of capacity illustrated in the case. It stated that 'a disabled person, and a person with a degenerative condition, is as entitled as anyone else to the protection of this presumption of capacity' (2012, para. 69). When decisions about changing accommodation for a person with diminished capacity are being made, the MCA provides for an advocate, called an Independent Mental Capacity Advocate (IMCA), where no family or friend is available. O'Keeffe believes that to force older people to live out their lives in institutional care against their wishes, 'potentially violates one of the most fundamental human rights – that of personal liberty – and is a decision which calls for robust legal standards and close scrutiny' (O'Keeffe, 2008).

Conclusion

The national demographic changes present an important opportunity for an examination of laws applying to older people, particularly older women, in order to ensure the optimum compliance with human rights standards and to reduce marginalisation. Reform of restrictive capacity laws based on proxy decision-making, often with no consideration of the wishes of the person concerned, is a key element in ensuring the visibility and voice of older people. The link between diminished mental capacity and deprivation of liberty requires specific attention. Supporting and enabling people to make their own decisions should be a normal element of good practice in any care environment. This might include specific communication strategies: ensuring information is in an accessible form, providing information over time and repeating it, or waiting to see if the person regains capacity to make the decision. The ADM Bill is expected to meet human rights standards and create a more equitable environment for older people and so it stands to make an important difference provided we are aware of the pitfalls and address them.

There is evidence from England and Wales that, despite training, those assessing capacity are not adhering to the requirements of the law, resulting in detrimental outcomes for the people involved. Assessing a person's capacity to return home or to move into a care environment will require a more specific focus on the issues at stake. Community supports are essential to ensure there is some choice offered so a real decision can be made. We have a long way to go and legislators and policy-makers should be prepared to listen and learn from the mistakes in other jurisdictions. In the context of this relatively innovative legislation, research findings from other countries are worthy of serious consideration.

References

Ahern, D., Doyle, M. and Timonen, V. (2007) 'Regulating home care for older people: the inevitable poor relation?', *Dublin University Law Journal*, 14(1): 374.

Bach, M. and Kerzner, L. (2010) *A New Paradigm for Protecting Autonomy and the Right to Legal Capacity*. Toronto: Law Commission of Ontario.

Cahill, S., O'Shea, E. and Pierce, M. (2012) *Creating Excellence in Dementia Strategy: A Research Review for Ireland's National Disability Strategy*. Dublin and Galway: DSIDC's Living with Dementia Research Programme.

Council of Europe (1999) *Principles Concerning the Legal Protection of Incapable Adults*. Recommendation No R (99) 4.

Council of Europe (2009) *Principles Concerning Powers of Attorney and Advance Directives*. Recommendation No (2009) 11.

Council of Europe (2010) *Recommendation of the Committee of Members to member states on the Protection of the Human Rights and Dignity of Persons with Mental Disorder*. Recommendation No R (2004) 10.

Council of Europe Steering Committee for Human Rights (2013) *Position Statement Concerning the CDDH Drafting Group on the Human Rights of Older Persons (CDDH-AGE)*. Strasbourg.

CSO (Central Statistics Office) (2011) *Census of Population 2011*. Dublin.

Department of Health (2010) *Quality Outcomes for People with Dementia: Building on the Work of the National Dementia Strategy*. London.

Department of Justice (2008) *Scheme of a Capacity Bill*. Dublin.

Dhanda, A. (2012) 'Universal legal capacity as a universal human right', in M. Dudley, D, Silove and F. Gale (eds), *Mental Health and Human Rights: Vision, Praxis and Courage*. Oxford: Oxford University Press, pp. 177–88.

Donnelly, M. (2010) *Healthcare Decision-Making and the Law: Autonomy, Capacity and the Limits of Liberalism*. Cambridge: Cambridge University Press.

Emmett, C., Poole, M., Bond, J. and Hughes, J. (2013) 'Homeward bound or bound for a home? Assessing the capacity of dementia patients to make decisions about hospital discharge: comparing practice with legal standards', *International Journal of Law and Psychiatry*, 36: 73.

Equality Authority of Ireland (2001) *Implementing Equality for Older People*. Dublin.

European Agency for Fundamental Rights (2013) *Legal Capacity of People with Intellectual Disabilities and Persons with Mental Health Problems*. Vienna.

European Coalition for Community Living (2012) *Position Paper: The Right of Disabled Children to Live in the Community*. Brussels. Available at www.enil.eu/wp-content/uploads/2012/07/Position-Paper_The-right-of-disabled-children-to-live-in-the-community.pdf (accessed 12 June 2015).

Global Alliance for the Rights of Older People (2014) *Report of the Independent Expert on the Rights of Older People*. First Annual Report to the Human Rights Council. A/HRC/27/46. Available at http://ap.ohchr.org/documents/alldocs.aspx?doc_id=23840 (accessed 11 June 2015).

Grover, A. (2011) 'Old age ... is it bad for your rights?', Statement of the Special Rapporteur on the Right to Health on International Day of the Older Person, 1 October, Geneva.

Hammarberg, T. (2011) 'Disability rights: from charity to equality', *European Human Rights Law Review*, 6: 1.

Help Age International (2009) *Strengthening Older Peoples' Rights: Towards a*

UN Convention. Available at: http://social.un.org/ageing-working-group/documents/Coalition%20to%20Strengthen%20the%20Rights%20of%20Older%20People.pdf (accessed 4 June 2015).

Herring, J. (2009) *Older People in Law and Society*. Oxford: Oxford University Press.

House of Lords (2014) *Report of the Select Committee Review of the Mental Capacity Act 2005: Post-legislative Scrutiny*. London.

HSE (Health Service Executive) (2013) *National Consent Policy*. Dublin.

Hunt, P. (2005) *Annual Report to the Human Rights Commission by the UN Special Rapporteur on the Right of Everyone to the Enjoyment of the Highest Attainable Standard of Physical and Mental Health*. E/CN.42005/51. Geneva.

Johnson, J. and Slater, R. (1993) 'Ageism: concept and definition', in J. Johnson and R. Slater (eds), *Ageing and Later Life*. London: Sage, pp. 200–6.

Lewis, O. (2012) '*Stanev* v. *Bulgaria*: on the pathway to freedom', *Human Rights Brief*, 19(2): 1–6.

LRC (Law Reform Commission) (2003) *Law and the Elderly*. Dublin: Law Reform Commission.

LRC (Law Reform Commission) (2006) *Vulnerable Adults and the Law*. Dublin: Law Reform Commission.

Mégret, F. (2011) 'The human rights of older persons: a growing challenge', *Human Rights Law Review*, 11(1): 37.

Mendez, J. (2013) *Report of the Special Rapporteur on Torture and Other Cruel, Inhuman or Degrading Treatment or Punishment*. A/HRC/22/53. Geneva.

Murphy, K., O'Shea, E., Cooney, A. and Casey, D. (2007) *The Quality of Life of Older People With a Disability in Ireland*. Dublin: National Council on Ageing and Older People in Ireland.

Oborne, C. and Hooper, R. (2002) 'An indicator of appropriate neuroleptic prescribing in nursing homes', *Age and Ageing*, 31: 435.

O'Keeffe, S. (2008) 'A clinician's perspective: issues of capacity in care', *Medico-Legal Journal of Ireland*, 14(2): 41.

Parker, C. and Clements, L. (2008) 'The UN Convention on the Rights of Persons with Disabilities: a new right to independent living?', *European Human Rights Law Review*, 4: 508.

Parliamentary Assembly of the Council of Europe (2012a) *Recommendation 1993 of the Parliamentary Assembly of the Council of Europe to the Committee of Ministers on Protecting Human Rights and Dignity by Taking into Account Previously Expressed Wishes of Patients*. Available at: http://assembly.coe.int/Main.asp?link=/Documents/AdoptedText/ta12/EREC1993.htm (accessed 11 June 2015).

Parliamentary Assembly of the Council of Europe (2012b) *Resolution 1859 of the Parliamentary Assembly of the Council of Europe on Protecting Human Rights and Dignity by Taking into Account Previously Expressed Wishes of*

Patients. Available at: http://assembly.coe.int/Main.asp?link=/Documents/AdoptedText/ta12/ERES1859.htm (accessed 11 June 2015).

Quinn, G. (2009) 'Resisting the "temptation of elegance": can the Convention on the Rights of Persons with Disabilities socialise states to right behaviour', in O. Arnardottir and G. Quinn (eds), *United Nations Convention on the Rights of Persons with Disabilities: European and Scandinavian Perspectives*. Brill: International Studies in Human Rights, pp. 215–56.

Royal College of Physicians (1997) *Medication for Older People*, 2nd edn. London.

Sugarman, J., McCrory, D.C. and Hubal, R.C. (1998) 'Getting meaningful informed consent from older adults: a structured literature review of empirical research', *Journal of the American Geriatrics Society*, 46(4): 517.

Tedstone-Doherty, D., Walsh, D. and Moran, R. (2007) *Happy Living Here: An Evaluation of Community Residential Mental Health Services*. Dublin: Mental Health Commission and Health Research Board.

UN DESA (United Nations Department of Economic and Social Affairs) (2012) *World Population Prospects: The 2010 Revision*. New York: United Nations.

United Nations (1991) *Principles for Older Persons*. A/RES/46/91.

UN OHCHR (United Nations Office of the High Commissioner for Human Rights) (2011) *Normative Standards in International Human Rights Law Relating to Older People: An Analytical Outcome Paper*. Geneva.

UN OHCHR (United Nation Office of the High Commissioner for Human Rights) (2012) *Report of the UN High Commissioner for Human Rights*. E 2012/51. Geneva.

Williams, V., Boyle, G., Jepson, M., Swift, P., Williamson, T. and Heslop, P. (2012) *Making Best Interests Decisions: People and Processes*. London: Mental Health Foundation.

WHO (World Health Organisation) (1999) *A Life Course Perspective of Maintaining Independence in Older Age*. Geneva: WHO/HSC/AHE/99.2.

8

Legal and ethical considerations in involuntary admissions to long-term care

Shaun T. O'Keeffe

Introduction

One of the greatest fears of older people is leaving their home and spending the end of their life in a nursing home. In a study of older Irish people living in the community, 87% wanted to remain in their own homes and half said they would not accept nursing home care even if they could no longer live independently (Garavan et al., 2001). Nevertheless, at any time about 5% of those over 70 years reside in a nursing home; overall, about a quarter of men and a half of women will reside in a nursing home prior to death (O'Shea et al., 2008).

Why is there such a discrepancy between the preferences of older people and what actually happens? When faced with the reality of losing independence, it is common for people to decide voluntarily, even if reluctantly, to go into a nursing home after considering their circumstances and the available supports. However, many, perhaps even a majority, of nursing home admissions are better described as 'quasi-voluntary' ('apparently but not really or superficially' voluntary) and a substantial minority of admissions are overtly involuntary (McAuley and Travis, 1997).

This chapter discusses the troubling legal and ethical issues raised by such cases. Current practice and the existing legal framework for involuntary admissions are discussed and it is argued that there is a need for safeguards in relation to such admissions in Ireland. The next part of the chapter deals with decision-making regarding possible involuntary nursing home admission. This includes consideration of how a functional assessment of capacity in such cases should be approached and the arguments for and against involuntary admission in the person's 'best interests'.

Quasi-voluntary admission to nursing homes

There are a number of aspects – each on a continuum from the acceptable to the unacceptable – to decision-making in such cases that might call into question the voluntariness of the person's decision to go into a nursing home. These include lack of involvement in planning, lack of choice and pressure from others.

Lack of involvement in planning

The common descriptions of 'placement' or of someone 'being placed' or 'being put' in a nursing home underline the frequent passivity of the person themselves. It is often the case, of course, that the lack of involvement of the person themselves is due to the same reason that a nursing home is under consideration, namely the severity of physical or cognitive problems and the fact that many admissions to nursing homes are precipitated by a sudden severe illness. However, family and healthcare professionals often fail to inquire about the person's values and preferences or fail to incorporate such preferences into planning for future care (Kane and Kane, 2001). This is troubling ethically. Also, the impact of admission to a nursing home is dependent on the degree of perceived control over entry: those who feel involved in the decision suffer less (Vlosky et al., 2001).

Lack of choice

Admission to nursing home care may be presented as the only possible option to deal with the care needs of a person. It is important that 'possible' not be conflated with 'reasonable' or 'realistic'. There are differences between care needs that (1) cannot possibly be met, (2) cannot be met because of deficits in the local support services, and (3) would best – whether most safely or most cheaply or with least cause for anxiety for family and healthcare professionals – be provided in a skilled nursing setting.

Social workers engaged in discharge planning in acute hospitals acknowledge a conflict between their duty to the person and that to the 'system' that aims for efficient discharge of patients. This is certainly a concern in an Irish healthcare system with overcrowding in emergency departments, delayed hospital discharges and often inadequate community supports.

Pressure from others

The distinction between strongly urging a person of the wisdom of entering a nursing home and using undue pressure or duress is not always straightforward. If people have care needs that cannot be met outside of a nursing home, it is reasonable and necessary to inform them of this fact. However, even if a person has considerable needs that cannot be met by the public health services, a discharge home can often be achieved if either (1) they can afford to buy and can access sufficient private care, or (2) if there is constant support and supervision by family and others close to them. The second is generally the cause of the most difficult conflicts in deciding where someone should live.

Many families do provide extraordinary care to enable people to remain in the community (see Murray, Chapter 3). The role of carer is often a difficult and exhausting one. Carers may have other responsibilities, such as to their own family; the physical demands can become too great; carers of very old people in particular will often themselves be aged and experiencing health problems; and supports such as respite breaks may be inadequate. The dynamics of individual families may also be a consideration. If the role of caring falls on one person, they may resent the lack of help from others in the family; on the other hand, inheritance issues – 'he's getting the house/farm so he should look after Dad' – are sometimes a consideration.

Conflicts between the person and those close to them are often stressful for them and for staff. Certainly older people generally prefer to stay at home but 'I don't want to be a burden on my family' is also a common priority. Family members who feel that a discharge home would place an unreasonable burden on them must be free to, and indeed encouraged to, express this view to the person. The person must also be free to express their views of what they see as their family's obligations.

However unpleasant and distressing these discussions may be – perhaps involving pleading, tears and raised voices – they cannot *not* happen in these circumstances. The role of the healthcare professional during such discussions is not easy: even when they sympathise with the views of family members, it is important that they are aware of the asymmetry of power, with perhaps several family members and professionals ranged against a person who is physically or mentally frail, and that the person is not browbeaten into agreeing to nursing home care.

Involuntary admission to nursing homes: current practice

At present, most involuntary admissions to and detentions in nursing homes are informal, with no oversight and no safeguards for those detained (or for staff in the nursing homes). This situation is, I will argue, unethical and unlawful.

Frequency of informal involuntary nursing home admissions

One UK study (Macdonald et al., 2004) (conducted prior to the introduction of mental capacity legislation) found that 6.1% of randomly selected residents of non-specialist nursing homes were prevented from leaving, of whom more than half had the mental capacity to decide whether to remain. Thus, about one in 30 residents were, *de facto*, unlawfully detained. It is likely that a similar situation currently applies in Irish nursing homes. Extrapolating from the approximately 12,000 annual deprivation of liberty applications in England (Care Quality Commission, 2014) suggests that the Republic of Ireland (with a population size less than a tenth of England) would have about a thousand such cases a year, although not all would involve a dissenting person – that is, someone who, whether or not they may have capacity, disagrees with the detention.

Mechanisms of admission

Hospital staff will be familiar with the 'engineered' acute hospital admission for the purpose of getting someone into a nursing home when they do not want to go. The admission to the acute hospital is often seen as having 'changed the facts on the ground': the person is now in a place of safety where staff have a duty of care not to discharge them back to an unsafe location and a responsibility to organise placement in a home.

Another approach is to persuade the person to enter a nursing home 'for a week or two' or 'to see if you would like it'. Sometimes the suggestion is genuine; often, there is no intention of allowing discharge. Marley (2013) is illuminating on what she calls 'compassionate deception':

> You can convince the person to go for a limited period of time, such as a week. Then you stretch it out to two weeks, then three ... You may also make arrangements for a facility to allow you to take the person there, saying you're going to visit someone there ... Then when you leave, don't take them with you. You will probably feel terribly guilty, but the person will almost certainly adjust.

Similar deceptive practices may be used by both hospital staff and families when people won't agree to nursing home care. They will be sent for 'convalescence' in a nursing home without any plan or practical means of discharge when that period ends.

Detention in the nursing home

In most nursing homes access to the outside world is via a locked door. While there is an obvious need to prevent unauthorised people getting in to the home, another goal is to prevent some residents from leaving. Visitors to nursing homes will be familiar with residents waiting by the door, often attended by vigilant staff, asking to be let out or to go home.

The residents who might be detained in this way are not a homogenous group. For some, detention may seem reasonable: some people with advanced dementia walk obsessively and without purpose; for others, the 'home' they want to return to means their original family home with their long-dead parents. Others, however, want to return to their own home and are prevented from doing so. At worst, if the resident vigorously asserts their wish to leave or attempts to leave physically they may be regarded as disruptive, aggressive or a risk to themselves, or others, and may receive psychoactive medication on that basis.

Detention in a nursing home does not always require a locked door. It is sometimes argued that the fact that the person cannot make their own arrangements to get home because of cognitive difficulties suggests that they lack capacity to decide whether to be at home. In fact, this changes the capacity question to one about the ability to arrange transport home! A second problem is that if someone with significant care needs is to go home successfully, it should be a 'planned discharge' with appropriate supports. A nursing home might argue that someone with such needs cannot just be allowed to walk out the door without such plans. In hospitals, this is the job usually of social workers working with members of the multi-disciplinary team. Few nursing homes have access to equivalent staff with the skills or willingness to arrange a complex discharge. The resident who wishes to leave is trapped: there is no way to arrange a credible discharge plan, and a desire to leave without such a plan will suggest irrationality.

Involuntary admission to nursing homes: legal framework

Current legal framework

At present the most common formal mechanism for involuntary detention in a nursing home is by taking the person into Wardship under the Lunacy Regulation (Ireland) Act 1871. Proceedings can be brought on the grounds that the individual requires to be protected from an identified risk of harm, and an order may be made that the person be detained in a long-term care facility (Law Reform Commission, 2005: 80). There is no review requirement in such cases and the Law Reform Commission (2005: 92) has noted:

> It is arguable that statutory provision for a person who has been made a Ward of Court to apply to the High Court to be discharged from wardship does not constitute an adequate review mechanism to address continuing detention in a long stay care facility or psychiatric residence having regard to case-law concerning Article 5 of the ECHR (European Convention on Human Rights).

An alternative approach is through the *parens patriae* jurisdiction of the High Court which involves the court acting in the best interests of an incapacitated adult. In *HSE* v. *O'B* (2011) IEHC 73, Birmingham J noted the need for safeguards and review: '[t]he orders proposed involve a serious interference with the right to liberty and that interference, if it is to be contemplated at all, must be reviewed on a regular basis and if it is to be continued will have to be justified on a regular basis' (2011, para. 25).

Finally, it is open to the donor of an Enduring Power of Attorney (EPA) under the Powers of Attorney Act, 1996 at section 4(1) to provide for his or her attorney to be given power over personal care decisions including where and 'with whom the donor should live'. There are some indications that in practice this is being interpreted as permitting involuntary placement in a nursing home, again with no adequate review or appeal mechanism. It is arguably unlikely that the potential for an EPA to be used in this way is highlighted to or understood by the donors.

The need for safeguards in relation to the deprivation of liberty in Ireland

Article 5(1)(e) of the ECHR states that no one shall be deprived of his or her liberty except 'in accordance with a procedure prescribed by law', while Article 5(4) states '[e]veryone who is deprived of his liberty … shall be entitled to take proceedings by which the lawfulness of his detention shall be decided speedily by a court'.

The important judgment of the European Court of Human Rights (ECtHR) in *HL* v. *United Kingdom* (2005) 40 EHRR 761, also known as the 'Bournewood case,' confirmed that detaining people in settings such as nursing homes where healthcare professionals 'exercise complete and effective control over [their] care and movements [and people are] under continuous supervision and control and … not free to leave' (2005, para. 91) (irrespective indeed of whether or not they are actively seeking liberty) is an unlawful deprivation of liberty under the ECHR unless a legal procedure has been followed and there is ready access to a procedure to appeal the detention.

While this decision represented an apparent shift from the decision in *HM* v. *Switzerland* (2004) 38 EHRR 314, in which it was held that placing an elderly woman in a nursing home to ensure medical care and satisfactory living conditions did not amount to a deprivation of liberty within the meaning of Article 5, distinguishing features between the cases were noted (2005, para. 93) such as that HM subsequently agreed to stay in the nursing home which 'was an open institution which allowed freedom of movement and encouraged contacts with the outside world'. Furthermore, the more recent decision in *Stanev* v. *Bulgaria* (2012) 55 EHRR 22, affirms the rights of individuals as contained in Article 5 in the context of admission to care homes.

The Supreme Court in *EH* v. *St Vincent's Hospital* [2009] IESC 46 (as followed by the High Court in *MK* v. *Clinical Director of St Patrick's University Hospital* [2013] IEHC 409) found that voluntary patients in psychiatric units, who are also not entitled to safeguards under the Mental Health Act 2001, are not deprived of their liberty in a situation of informal detention. In considering the relevance of these decisions to people who are informally detained in nursing homes, it is important to consider the particular facts of these cases: the period at issue was ten days in both *EH* and *MK* after which all of the statutory protections and procedures of the Mental Health Act 2001 were fully restored, and it was common cause that both patients were suffering from serious mental illness. Kearns J stated in *EH* that '[t]o the extent that the applicant was at any time denied the benefit of certain procedural protections, it is absurd and unreal to suggest that she was removed at any point from the protection of the Act of 2001' (2009, para. 46).

People formally detained under the Mental Health Act 2001 are detained for a certain time period with automatic review and are entitled to legal representation, to communicate with the Inspector of Mental Health Services, to have the detention reviewed by a tribunal and to appeal to the Circuit Court against a decision of a tribunal (see Whelan, Chapter 14). In contrast, those informally detained in a nursing home have none of these safeguards and have no due process or reasonably accessible procedure for appeal. Compared to the 'mere technical defects' raised in *EH* (2009, para. 50), the problems for those involuntarily detained in nursing homes seem consistent with what O'Higgins CJ described in *State (McDonagh)* v. *Frawley* [1978] IR 131 as 'such a default of fundamental requirements that the detention may be said to be wanting in due process of law' (1978, para. 136), and it seems probable that this current Irish practice is in breach of the ECHR.

At present, there is no information on possible deprivation of liberty safeguards in Irish legislation, although these are essential. There is no fair basis for saying that people detained in a nursing home – a detention which, given the age of many of those detained and the progressive nature of many of the conditions that have triggered detention, will often be for the rest of the person's life – should receive no scrutiny at all.

This does not mean that the same procedure as is required for involuntary admission to an approved centre under the Mental Health Act 2001 needs be followed. The UK government, in its response to the Bournewood case, considered extending the provisions of its mental health laws to those lacking capacity but ultimately opted for a new 'protective care' system where authority for a person's detention is provided by clinician assessors rather than by a court or tribunal. The safeguards introduced, which are known as the Deprivation of Liberty Safeguards, are admittedly complex and time-consuming and concerns have been expressed that they are poorly understood in many nursing homes and hospitals (Richardson, 2010). Nevertheless, the overall impact of this approach seems to have been positive and cases, such as the widely reported Court of Protection case of *Westminster City Council* v. *Sykes* [2014] EWHC B9 (COP) attest to the nuanced and compassionate decision-making that can result.

Decision-making regarding involuntary nursing home admissions

The Assisted Decision-Making (Capacity) Bill 2013 when enacted will introduce some important principles, including a functional (decision-specific) approach to capacity, a rebuttable presumption of capacity, use of the least restrictive interventions possible for those who may lack capacity and an emphasis on the will and preferences of such people.

In contrast to the 'all or nothing' approach to capacity exemplified by wardship, the functional approach to capacity is intended to maximise the ability of people with cognitive difficulties to make their own decisions. It is important that this spirit is respected in the interpretation and implementation of capacity legislation by healthcare professionals, by courts and in any codes of practice drawn up to guide decision-making.

Decisions that someone lacks capacity to decide where they should live *and* that as a result they should be detained involuntarily in a nursing home must be discussed separately. The fact that they are separate issues is often misunderstood and it is common to find the attitude among healthcare professionals of 'if they lack capacity surely we can decide'.

Functional assessment of capacity to decide where to live

The issue of capacity is often poorly understood by healthcare staff. Misuse of cognitive testing is one common problem. Screening (not diagnostic) tests for dementia are sometimes misinterpreted as providing definitive evidence about capacity. Most are highly influenced by verbal skills and educational levels, and the questions asked such as naming the Taoiseach are not relevant to any likely healthcare decision. The presumption of capacity is often disregarded in practice with dementia, for example, being seen in effect as reversing that presumption and meaning 'convince me you have capacity'. As Molloy et al. (1999) have stated, 'the onus is on society to show that an adequate trigger exists to challenge [this presumption]' (1993: 23). Staff often worry that they will be blamed if a person goes home and something goes wrong. This may lead them to request capacity assessments whenever people are taking risks as an insurance against criticism.

Finally, there is often a belief that a capacity assessment is a simple affair, even when the issue is as monumental as possibly depriving someone of their liberty. The importance of maximising capacity to make any decision by taking time to educate the person, by waiting until delirium has resolved and of encouraging and facilitating their involvement in decision-making are often poorly understood.

Applying the functional test

Clinicians should be honest about the purpose of the assessment if there is a real chance that a finding of incapacity may lead to loss of liberty (O'Keeffe, 2008). The Assisted Decision-Making (Capacity) Bill 2013 states that somebody lacks capacity to make a decision if he or she is unable: (1) to understand the information relevant to the decision, (2) to retain that information, (3) to use or weigh that information as part of the process of making the decision, or (4) to communicate his or her decision.

For decisions regarding where to live, the relevant information for a person concerns (1) his or her disabilities and care needs, (2) any relevant supports or lack of supports, and (3) the reasonably foreseeable consequences of any options, that is the benefits and hazards of remaining at home *and* the benefits and hazards of nursing home care. It is important, as Munby J stated in *Re MM (an adult)* [2007] EWHC 2003 (Fam), that the risk of future harm 'is a real possibility, rather than a merely fanciful risk, of such harm'.

If someone has significant memory problems, they may have difficulty recalling problems that have arisen and feel that others reporting them are being untruthful or are greatly exaggerating such problems. It is essential that an assessor make every effort to persuade the person to accept the facts, including an explanation that failure to so do may impact on the outcome of assessment.

Any uncertainty should be honestly presented by the assessor. An assertion that failure to give a blood transfusion to someone with severe haemorrhaging, for example, carries a high risk of death can be given with a high level of certainty. In contrast, falls risk prediction cannot generally be made with anything like the same degree of confidence, and there is little evidence that admission to a nursing home – unless it involves a usually unacceptable degree of restraint – will reduce the risk of falls.

Capacity assessment is not a memory test: information need be retained only for long enough to weigh it in the balance in reaching a decision. Reaching an identical decision following each discussion even if the information provided and discussion is forgotten a few minutes later is a sign of consistency of reasoning.

For some people going home irrespective of the risks or difficulties is a non-negotiable preference. It is certainly easier for an assessor to agree that someone is weighing the information provided if the person engages in or can provide an 'on the one hand, but on the other' type of explanation of their thought processes. However much a desire to go home 'no matter what' may be regarded as unrealistic or very unwise, it is a commonly held view rather than one that is so unusual or eccentric that it would reasonably call someone's rationality into question. The assessor should seek any general views or personal philosophy or experiences that would show the reasoning involved: a poor experience with a nursing home, a statement – or agreement – that they would value liberty over security or quality of life over duration of life or would rather run the risk of an unpleasant death at home than live safely in a home would all be helpful. Most people who refuse a nursing home are clear and consistent in their views. A lack of clarity or consistency reasonably raises questions about capacity.

Assessment of best interests in involuntary admission to a nursing home

'Best interests' has in the past been used as a shortcut or mechanism to disregard people's preferences regarding their own care. In contrast, it is important to consider 'best interests' in a broad sense, including the person's view of what a good life means to them. This approach is reflected in the guiding principles set out in the Assisted Decision-Making (Capacity) Bill 2013. People, even if lacking capacity, are generally the best judges of what is in their interests; it is not just a matter of 'safety first' or what is medically recommended. Many people value liberty above safety: the popularity of winter sports and other potentially dangerous pursuits are examples. A risk that something very bad might happen is intrinsic to living alone with any degree of frailty. However, while ordinary prudence might reduce some of these risks, it is also true than a life dominated by safety and by risk-aversion is no life for many people. As was noted by Eldergill J in *Sykes*, '[s]everal last months of freedom in one's own home at the end of one's life is worth having for many people with serious progressive illnesses, even if it comes at a cost of some distress' (2014, para. 10). Finally, it is necessary to consider the very real hazards of nursing home care. Some of the relevant arguments in respect of admission are outlined below.

Arguments in favour of involuntary admission

In most cases, involuntary admission of a person to a nursing home is considered, with the best of motives, by concerned healthcare professionals and those close to the person because the person is experiencing great difficulties in caring for themselves. The most common reason for an involuntary placement is because someone has advanced dementia, most commonly Alzheimer's disease. In particular, the development of behavioural and psychological problems, occurring in up to two thirds of sufferers at some stage, are often difficult to manage even with maximum support from specialist services, especially if they lead to resistance to or refusal of supports.

Difficulties that may result include deterioration of living quarters into squalor, a fire hazard due to burning of pots, failure to take adequate food or fluids, inability to manage essential medications, lack of personal cleanliness, wearing dirty and sometimes wet clothes, getting lost, failing to manage money and vulnerability to financial abuse, risk of falls due to poor safety awareness, constant calls for help to family members or health professionals and disturbed sleep.

This is a gloomy set of problems and the argument that in some cases the only practical approach may be admission to a nursing home is a strong one. Admission to a skilled nursing facility will not eliminate or mitigate all problems, but it should, at a minimum, ensure access to basics such as food, water, warmth, shelter and basic security.

Potentially misleading arguments in favour of involuntary admission

Some of the problems mentioned above can be managed with less restrictive interventions than involuntary admission such as, for example, by taking control of finances. Others will not be solved easily even by involuntary admission, for example, refusal to be bathed or to take medications.

There is also a danger that the problems will be exaggerated or misinterpreted when trying to ensure placement in a nursing home. 'Wandering' is an example of a common trigger leading to admission to a nursing home. However, 'wandering' is not a diagnosis (Flaherty et al., 2002) and a blanket solution of involuntary admission is not appropriate or reasonable. Some people with advanced dementia will walk about aimlessly. Getting lost is almost inevitable if they leave their home, and some safety measure or restriction will be needed. Others have always enjoyed and continue to enjoy going out for a walk. Some may have difficulty finding their way home if their sense of direction is impaired, or they may show poor judgement in dressing for bad weather, but many have no difficulties. Dementia may interfere with the sleep/wake cycle, and sometimes people get up in the middle of the night and walk to the shops or the church only to be surprised to find them closed and empty. They often return home safely, albeit in a puzzled state, after such nocturnal excursions.

Those living in a local community, where they are well known, will usually experience considerable kindness, understanding and help if they have difficulty getting home. Indeed the Dementia Friendly Communities project of the Alzheimer Society of Ireland will encourage this approach. Nevertheless, every year, people with dementia will get lost causing much worry to those close to them, and some tragically will die as a result.

Another danger is that it is easy to judge people at their worst rather than their best. People with dementia are particularly prone to episodes of acute confusion (delirium) during acute illness. Delirium will almost always be worse in environments, including hospitals, other than the person's own home. It is unfair to judge their abilities based on what is for them a disadvantageous situation.

Arguments against involuntary admission

For someone who does not want to be there and is not allowed to leave, a nursing home is not the idealised, theoretical place of safety common to arguments in favour of detention but an actual physical institution with, notwithstanding all genuine efforts in favour of homeliness, the inevitable characteristics of a 'total institution': 'a place of work and residence where a great number of similarly situated people, cut off from the wider community for a considerable time, together lead an enclosed, formally administered round of life' (Goffman, 1961: 17).

The person who enters and remains voluntarily may chafe at some of the inevitable restrictions and compromises necessary in a communal setting; the emotions of someone who did not enter freely and cannot leave are, even if the person cannot express them clearly, likely to be more extreme. All the emphasis on maintaining autonomy within the nursing home – on how many metaphorical internal doors are open – matters little in the face of forced detention when the door to the outside world is literally closed.

There are some particular hazards of nursing homes for those with dementia. Home is familiar territory, a repository of memories, and where people will usually feel most comfortable, most oriented and most able to cope with daily activities. It is not surprising that nursing home placement is often associated with accelerated short-term cognitive decline in Alzheimer's disease (Wilson et al., 2007). Admission to a nursing home can cause a worsening of quality of life. One survey of admissions to nursing homes (Scocco et al., 2006) reported that 'participants expressed feelings of loneliness and marginalization' and 'psychiatric symptoms worsened and quality of life was perceived more poorly'. In a community setting, the person with dementia is often the centre of attention, even if to an excessive and unsustainable degree, for family and healthcare staff. In contrast, as Caplan (1990) has noted, staff in nursing homes 'are constantly faced with the challenge of weighing the interests of the individual resident against the interests and needs of the entire nursing home community'. Thus interventions, such as antipsychotic or sedative medication, might be considered for the sake of others. The same interventions might also be considered in these circumstances if the person were at home, but at least the beneficiary would be someone close to them rather than a group of strangers. One reason sometimes given for admission to a nursing home is that the person will receive better medical care. This is not always the case. Nursing home residents often have poorer access to hospital facilities, such as chronic disease management clinics, than those in the community. Antipsychotic medications increase mortality and cause strokes, among other problems. While such medications have a role in treating distress caused by problems such as psychosis, it is a consistent finding that approximately 50% of use in nursing homes is for inappropriate indications, often to ensure the smooth running of the institution or to lessen disruption for others (Murphy and O'Keeffe, 2008). Ultimately, and probably as a result of the factors above, there is evidence that life expectancy is shorter in people with Alzheimer's disease admitted to long-term care (McClendon et al., 2006).

Who else counts?

What about those close to the person, especially when they have been striving to keep the person at home, who may be experiencing exhaustion, depression, endless worry and even physical decline as a result of the caring role? Is their only role to reflect and interpret the preferences of the patient?

Whatever about the law, it is difficult not to conclude, however uncomfortable the thought, that there is some kind of moral metric when considering the ethical claim of others to a voice in decision-making. The same unspoken metric often underlies the value judgements made and the sympathy felt (or withheld) by healthcare staff when considering the views of those close to a person who may lack capacity. Factors that underlie such judgements as to whether somebody 'deserves' to have a say include the nature and closeness of the relationship between the person and the claimant, the degree to which the claimant has been involved personally in caring for the person, the quality of the care provided, the impact, if any, of the caring role on the health and well-being of the claimant, any potential interests and even the 'worthiness' of the person.

Two theoretical (although realistic and common) examples illustrate this point. Mr A has become more demented. His wife has cared for him with obvious devotion but has recently had to get up several times every night to try to coax him back to bed. She has now developed health problems and feels she cannot go on with the caring role. She feels guilty that she cannot do what she had always hoped to do and to mind her husband at home. He refuses to consider nursing home care. Mr B is a single man who lives alone and has progressive dementia. His only relative is a niece who lives a few miles away and has not been involved in his care. Recently he has been seen walking outdoors at night in his pyjamas by neighbours who have been ringing up his niece to see what can be done. She urges that he be admitted to nursing home care. He refuses to leave his home.

There are many carers such as Mrs A. It is understandable that healthcare staff will sympathise with her and that books on caring for those with dementia will urge people like her not to feel guilty if they do pursue nursing home care. The views of Mr B's niece will probably command less respect from healthcare staff. This is not to imply that she could or should do more for her uncle, only that she has not 'earned' the right to be a major determinant of her uncle's future.

When a person's care needs impose a significant burden on those close to them, it can be difficult, if not impossible, to disentangle their relative interests when the issue of nursing home care is raised. A carer who is exhausted by and no longer able to fulfil the role of caring has needs of their own; this is especially true if, as in the case of a spouse living in the same house, they cannot readily disengage from the caring role. One approach, consistent perhaps with a communitarian approach to ethics, is to regard a carer like Mrs A and the person they care for as a long-standing and mutually supportive unit. As a unit, there can be no conflicts of interest and, in the example provided, the best interest of the unit is served by placement of Mr A in a home. This is tempting but I would argue that it is more honest to avoid any confusion of terms and to accept that a conflict of interest is just that and that Mr A's interests may diverge from those of Mrs A (see Murray, Chapter 3).

Conclusion

Healthcare professionals, including doctors, nurses and allied health professionals, play an important role when problems arise about where someone should live. Certain specialties such as geriatric medicine and psychiatry are likely to become involved in trying to find a solution and to be asked for 'capacity assessments'. It is important that every effort is made to enable a person with cognitive difficulties to make their own decision even if it seems unwise.

Healthcare professionals have expertise regarding healthcare matters. This does not translate into any expertise on what individuals regard as a good or acceptable life for themselves, including deciding where they should live. Unfortunately, some healthcare professionals have been quick to appropriate the area of personal space into medical terminology, to move from 'these are the risks that they will face at home' through 'they are not safe to go home' or 'they failed the home visit' to 'they should not go home'.

There are undoubtedly circumstances where admission to and detention in a nursing home seems justified. However, such circumstances are no excuse for ignoring the seriousness of a decision to deprive somebody of their liberty or for facilitating or turning a blind eye to unlawful admission and detention. Healthcare professionals have a duty to ensure that involuntary admission to a nursing home of a dissenting person only occurs through a legal mechanism, irrespective of the inconvenience or expense to the healthcare system.

At present, involuntary admission and detention of people in a nursing home often occurs without any legal process or right to appeal. It is unacceptable that such detentions should not receive the same degree of scrutiny as detentions under mental health legislation. Capacity legislation and deprivation of liberty safeguards will help to resolve this problem only if implemented by healthcare professionals and by courts in a way that respects where possible the strong preferences of people to remain at home.

References

Caplan, A.L. (1990) 'The morality of the mundane: Ethical issues arising in the daily lives of nursing home residents', in R.A. Kane and A.L. Caplan (eds), *Everyday Ethics: Resolving Dilemmas in Nursing Home Life*. New York: Springer, pp. 37–50.

Care Quality Commission (2014) *Monitoring the Use of the Mental Capacity Act Deprivation of Liberty Safeguards in 2012/13*. London: Care Quality Commission.

Flaherty, G., Tobin, T.S. and Silverstein, N.M. (2002) *Dementia and Wandering Behavior: Concern for the Lost Elder*. New York: Springer.

Garavan, R., Winder, R. and McGee, H. (2001) *Health and Social Services for Older People (HeSSOP). Consulting Older People on Health and Social Services: A Survey of Service Use, Experience and Needs.* Dublin: National Council on Ageing and Older People.

Goffman, E. (1961) 'On the characteristics of total institutions', in D. Cressey (ed.), *The Prison: Studies in Institutional Organization and Change.* New York: Holt, Rinehart and Winston, pp. 68–106.

Kane, R.L. and Kane, R.A. (2001) 'What older people want from long-term care, and how they can get it', *Health Affairs*, 20(6): 114.

Law Reform Commission (2005) *Consultation Paper on Vulnerable Adults and the Law: Capacity.* Dublin: Law Reform Commission.

Macdonald, A.J., Roberts, A. and Carpenter, I. (2004) 'De facto imprisonment and covert medication use in general nursing homes for older people in South East England', *Aging Clinical and Experimental Research*, 16(4): 326.

Marley, M. (2013) *Convincing a Loved One to Go to a Nursing Home.* Available at: http://caregiver.com/articles/print/convincing_nursing_home.htm (accessed 4 June 2015).

McAuley, W.J. and Travis, S.S. (1997) 'Positions of influence in the nursing home admission decision', *Research on Aging*, 19(1): 26.

McClendon, M.J., Smyth, K.A. and Neundorfer, M.M. (2006) 'Long-term-care placement and survival of persons with Alzheimer's disease', *The Journals of Gerontology Series B*, 61(4): 220.

Molloy, W., Strang, D. and Darzins, P. (1999) *Capacity to Decide.* Ontario: New Grange Press.

Murphy, J. and O'Keeffe, S.T. (2008) 'Frequency and appropriateness of antipsychotic medication use in older people in long-term care', *Irish Journal of Medical Science*, 177(1): 35.

O'Keeffe, S.T. (2008) 'Clinician's perspective on issues of capacity in care', *Medico-Legal Journal of Ireland*, 14: 41.

O'Shea, E., Murphy, K., Larkin, P., Payne, S., Froggatt, K., Casey, D., Ní Léime, Á. and Keys, M. (2008) *End- of-life Care for Older People in Acute and Long Stay Care Settings in Ireland.* Dublin: National Council on Ageing and Older People.

Richardson, G. (2010) 'Mental capacity at the margin: the interface between two acts', *Medical Law Review*, 18: 56.

Scocco, P., Rapattoni, M. and Fantoni, G. (2006) 'Nursing home institutionalization: a source of eustress or distress for the elderly?', *International Journal of Geriatric Psychiatry*, 21(3): 281.

Vlosky, D.A., Bruin, M., Draughn, P.S. and Tiller, V. (2001) '"Say-so" as a predictor of nursing home readiness', *Journal of Family and Consumer Sciences*, 93(1): 59.

Wilson, R., McCann, J., Li, Y., Aggarwal, N., Gilley, D. and Evans, D. (2007) 'Nursing home placement, day care use, and cognitive decline in Alzheimer's disease', *American Journal of Psychiatry*, 164(6): 910.

III
REGULATING RESEARCH

9

Retention and use of human biological samples: the Guthrie card example

Deirdre Madden

Introduction

The retention and use of human biological samples raises interesting and challenging ethical and legal issues including compliance with principles of autonomy and privacy as well as the provisions of data protection law. However, in addition, there are wider competing public interests in this context due to the potential value of such samples for diagnostic purposes, clinical research and innovation and public health and epidemiology. This chapter will explore these issues through the lens of one specific example of the use of biological samples, namely the acquisition, retention and use of newborn screening cards, also known as Guthrie cards.

In 2009, a complaint was made to the Irish Data Protection Commissioner in relation to the retention of the newborn screening cards without consent, contrary to the Data Protection Acts of 1988 and 2003. The Commissioner upheld the complaint and a new policy in relation to the cards was subsequently agreed between the Health Service Executive, Department of Health and Data Protection Commissioner to the effect that, in the future, specific consent should be obtained for the retention of the cards for a ten-year period after which they would be disposed of. In relation to the existing archive of cards, it was agreed that the retention of samples without consent clearly contravened both EU and national data protection legislation and those cards must therefore be disposed of. The Minister for Health subsequently ordered the destruction of the cards unless individuals requested them back. There were calls from clinicians and researchers to retain the cards as a valuable medical resource for diagnosis and research as a result of which the Minister paused the destruction order pending advice from the Attorney General. At the time of writing, approximately 30,000 cards have been returned to those who requested them and the Attorney General's advice has not been made public. The future of the existing archive therefore remains uncertain.

This chapter will consider the ownership of newborn screening cards and the blood spots retained on them, the role of consent to the use of these cards and relevant data protection provisions which have resulted in challenges to their retention. The issues raised here also have relevance for biobanks and other existing archives of retained biological samples in hospitals and research facilities as similar questions arise in relation to those collections. The chapter concludes by recommending that legislation be introduced to exempt the newborn screening card collection from data protection legislation and to put in place a clear and robust governance framework to ensure that individual rights are protected to the greatest extent possible. These recommendations are also relevant to other collections of biological samples in which a strong argument exists for their retention for diagnostic purposes as well as for public health.

Use of newborn screening cards in clinical diagnosis and research

Newborn screening for Phenylketonuria (PKU) was introduced in Massachusetts in the United States in 1962 and less than four years later Ireland started its national newborn screening programme for PKU. The screening is based on a small sample of blood which is drawn from the heel of the infant a few days after birth, known as the heel prick test. The sample of blood taken from the baby is stored on a piece of filter paper known as a Guthrie card. The card also contains information for identification, such as the baby's name, mother's name, date and place of birth. In addition to their primary diagnostic purpose, these cards may be used for a range of secondary purposes such as confirmation of laboratory tests, development of new screening tests, public health research, genetic testing of siblings of a deceased person, and assisting in forensic investigations. Some of these uses require identified samples while others can use anonymised samples. The National Newborn Bloodspot Screening currently stores screening cards from heel prick tests carried out since 1984.

Screening cards can be used in clinical diagnosis of a number of medical conditions in addition to PKU, such as congenital viral infections that can cause deafness and neurological disability. The cards may also be beneficial for families who have had a child die in the past from a progressive but unexplained neurological, endocrine or metabolic condition where medicine had not been able to diagnose the condition at the time. With modern advances in genetics, the card of the deceased child may be used to diagnose the fatal condition years later, which may be of significant interest to the family for the benefit of other siblings or reproductive planning. Margey et al. (2011) state that the cards may also be used in cases of Sudden Cardiac Death (SCD), which causes the deaths of at least 5% of young adults under the age of 35. Research in Ireland has shown that at least 25% of these deaths are due to previously unrecognised hereditary disorders of heart rhythm such as Long QT syndrome and other conditions (McGorrian et al., 2013). This has also been demonstrated in international studies (Behr et al., 2008). Unfortunately in many cases of SCD, blood samples were not taken at autopsy so the Guthrie card may be the only sample which could be used for genetic testing of the deceased person (Gladding et al., 2010; Skinner et al., 2011). This is relevant in order to ascertain if there is a specific genetic cause of the person's death so as to screen other family members for the same mutation and, if found, an appropriate clinical preventative treatment plan put in place.

The screening cards may also have important and valuable significance in medical research as they offer an archive which can be used in epidemiological studies. For example, studies of screening cards were carried out to ascertain the frequency in Ireland of genetic conditions such as those which cause neural tube defects (Mynett-Johnson et al., 2002; Kirke et al., 2004). Such information was then used in public health intervention programmes to inform women of childbearing age of the importance of folic acid supplementation. Archived screening cards were also successfully used in research into the hereditary condition haemochromatosis (Byrnes et al., 2001). This information has been used to increase awareness of the condition among the medical and nursing profession and the public, leading to earlier and more successful interventions. Similarly the cards have been used in international studies to study the frequency of gene variants associated with autism and leukaemia and it is expected that with the development of epigenetics, researchers will be able to use these cards to gain better understanding of diseases including cardiovascular disease, cancer, neurological disorders and diabetes.

Ownership and control of biological samples

The practice of retention of screening cards varies internationally. Some countries such as Denmark and Sweden store cards indefinitely for audit and research purposes. Others, such as France and most states in the United States, destroy the cards soon after testing is complete. New Zealand and Australia have policies allowing the cards to be retained for a variety of times ranging between two years to indefinitely. Questions arise in relation to who owns the cards and the blood spots? Who may access them and under what conditions? What uses are permissible beyond the initial diagnosis? Bowman and Studdert (2011) argue that there are no straightforward answers to these questions in Ireland and many other countries due to the absence of a specific legal framework governing the cards, leaving rules regarding ownership, storage and use to be drawn from a complicated mix of directly and indirectly related laws.

Uncertainties regarding the ownership of screening cards have led to a number of controversies around the world in recent years. For example, in 1997 police in Western Australia obtained a court order allowing them to test DNA from blood spot cards as part of an investigation into alleged incest (Pennells, 1997). The incident prompted public outcry that eventually led to the destruction of all cards older than two years (Office of the Victorian Privacy Commissioner, 2002). In another example, in Victoria, a mother who became concerned about storage of her children's cards requested their return and received those for children who were not hers, sparking concern and public debate about oversight of the state's screening programme (Lawson and Smith, 2001). In New Zealand, use of the cards for forensic purposes such as paternity testing (*H* v. *G* (2000) 18 FRNZ 572) raised public concerns, and in the United States, the Texas Civil Rights Project sued the state on behalf of five parents over storage and use of screening cards which led to the destruction of 5.3 million cards that had been in storage up to 2009 (May, 2010). Bowman and Studdert (2011) say that the common element in these controversies is the public apprehension that they provoke:

> Critics charge that the retention of cards, followed by the secondary use of blood spots without the consent of the child or parents, effectively creates a national biobank. In the absence of explicit legislation establishing such a repository, it is decried as a kind of 'biobank by stealth'. The types of legal protections that regulators would normally point to in assuaging such concerns – clear restrictions on access and use, well defined property rights, and preservation of patient autonomy through informed consent – are often missing, or lack clear application to NBS programs. (2011: 319)

In examining the question of who owns the samples and cards, it is important to look at the ownership of biological samples more generally.

Are biological samples property?

Human tissue is commonly removed from the body in the course of diagnosis or treatment. Blood or bone marrow may be drawn for diagnostic examination. Small pieces of tissue or biological specimens may be taken by biopsy for pathological examination and diagnosis, and larger amounts of tissue may be removed surgically during operations for malignant or other disease. Good practice normally dictates over-collection of such tissue and there may often be leftover tissues after sampling, diagnosis and therapy. This may be discarded as clinical waste, but may alternatively be archived and made available for scientific research, medical training, audit of laboratory procedures and scholarship. In all pathological archives, the material is stored anonymously and may be identified only by laboratory number. Therefore, if the material is used for research purposes, anonymity is assured. However, this is reversible so that patient identity may be established by the pathologist linking the material with confidential diagnostic records if, for example, the research reveals information that is relevant to the care and treatment of the individual patient and contact with the patient is thus considered appropriate.

The legal status of archived human tissue in Ireland is at the present time uncertain (Madden, 2004) and the promised Human Tissue Bill to deal with this and other issues is long overdue. In relation to the question of whether such specimens would be considered property, Madden argues:

> The legal answer given to the question may depend on the context in which the question is raised before a court as well as the purposes and circumstances in which the tissue was originally taken, used and retained. The court would undoubtedly be cognisant not only of patients' rights to autonomy, privacy and dignity, but also the substantial public interest in the activities of treatment, archiving, research and teaching. (2004: 76)

At common law the courts have traditionally taken the view that there is no ownership in the human body, its parts and tissue (Creagh, 2001). The approach has been to treat tissue as *res nullius* (a things belonging to no one) unless it has been transformed by skill and expertise into a different product such as an anatomical specimen. The property rights would then be accorded to the person who applied the skill or technique to the tissue.

In recent years there has been an inexorable movement in healthcare towards a greater recognition of the right of autonomy which may also influence the way in which this issue is now considered. The question is therefore perhaps less one relating to property rights and more relating to personhood and privacy. As Atherton (2003) points out:

> [T]he problem, at its most fundamental level, is not so much a question of property models or any other models, but rather one of control. The real questions are now not so much whether the answers should be found through the law of property, tort or contract, but rather who is given the control and how far that control goes. (2003: 183)

Impact of Moore *v.* Regents of University of California

Until recently, no one cared too much about what was left on the barber's floor or the operating theatre, as these things were not of sufficient value to provoke disputed property claims (Harris, 1996). That situation is now changing with the recognition of the commercial value of separated body parts and tissue and an increased concern with privacy and data protection (Nuffield Council on Bioethics, 1995). In *Moore* v. *Regents of the University of California* [1988] 249 Cal Rptr 494 (Court of Appeals); [1990] 272 Cal Rptr 146 (Cal Sup Ct), a patient's spleen cells as well as blood samples and other bodily substances were removed, stored and used to develop a profitable cell-line without his knowledge or consent. Moore took legal action against the university for the tort of conversion (acting in a way contrary to the rights of the owner of property), breach of fiduciary duty and lack of informed consent. On the latter two grounds, Moore was successful; however, on the issue of whether Moore or the university owned the excised tissue, the California Supreme Court found in favour of the university. The court found that there was no precedent for the recognition of such a claim and that, once excised from the body, the patient loses any legal interest in the tissue. The majority judgments appear to have been largely grounded in a utilitarian argument that to hold otherwise would threaten to halt important medical research, as, unless the researchers had an economic interest in the research, there would be no incentive to them to carry out such work. If patients had ownership rights over the tissue, researchers would be greatly restricted in their ability and willingness to carry out important research, as they might fear the imposition of civil liability.

A privacy argument was also put before the court, to the effect that Moore did not validly consent to the removal of his tissue since he was not made aware of the uses to which it would be put. Therefore, carrying out a medical procedure on a patient without informing him of all its consequences was an invasion of his privacy and he should be regarded as owner of all that was excised. Otherwise, there could always be justification of invasion of privacy in the name of science. The California Supreme Court held that privacy rights could be sufficiently safeguarded by the imposition of duties of disclosure on medical practitioners. If the employees at the medical centre in this case were aware of its potential when they removed the tissue, and did not inform Moore of such potential, Moore would have an action against them for breach of duty. The court took the view that, however one may wish to protect patients' privacy and dignity, the solution is not to accord ownership rights to the patient in the excised tissue. Although not explicitly stated as such, the court appears to have taken the view, perhaps on utilitarian grounds, that a patient's consent to surgery entails an abandonment of any claims over the removed tissue. Thus, there is no claim for breach of property rights and the issue becomes one of ensuring that a valid and effective consent has been given (Madden, 2004).

If we therefore take the view of the California Supreme Court that the crux of the issue lies not in ownership or property rights *per se* but rather the locus of control and decision-making authority (which may of course be regarded as quasi-property rights), we need to examine how principles of informed consent might apply in this context. There are a number of options available to deal with the issue of informed consent. First, it could be argued that it is inherent in any consent to treatment that tissue removed in the course of treatment will be regarded as having been abandoned by the person from whom it was removed. Although it might be said that the ownership of the tissue must initially vest in the patient, consent to its removal entails that, unless the patient continues to exert an ownership interest in it, the user of the tissue acquires the right to possess and possibly own the tissue (Nuffield Council on Bioethics, 1995: 77). The theory of abandonment upon which this argument rests suggests that in consenting to medical treatment, the patient waives all rights in respect of tissue excised as part of that treatment for accepted uses of audit, research and medical training in recognised universities and medical schools. Consent for such uses is thus taken to be implicit in the knowledge of such use and the failure to object (Medical Research Council, 2001; Price, 2003). For all other uses, it may be argued that explicit consent by the patient is necessary. However, it is important to note that the abandonment approach is problematic as it may be difficult to interpret patients' actions as an intentional abandonment, particularly where a commercial and valuable exploitation is anticipated. The common law has tended to restrict abandonment theories to theft and wrecks, and may not extend beyond those categories.

A second option is that tissue removed in circumstances other than treatment, which is voluntarily donated, will be regarded as a gift. This does not imply that conditions may not be attached as to the uses to which the gift may be put, and there is an underlying assumption that nothing would be done that might be detrimental to the donor (*Washington University* v. *Catalona et al.* 437 F Supp 2d 985 (US Dist 2006)). A third option is that, where tissue is removed voluntarily and intended to be kept for the donor, the donor would be able to claim that tissue on the strength of the agreement under which it is kept. A final option is that, where tissue is removed without explicit knowledge and consent (as in *Moore*), any claim by the patient will revolve around the validity of any general consent given and whether consent to removal and retention of the tissue could be said to have been implied in the circumstances. The Nuffield Council on Bioethics suggest that legal claims by persons from whom tissue is removed should proceed on the basis of the consent given to the procedure rather than a claim in property (Nuffield Council on Bioethics, 1995: para. 9.15). However, the recommendations of the Nuffield Council have been criticised as an ad hoc measure that mixes property and non-property analyses to the public policy issue at stake here (Matthews, 1995; Grubb, 1998).

Property arguments have also arisen in relation to reproductive material. In *Yearworth* v. *North Bristol NHS Trust* [2009] 3 WLR 118, 107 BMLR 47, the Court of Appeal acknowledged that the law has traditionally been silent about property rights in parts or products of the human body but with the increased recognition of their commercial value and significance, this has changed in recent years. The court took the view that 'developments in medical science now require a re-analysis of the common law's treatment of an approach to the issue of ownership of parts or products of a living human body, whether for present purposes (viz. an action in negligence) or otherwise' (2009, para. 45). The decision is regarded by many as 'an important turning point in medical jurisprudence. For all of its qualifications and lack of legal authority, it signals a sea change in judicial attitude towards patients' rights' (Mason and Laurie, 2010: para. 14.34). Mason and Laurie take the view that it offers a degree of empowerment for patients over material taken from their bodies should they choose to exercise it but they query how far such rights may go in light of competing claims such as those raised in the name of science in the *Moore* case. Similarly Bowman and Studdert say on one view of the decision in *Yearworth*, it simply dealt with an unusual situation but on another view, 'the courts are laying the groundwork for stronger proprietary rights in human tissue' (Bowman and Studdert, 2011: 320).

It remains to be seen whether and to what extent the Irish courts will take a similar view to that outlined above. There are no Irish cases on this issue and it may be that, in keeping with the antipathy towards recognition of property rights in the human body shown by the courts elsewhere, an Irish court would choose to deal with instances in which such claims are made by preferring a consent and control model. In this sense, the question of ownership of blood spot cards and the tissue retained on the cards would centre not on property rights but rather on respect for autonomy, informed consent and privacy.

Regulating the use of screening cards

Valid consent

In any healthcare intervention informed consent must be obtained from the person, or someone with legal authority to act on their behalf, before starting the medical treatment or investigation (Health Service Executive, *National Consent Policy*, 2013). This requirement is consistent with fundamental ethical principles, with good practice in communication and decision-making and with national health and social care policy. The need for consent is also recognised in Irish and international law. The ethical rationale behind the importance of consent is the need to respect the person's right to self-determination (or autonomy) – their right to control their own life and to decide what happens to their own body. In the case of children, it is important that respect for their autonomy is integrated into decision-making in the same way as for adults. However, where the child is an infant who is unable to make decisions for him/herself, parents or legal guardians may consent to medical procedures for the child as they have primary responsibility to act in the best interests of their child and to care for the child in a manner that respects the child's dignity and well-being.

In order for consent to be valid, the patient must have received sufficient information in a comprehensible manner about the nature, purpose, benefits and risks of the intervention; must not be acting under duress; and must have the capacity to make the particular decision. When applied to the decision as to whether or not to conduct screening on a child, it might be expected that parents would require certain information in order to comply with the requirements of informed consent, such as the purpose of the test, its accuracy, how it is carried out, any risks for the child, how long the sample will be stored for and who will have access to the test results and the blood sample and for what purposes. At the time the newborn screening programme was introduced in the 1960s, implied consent was the norm in common clinical practice. Therefore the information outlined above was not commonly sought by parents or offered by those carrying out the screening. As clinical practice changed over the years, the procedure for consent also evolved and explicit consent is now sought from parents since 2011.

Difficult issues arise in relation to the retention of material originally obtained and stored without consent at a time when consent was not a common practice. In the UK the Human Tissue Act 2004 provides that consent must be obtained for the storage or use of human tissue for a scheduled purpose. However, the consent requirements of this Act are not retrospective. This means that legally it is not necessary to have obtained consent to store or use an 'existing holding' for a scheduled purpose. An existing holding is defined as material from the living or deceased that was already held at the time the 2004 Act came into force on 1 September 2006. Ireland does not have any human tissue legislation in place to deal with issues relating to the removal, retention and use of biological material either from deceased or living persons. The Madden *Report on Post-mortem Practice and Procedure* (2005) which dealt with the issue of retention of the organs of deceased children following post-mortem examinations without the knowledge or consent of their parents stated that:

> [I]t is clear that human tissue legislation is urgently required to deal with issues relating to removal, storage and uses of human biological material from the living and the deceased. Provision should be made in such legislation to facilitate and encourage medical education and training, and approved medical research, while maintaining the principle of respect for the donor, the deceased person and the bereaved. (Madden 2005: 151)

Following the recommendations contained in this Report, a draft Human Tissue Bill was published which aimed, *inter alia*, to regulate the removal, retention, storage, use and disposal of human tissue from deceased persons. A public consultation exercise was carried out by the Department of Health but, at the time of writing, the Bill has not yet been published.

Data protection

The Data Protection Directive 1995 (Directive 95/46) was implemented in Ireland in the Data Protection Act 1998 as amended by the Data Protection (Amendment) Act 2003 (DP Acts). Under the DP Acts, 'personal data' is data that relates to an identified or identifiable individual. Such data may only be collected and processed in accordance with data protection legislation unless it is rendered fully anonymous. Provisions relating to fair obtaining and lawful processing must also be complied with in relation to such data. One of the issues that arise here includes consideration of whether identifiable tissue retained by a hospital or laboratory comes within the definition of personal data for legal purposes. There seems to be a divergence of views in Europe on this issue. For example, the definition of personal data in German data protection legislation (Federal Data Protection Act, 2009) includes data linked to human biological materials as 'health data' and 'special types of personal data', and specific protection of these kinds of data is laid down by the legislation. However, the biological material itself is not included in its scope and it appears that newborn screening cards are retained as they are not viewed as contravening data protection law. It is unclear whether the DP Acts apply to biological material. The definition of personal data in the legislation is 'data relating to a living individual who is or can be identified either from the data or from the data in conjunction with other information that is in, or is likely to come into, the possession of the data controller'. The question therefore seems to be whether the identity of the individual can be obtained either from the biological material/tissue sample or from the sample in conjunction with other information in or likely to come into the possession of the data controller. If so, it is covered by the legislative definition.

States are obliged under the Data Protection Directive to prohibit the processing of data concerning health. Article 2 of the Directive states that processing of personal data means any operation or set of operations which is performed upon personal data, whether or not by automatic means, such as collection, recording, organisation, storage, adaptation or alteration, retrieval, consultation, use, disclosure by transmission, dissemination or otherwise making available, alignment or combination, blocking, erasure or destruction. An exception to this prohibition is allowed where processing of the data is required for the purposes of preventive medicine, medical diagnosis, the provision of care or treatment, or the management of healthcare services, and where those data are processed by a health professional subject to the obligation of professional secrecy. The DP Acts in Ireland extended this exception to include medical research. Legitimate processing of personal data can therefore only take place where data quality principles are complied with and at least one of the conditions for processing is met. While consent of the data subject is provided as one of these conditions, consent is not essential provided the data quality principles are adhered to and one of the other conditions is met. Therefore, although it may be considered best practice to obtain consent, it is legally acceptable to rely on non-consent alternatives even if consent would be practicable and not inappropriate.

How do the Directive and the DP Acts apply to existing collections of biological samples, such as newborn screening cards, for which consent was not obtained in the past? Clearly, many of these samples and cards were collected and retained prior to the introduction of the Directive and thus a question arises as to whether the Directive operates retrospectively. Moreover, the Directive does not apply to deceased persons so its provisions have no relevance to those whose cards have been retained and are no longer still living.

Where the DP Acts apply, medical data comes within the category of 'sensitive' personal data. This means that processing of this data must comply with sections 2, 2A and 2B. Therefore the first challenge is to ensure that the retention of the samples and cards satisfies section 2(a) which means establishing that the data was obtained and processed fairly. Fair processing requirements are set out in section 2D and include a requirement that the data subject be informed of the identity of the data controller and the purpose or purposes for which the data are intended to be processed. It appears to be the case that in Ireland historically this information was not given to parents of infants undergoing the screening test (until the new policy was introduced in 2011 in light of the controversy explained in the Introduction) and therefore section 2(a) is not satisfied. Although there are exceptions in the DP Acts, which allow for the processing of personal data without consent under certain circumstances, these exceptions only apply where the data has been obtained fairly in compliance with section 2(a).

Guidelines issued by the Data Protection Commissioner in relation to research in the health sector state that anonymised and pseudonymised use of data does not need consent (Office of the Data Protection Commissioner, 2007). The application of these guidelines in relation to existing collections of biological samples or screening cards would mean that, if anonymised, they could be used for research purposes without consent. However, some of the potential valuable uses of the cards require the possibility of identifiable data being made available in order, for example, to identify a genetic cause for Sudden Cardiac Death in a family member.

The *National Consent Policy* (Health Service Executive, 2013) states that archived material or data may be used for research without consent where the material/data is not identifiable and there is no potential harm to the person from whom the material/data was obtained. It also states that where the material is identifiable, a research ethics committee may waive the consent requirement if the use of the material/data without consent is unlikely to adversely affect the welfare of the individual involved; the researchers will take appropriate measures to protect the privacy of individuals and to safeguard the material/data; they will comply with any known preferences of the individuals in relation to their material/data; and it is impossible or impractical to seek consent from individuals to whom the material/data relates. It may therefore be possible, in compliance with these criteria, to satisfy the requirements of the Policy in seeking access to biological samples for research purposes.

A further noteworthy provision here is section 8 of the Data Protection (Amendment) Act 2003 which provides that any restrictions in the Act on the prohibition on processing do not apply, *inter alia*, if the processing is 'required by or under any enactment or by a rule of law or order of a court'. Therefore it is possible that the Minister for Health could decide to introduce specific legislation dealing with the retention of screening cards through, for example, the proposed Human Tissue Bill. This legislation could effectively exempt this collection, and others, from the provisions of data protection provisions in the interest of the common good and could introduce a structured governance framework as discussed below to ensure that individual rights are protected as much as possible.

Governance

In Ireland, the lack of a governance framework for the retention of biological samples and newborn screening cards has threatened the operation of the screening programme and the acknowledged importance and value of the retention of these cards for public health. The options open to legislators and policy-makers are to enact a specific statute tailored to govern the programme in Ireland, such as through the long-awaited Human Tissue Bill; or to apply current law and practice to consent and collection procedures. The difficulty with the latter option is that, although it may be attractive to rely on existing concepts and policies, their application in this context is problematic given the challenges posed by data protection law. Even with an excellent informed consent policy in place, long-term storage and secondary use of blood spots collected from newborn infants 'raise broader questions for society about accountability, transparency, agency and privacy. A fragmented regulatory approach in which discrete aspects of NBS programs are dealt with by discrete laws, risks losing sight of the forest through a focus on the trees' (Bowman and Studdert, 2011: 321).

Bowman and Studdert argue that a dedicated legal regime should be developed which, although it would lead to stricter requirements for informed consent at the collection stage, would not necessarily lead to restrictive rules on secondary uses as there is generally strong public support for health research. A coherent legal framework should be developed which would reflect a considered balance between the rights of parents and children, community attitudes to the storage and use of biospecimens, and the interests of all citizens in high-quality healthcare. The Committee of Ministers of the Council of Europe published a Recommendation in 2006 on research on biological materials of human origin which emphasises the balance to be sought between the realisation of human rights and fundamental freedoms, protection of privacy, dignity, identity and integrity of individuals on the one hand and the importance of progress in medical and biological sciences obtained through biomedical research, knowledge and discovery on the other. Article 14 recommends that collections of biological materials should follow certain principles including: the designation of the person responsible for the collection; the specification of the purpose of the collection; principles of transparency and accountability in governance arrangements; appropriate documentation of samples and the relevant consent given; clear conditions regarding access to and use of the samples; and appropriate quality assurance measures. Principles for such a framework have also been developed by a number of expert groups in Australia (Human Genetics Society of Australia, 2000), Scotland (Laurie et al., 2014), and Ireland (Royal College of Physicians of Ireland, 2013).

Conclusion

The value and significance of the newborn screening cards is clear both for clinical diagnosis and for research. However, the frameworks which govern access to and use of the cards are different for each of these purposes. Irish law does not appear to consider that human biological material removed from the body is the property of the individual and therefore issues of authorisation of access to and use of the material must fall within an alternative model such as informed consent and/or data protection and privacy provisions.

In the context of medical research, it is possible to conduct research in the absence of consent if the material is not identifiable and its use is unlikely to cause substantial damage or distress. However, in the context of medical diagnosis such as for Sudden Cardiac Death, linkage to the identity of the individual is necessary in order to protect the health of related persons. In the context of the controversy that has arisen in Ireland in relation to the retention of the screening cards (as outlined in the Introduction), since the parents of the children who underwent the blood spot test were not informed that the blood spots were going to be retained for a specific purpose, the 'fair obtaining' requirement of the Data Protection Act 2003 may not be met. Therefore it may be that the only way in which identifiable blood spot cards could be retained would be under section 8 of the Act where the Minister for Health could introduce specific legislation dealing with the retention of screening cards, together with an appropriate governance framework to regulate access to and use of the cards for diagnosis and research. It would be valuable if such legislation also dealt with other archived collections of biological samples for which consent was not obtained but which provide important sources of information for research and public health.

References

Atherton, R. (2003) 'Who owns your body?', *Australian Law Journal*, 77: 178.

Behr, E.R., Dalageorgou, C., Christiansen, M., Syrris, P., Hughes, S. and Tome Esteban, M.T. (2008) 'Sudden arrhythmic death syndrome: familial evaluation identifies inheritable heart disease in the majority of families', *European Heart Journal*, 29(13): 1670.

Bowman, D. and Studdert, D. (2011) 'Newborn screening cards: a legal quagmire', *Medical Journal of Australia*, 194(6): 319.

Byrnes, V., Ryan, E., Barrett, S., Kenny, P., Mayne, P. and Crowe, J. (2001) 'Genetic hemochromatosis, a Celtic disease: is it now time for population screening?', *Genetic Test*, 5: 127.

Council of Europe (2006) *Recommendation of the Committee of Ministers to Member States on Research on Biological Material of Human Origin.* Recommendation (2006) 4.

Creagh, C. (2001) 'Property in the living body', *Bar Review*, 209.

Directive 95/46 of the European Parliament and of the Council of 24 October 1995 on the protection of individuals with regard to the processing of personal data and on the free movement of such data, [1995] OJ L 281/31.

Federal Data Protection Act (2009) (BDSG) in the version promulgated on 14 January 2003 (Federal Law Gazette I, p. 66), last amended by Article 1 of the Act of 14 August 2009 (Federal Law Gazette I, p. 2814), in force from 1 September.

Gladding, P.A., Evans, C.-A., Crawford, J., Chung, S.K., Vaughan, A. and Webster, D. (2010) 'Posthumous diagnosis of long QT syndrome from neonatal screening cards', *Heart Rhythm* (official journal of the Heart Rhythm Society), 7(4): 481.

Grubb, A. (1998) '"I, me, mine": bodies, parts and property', *Medical Law International*, 3: 299.

Harris, J. (1996) 'Who owns my body?', *Legal Studies*, 16: 55.

Health Service Executive (2013) *National Consent Policy*. Dublin.

Human Genetics Society of Australia (2000) *Retention, Storage and Use of Sample Cards from Newborn Screening Programs*. Sydney.

Kirke, P.N., Mills, J.L., Molloy, A.M., Brody, L.C., O'Leary, V.B. and Daly, L. (2004) 'Impact of the MTHFR C677T polymorphism on risk of neural tube defects: case-control study', *British Medical Journal*, 328(7455): 1535.

Laurie, G., Hunter, K. and Cunningham-Burley, S. (2014) *Storage, Use and Access to the Scottish Guthrie Card Collection: Ethical, Legal and Social Issues.* Edinburgh: Scottish Government Social Research.

Lawson, C. and Smith, R. (2001) 'Protecting genetic material and genetic information: a case study of Guthrie cards in Victoria', *Journal of Law and Medicine*, 9: 21.

Madden, D. (2004) 'Legal status of archived human tissue', *Medico-legal Journal of Ireland*, 10(2): 76.

Madden, D. (2005) *Report on Post-mortem Practice and Procedure*. Dublin: The Stationery Office.

Margey, R., Roy, A., Tobin, S., O'Keane, C.J., McGorrian, C., Morris, V. (2011) 'Sudden cardiac death in 14–35 year olds in Ireland from 2005 to 2007: a retrospective registry', *Eurospace*, 13(10): 1411.

Mason, K. and Laurie, G. (2010) *Law and Medical Ethics*, 8th edn. Oxford: Oxford University Press.

Matthews, P. (1995) 'A man of property', *Medical Law Review*, 3: 251.

May, M. (2010) 'Destroying newborn blood samples threatens birth defect research', *Nature Medicine*, 16: 140.

McGorrian, C., Constant, O., Harper, N., O'Donnell, C., Codd, M. and Keelan, E. (2013) 'Family-based cardiac screening in relatives of victims of sudden arrhythmic death syndrome', *Eurospace*, 15(7): 1050.

Medical Research Council (2001) *Human Tissue and Biological Samples for Use in Research*. London: MRC Ethics Series.

Mynett-Johnson, L.A., Keenan, C., Black, I.L., Livingstone, W.J., Lawler, M. and Roche, H.M. (2002) 'Thermolabile methylenetetrahydrofolate reductase (C677T): frequency in the Irish population', *Irish Journal of Medical Sciences*, 171(1): 37.

Nuffield Council on Bioethics (1995) *Human Tissue: Ethical and Legal Issues*. London.

Office of the Data Protection Commissioner (2007) *Guidelines on Research in the Health Sector*. Portarlington.

Office of the Victorian Privacy Commissioner (2002) *Submission to the Forensic Procedures Review Committee on its Review of Part 1D of the Crimes Act 1914 (Cth)*. Melbourne: Privacy Victoria.

Pennells, S. (1997) 'Police test worry', *AMA, The West Australian (Perth)*, 2 August.

Price, D. (2003) 'From Cosmos and Damian to Van Velzen: the human tissue saga continues', *Medical Law Review*, 11: 1.

Royal College of Physicians of Ireland (2013) 'Newborn screening blood spot cards: submission to the Minister for Health', unpublished.

Skinner, J.R., Crawford, J., Smith, W., Aitken, A., Heaven, D. and Evans, C.-A. (2011) 'Prospective, population-based long QT molecular autopsy study of postmortem negative sudden death in 1 to 40 year olds', *Heart Rhythm* (official journal of the Heart Rhythm Society), 8(3): 412.

10

A moral gap? Examining Ireland's failure to regulate embryonic stem cell research

Ciara Staunton

Introduction

Developments in human biotechnology have created new ethical concerns. Just as the early years of organ transplant technology brought about a change in our concept of death, developments in embryology are challenging our concept of what constitutes life. Progress in medical science has now made it possible not only to create an embryo in a laboratory, but to destroy that same embryo in the course of medical research. While there is great potential for advancement in regenerative medicine, the fact that the embryo must be destroyed has resulted in embryonic stem cell research (ESCR) being described as the most contentious bioethical issue of recent times (Varmus, 2010).

At the heart of the debate on ESCR is the status of the embryo. For some, ESCR can never be justified as an embryo is a human life and ESCR necessitates the destruction of human life (Congregation for the Doctrine of the Faith, 2008). Yet many disagree with this contention, arguing that defining human life has become much more difficult due to our increasing level of scientific information (Fitzgerald, 2003). Others still argue that the embryo is nothing more than a clump of cells (Goldstein, 2008). Alongside this ethical debate is the scientific promise of ESCR. Known as the 'ultimate cell' or the 'mother of all cells' (Singapore Bioethics Advisory Commission, 2002), it has the potential to grow into any cell in the body, can be engineered to produce new tissue or organs, and brings hope to those suffering from degenerative illness as well as incurable diseases (Editorial, 2004; Semb, 2005).

In the face of this scientific promise and ethical uncertainty, policy-makers are left with a difficult task of determining the legal status of the embryo and the development of ESCR policy. They must choose between affording the embryo full legal status which may help them avoid a potentially politically damaging debate on the right to life, or decide to promote the development of science with a policy that permits the destruction of the embryo. Yet despite numerous reports and judicial pronouncements on this issue, the Irish legislature has failed to address ESCR, leaving the embryo without regulatory protection. Such a situation can not necessarily be seen as representative of the views of the Irish public. Refusal by successive governments to resolve this issue has resulted in a system that, by default, could allow for embryo destructive research.

This chapter discusses the legal and ethical issues that arise in regulating ESCR in Ireland. Noting that the ethical debate is unlikely to be resolved, it will outline the three approaches Irish policy-makers may take: a restrictive approach, a permissive approach or an intermediate approach. An analysis of the current status of ESCR will demonstrate that although the Irish courts seem to support the intermediate approach, the lack of legislative guidance has left the embryo without legal protection. This chapter argues that it is time for a national discussion on the status of the embryo. Such a discussion is necessary for a regulatory framework that both protects the embryo and accommodates ESCR.

Ethical status of the embryo

The importance of establishing the moral status of the embryo lies in the fact that morality has long guided the law. It is argued that the law is only followed because it consists of morally binding principles which represent the ideals of society (St John-Steva, 1964). In a sense, moral and legal principles have a symbiotic relationship as moral principles are a quest for the ideal, for what society should be (Petit, 2010), while the law attempts to ensure that these ideals are implemented through sanctions if they are not followed.

Problems arise, however, when society cannot agree on moral principles, and policy-makers must accommodate these differing moral beliefs while providing for a coherent set of legally binding rules or principles. This difficulty is compounded by the increasingly pluralistic nature of society in recent years, which has made reaching a consensus much more difficult. Rawls has stated that:

> The political culture of a democratic society is always marked by a diversity of opposing and irreconcilable religious, philosophical, and moral doctrines. Some of these are perfectly reasonable, and this diversity among reasonable doctrines political liberalism sees as the inevitable long-run result of the powers of human reason at work within the background of enduring free institutions. (1993: 3)

While such plurality of views may be a hallmark of a modern democracy, policy-makers still face a stark challenge in regulating ESCR. Yet this challenge is not insurmountable. The focus should not be on resolving the debate on the status of the embryo, but rather on finding some consensus in Ireland. If there is a common morality that the embryo has moral status, then a convincing justification is necessary to destroy them for research purposes. Furthermore, the greater the moral status that society affords the embryo, the greater the justification required before the embryo can be destroyed for ESCR (Holm, 2002). So what could this common morality be?

Restrictive approach

If the common morality views an embryo as a human being from fertilisation then destroying it for research purposes would contravene the sanctity of life and therefore require a restrictive approach to ESCR. Such an approach is taken by some religions, notably the Catholic Church who teach that the embryo must be protected from conception (Congregation for the Doctrine of the Faith, 2008). Under such doctrines, it is professed that humans are made in God's image and this extends to the embryo. It is irrelevant that an increased understanding of the developmental process of an embryo has shown that the embryo does not in fact resemble a human being, as it is believed that 'no amount of embryological investigation could conceivably crack what is held to be an awesome mystery' (Evans, 1996: 31).

Others who favour the restrictive approach argue that an embryo has the same moral status as a human being, due to its potential to develop into a person. In some respects this potential is recognised by society as pregnant women are advised to take care of their health from the beginning of (and often prior to) their pregnancy. It is now also common for health warnings to appear on alcoholic drinks and cigarette packaging, advising women of the dangers of the product for their unborn child.[1]

A problem with ascribing moral status based on potential is that it is a potential only, a potential which may not be realised (Harris, 1985). In this sense, the oft-quoted comparison between the acorn and the tree has value: while the acorn has the potential to become a tree, it is not yet a tree and should not be treated as such. Similarly, in its opinion on the Ethical, Scientific and Legal Issues Concerning Stem Cell Research, the Irish Council for Bioethics (ICB) noted that every person has the potential to become a criminal but they are not treated as such until they do in fact commit the crime (ICB, 2008). Furthermore, Cohen argues that this potential to become a person exists in the reproductive context only and thus is not an issue in regenerative medicine such as ESCR. Cohen argues that an embryo only has moral status due to its potential to provide medical assistance to those already living (Cohen, 2007). According to this theory, full moral status cannot be afforded to every embryo as it was not intended that a live birth would result.

Even for those where a live birth was expected, an embryo may never become a person: it may become a hydatiform mole,[2] it may never implant due to a contraceptive barrier such as that of the intrauterine system (IUS), it may be frozen indefinitely in an IVF clinic (Singer and Dawson, 1988), or, if implanted, the foetus may spontaneously abort. Furthermore it is highly unlikely that an embryo will ever become a person as up to 80% of all embryos never implant due to 'natural wastage' (Teklenburg et al., 2010).

Permissive approach

On the other end of the spectrum is the permissive or liberal approach to ESCR. This is premised on the belief that only human beings have moral status. To be considered a person, an entity must have the capacity to be self-conscious or aware of themselves, have the capacity to be rational and the capacity to react to stimuli (Ford, 1988). The first criterion (i.e. the capacity for self-consciousness) requires that a person ought to be aware of themselves and their interaction with others and this recognition of self must be more than the presence of the ability to communicate (Grobstein, 1981) but include an ability to perceive others (Locke, [1689] 1959). The criterion of rationality states that personhood is limited to entities which have the capacity to think rationally or, as Locke defines it, to be an entity which is a 'thinking intelligent being' (Locke, [1689] 1959). The final criterion requires that entities react to stimuli such as pain or pleasure, warmth or cold.

An alternative to the aforementioned criterion is Lockwood's concept of 'brain life'. For Lockwood, it is only when an organism has a brain that it should have moral status. Prior to the formation of the brain the entity has the potential to become a human being, but for Lockwood, this potential is irrelevant. Lockwood is of the opinion that the notion of a 'brain life' is what should be used to determine the beginning of a human life as this is consistent with the concept of brain death, the time when a human being is thought to no longer exist. Thus Lockwood argues that unless another human being's interests are affected, it is morally permissible to engage in research on an embryo or developing foetus up to the point of brain development (Lockwood, 1985).

The problem with both approaches to defining a person is that there is the danger that they will exclude certain members of society. For example, following the self-consciousness/rationality criteria, to be a person potentially removes newborns, people with a disability or those in a coma from being a person, as they may not have the ability to interact with others or rationalise. Such a move would be contrary to United Nations Convention on the Rights of Persons with Disabilities (2006). It is also unclear what level of self-awareness or rationality is required. On the other hand, the third criterion (reaction to stimuli) has the ability to expand the definition of person to both plants and animals. Animals will react to extreme heat in much the same way as a person does and plants react to sunlight by growing towards it.

Under these criteria and Lockwood's concept of brain life, the embryo would have no moral status and thus would have no moral right to protection. Yet even in the most liberal regimes regulating ESCR, there is some legal protection afforded to the embryo.

Intermediate position

For many, the moral status of the embryo is unclear and it occupies an intermediate moral status. The gradualist approach is a manifestation of this position and it accords increasing moral status to the embryo as it develops. This approach acknowledges that no single stage of the development of the embryo is more important than the others, but rather each stage is important as the embryo cannot develop without all stages. While acknowledging that there is no definite point at which the embryo can be said to be a person, as the embryo develops and becomes closer to being a person, the moral status of the embryo increases. The approach has been likened to that of the colour spectrum. Just as it is unclear at which point a colour changes into another colour, it is unclear at which point an embryo changes from one stage of development to the next (Poplawski et al., 1991).

Following this approach, it would appear that the embryo has the lowest level of moral status at the one cell stage when the embryo is initially formed after fertilisation, and has the highest level of moral status prior to birth. As the embryo's chances of becoming a person increase upon implantation, the implanted embryo would have a higher moral status than that of the embryo *in vitro* or the unimplanted embryo *in vivo*.[3] Consequently, one could also assume that following this approach, the embryo prior to implantation has the lowest moral status. Thus if a choice had to be made between research on an eight-cell, unimplanted embryo and a 30-week foetus, research should be carried out on the eight-cell embryo rather than the 30-week foetus.

While it is clear that under the gradualist approach an embryo *in vitro* would have a lower level of moral status, this approach fails to indicate whether that means that destructive research may be carried out. Furthermore the approach offers no guidance on what moral status the embryo has at a particular point in its development, as opposed to its *relative* moral status. The approach provides guidance when faced with the choice of carrying out embryo-destructive research on embryos which are at different points in their development but not when faced with the question of whether ESCR should be permitted, or the question of what the moral status of the early embryo is.

Despite the lack of definitive guidance from this theory, it was adopted by the Warnock Committee (Department of Health and Security, 1984) and the Singapore Bioethics Advisory Commission (2002), perhaps because it is the most politically workable approach. With this approach, an implanted embryo would have more respect than an unimplanted embryo. In this way, respect is granted according to the stage of development of the embryo. The embryo may also be respected by ensuring that it is only used for essential research such as for life-saving therapies and not for cosmetic research. Thus, while the embryo may have substantial moral status, this may be outweighed by the potential of the research, provided only necessary research is carried out (Latham, 2009).

While 'respecting' the embryo is consistent with permitting some, albeit limited, research on the embryo (Parens, 2000; Meyer and Nelson, 2001; Johnson Kukla, 2001–2; Robertson, 1999) there is generally seen to be a cut-off point at which embryonic research is prohibited due to the increasing moral status of the embryo. This cut off point is often the formation of the primitive streak, which occurs around day 14. This point is seen as important as the primitive streak is necessary for brain function and also the formation of the central nervous system.

At its core, the intermediate approach is a political compromise, with due deference shown to the competing moral arguments on the status of the embryo. It also reflects the reality that the moral status of the embryo is in fact uncertain (Smith, 2006). One formulation of the compromise may be that ESCR is only permitted for research on serious illnesses, 'research that involves the destruction of embryos is permissible where there is good reason to believe that it is necessary to cure life-threatening or severely debilitating diseases' (Siegel, 1999: para. J-10). Although such compromises may be seen as ethically flawed and inconsistent, they reflect the political realities of the debate and arguably provide a middle ground between two opposing positions. In practice, the law does not have to deal with the moral status of the embryo, but the restrictions on ESCR research indicate the law's approach in this regard.

The challenge for policy-makers is how best to achieve this political compromise where there are three competing moral viewpoints to contend with: the liberal position, the conservative position and the intermediate position. Good policy dictates that the competing moral considerations of each group are recognised. In developing Irish ESCR policy, the legislature is obliged to consider the Constitution and, in addition, should consider the scientific potential of ESCR, public opinion, and should also draw on independent expert reports, such as the ICB Report of 2008.

The legal status of ESCR in Ireland

Until the decision in *Roche* v. *Roche* [2010] 2 IR 321, it was not clear whether an embryo *in vitro* constituted the 'unborn' and was therefore entitled to constitutional protection under Article 40.3.3. The consequences for IVF and embryos *in vitro* were not debated in depth at the time of the Eighth Amendment (which inserted Article 40.3.3. into the Constitution) despite the birth of the first child through IVF four years previously. That said, in the Seanad debates, Senator Catherine McGuinness did seek to insert the phrase 'which shall not include fertilised ovum prior to the time at which such ovum becomes implanted in the wall of the uterus' after the 'unborn' in the wording of the proposed amendment (*Seanad Debates*, 1983: vol. 100, col. 1092). Such a proposal would have clarified that the unborn was to apply to embryos *in vivo* only, leaving embryos *in vitro* outside of constitutional protection. However, this proposal was defeated, leaving the unborn undefined and it was accurately predicted that the Eighth amendment would need 'further legislation, amendments or litigations in the courts, either national or European' (Boyle, 1982: 10).

A number of independent reports have recommended the inclusion of a definition of the 'unborn' in the Constitution. In 1996, the Constitution Review Group (CRG) examined Article 40.3.3 and noted that 'unborn' could mean from fertilisation, implantation or some other point in time. The CRG suggested that the unborn could be defined as 'on the way to being born' or 'capable of being born' (CRG, 1996: 275). Had a definition been inserted into the Constitution, it would have clarified the status of ESCR and assisted reproductive technologies and provided legal guidance to researchers, scientists and clinicians working in this area.

The 2005 report of the Commission on Assisted Human Reproduction (CAHR) also referred to the uncertainty surrounding the definition of the unborn. While acknowledging that clarity would only come by way of a Supreme Court decision or a referendum (CAHR 2005), the CAHR (with one dissent) recommended that the embryo *in vitro* should not be protected under Article 40.3.3 and that ESCR should be regulated along with assisted human reproduction (AHR) which would be overseen by an independent regulatory authority (IRA) (CAHR, 2005). In 2008, the Irish Council on Bioethics made similar recommendations in its report *Ethical, Legal and Scientific Issues Concerning Stem Cell Research* (ICB, 2008). The Council was of the opinion that a failure to regulate this area undermines the moral value of the embryo and also hinders the development of this field of research in Ireland (ICB, 2008).

Roche *v.* Roche

The issue of ESCR finally came before the Supreme Court in *Roche* v. *Roche*. The case concerned a couple who underwent IVF treatment which resulted in the creation of embryos. The couple subsequently separated and Mrs Roche sought to implant some of the embryos into her womb, contrary to Mr Roche's wishes, arguing that the embryos constituted the 'unborn' and that implanting the embryos protected their right to life.

Both the High Court and Supreme Court stated that the embryo *in vitro* is not constitutionally protected under Article 40.3.3 and that the article applies only to embryos which are implanted *in utero*. The court stated that clarity as to the status of the embryo *in vitro* is necessary and that this must come from the Oireachtas. In the High Court, McGovern J criticised the lack of government action in this area, claiming that it left the embryos in a precarious situation. Furthermore, the lack of legislation since the publication of the CAHR Report has forced the courts to deal with complex issues which should be the subject of a regulatory regime established by the Oireachtas. In the Supreme Court, Murray CJ considered that the issue was not justiciable, stating that it is for the legislature to resolve such policy issues as it has 'initial responsibility for the protection and regulation of constitutional rights'. However, Denham J correctly noted that the court was being asked to interpret an article of the Constitution rather than engaging in philosophical debates on human life:

> This case is not about the wonder and mystery of human life. This is a court of law which has been requested to make a legal decision on the construction of an article of the Constitution of Ireland. The question raised is whether the term 'unborn' in the Constitution includes the three frozen embryos in issue in this case. It is a matter of construing the word in the Constitution to determine its constitutional meaning (at 367).

Although the court declined to state what status the embryo *in vitro* has in Irish law, McGovern J in the High Court and Geoghegan J in the Supreme Court seemed to favour the intermediate position on the status of the embryo, as both considered that the embryo is deserving of 'respect'. It is now for the legislature to state what that 'respect' means in law as the lack of regulations indicating how the embryo should be respected 'is undesirable and arguably contrary to the spirit of the Constitution' (at 393).

ESCR in Ireland

Two Irish universities, University College Cork (UCC) and Trinity College Dublin (TCD), have stated that embryonic stem cell research was permissible in their respective institutions (TCD, 2009; UCC, 2008) and drafted ethical guidelines in line with the recommendations of the ICB. Following on from this, in October 2010 Science Foundation Ireland (SFI, 2010) and the Health Research Board (HRB) announced that they would not consider grant applications that use embryonic stem cells, on direction from the Department of Health, who stated that it was preparing a regulatory framework for AHR that would encompass ESCR. To date, no regulations have been forthcoming but the funding policy remains in place and no public funds can be spent on ESCR. In 2014, the Irish Medicines Board licensed the Centre for Cell Manufacturing Ireland, which will supply adult stem cells for research (O'Kelly, 2014; O'Sullivan, 2014). By banning public funding of ESCR and providing this licence to supply adult stem cells, the government's policy appears to favour adult stem cell research.

Although, following the SFI and HRB decisions, state funding cannot be used for ESCR, the absence of a regulatory framework on a statutory footing means that there is currently no mechanism preventing researchers utilising private funding from carrying out ESCR in a manner which may not be in accordance with ethical best practice. Not only would this mean that the status of the embryo and its protection would vary according to individual researchers, but there would be no national oversight of ESCR (with the exception of the ethical guidelines that must be followed in research generally).

Towards a framework for regulation of ESCR

Although *Roche* makes it clear that the embryo *in vitro* has no constitutional protection, the legal status of the embryo and ESCR is uncertain. ESCR is not illegal, and the absence of any regulatory structure may enable the research to develop in an unregulated sphere with no legal or ethical oversight. To address this there is a need to resolve the status of the embryo and regulate for ESCR.

In order to introduce a coherent regulatory structure for ESCR, there is first a need for a public debate. The challenge with introducing ESCR regulation in Ireland is that, to date, the focus of debate in relation to embryos has been on the application of Article 40.3.3 and thus the discussion has largely been framed by the parameters of the abortion debate. Now that the Supreme Court has clarified that the embryo is not considered 'unborn', the focus should be on the specific issues relevant to ESCR. The potential of the research in the development of regenerative therapies and the dignity of those who need these therapies should also be considered in this debate.

Although this is a difficult and challenging subject matter that is fraught with ethical uncertainty, it *is* possible for this debate to be conducted in a mature and thoughtful manner and it *is* possible for a robust legal framework to emerge out of this debate. A useful example is found in the development of the United Kingdom regulatory process. The UK introduced a robust regulatory framework after a long process of debate (Gunning and English, 1983). It began with the Warnock Report in 1984 (Department of Health and Security, 1984), which was one of the first reports in the world to consider embryo research, and the 1987 White Paper Human Fertilisation and Embryology: A Framework for Legislation. It culminated with the passing of the Human Fertilisation and Embryology Act 1990 and accompanying secondary legislation that regulates ESCR and AHR. The legislation also established an independent regulatory authority (IRA), the Human Fertilisation and Embryology Authority (HFEA) that publishes a code of conduct and oversees the licensing system established in the Act. This strict but liberal system has been lauded as having 'engendered public confidence in the ethical development and use of human reproductive technologies' (Department of Health, 2005: para. 2.13).

Just as the recommendations of the Warnock Report formed a basis for the HFE Act 1990, the recommendations of the CAHR and ICB are a solid foundation on which to begin a national debate in Ireland. Both reports were comprehensive independent reports, free from political interference and based on legal and ethical reasoning. As with any discussion on the status of an entity so closely linked to human life, this debate will be complex and challenging. This is, however, not an insurmountable hurdle. The Protection of Life During Pregnancy Act 2013 was introduced after a period of intense public debate that heard from the legal profession, the medical profession as well as civil society groups. This process, during which various sections of Irish society were given an opportunity to contribute to the debate and potentially to impact on the development of the legislative framework, should be followed in the development of regulations for ESCR.

Both the CAHR and ICB reports recommended the establishment of a regulatory framework similar to that of the HFEA. The introduction of legislation and the establishment of an IRA is essential in the context of ESCR. Legislation would clarify the status of the embryo and outline the permitted boundaries of the research. Important issues to be addressed by the legislation would include whether only embryos left over after IVF treatment could be used, or if embryos could be created specifically for research purposes. An IRA would be a suitable body to oversee the implementation of the research and to publish a code of conduct to guide researchers and clinicians. ESCR is an ever developing science and the law alone is ill equipped to keep pace with the changes in science (Koops et al., 2009). An IRA can quickly update its code of conduct in line with scientific developments and advise the government when any new technology necessitates a change in the law. This is crucial as developments in technology can undermine basic assumptions upon which a particular statute was based (Sunstein, 1990). The HFEA has fulfilled this role in the UK since 1990 and although problems have arisen from time to time, overall it has served the regulatory system well (Callus, 2011; Department of Health, 2005).

During the debates on the HFE Act 1990 in the UK, it was noted that 'legislation is necessary not only to regulate research on embryos and to protect the integrity of reproductive medicine, as well as the legal position of the scientist or clinician, but to take account of social and ethical considerations' (HC Deb, 1990: col. 938). The evolution and development of the system in the UK has illustrated that this is indeed correct and the introduction of a similar system in Ireland that is reflective of our societal beliefs can ensure that there is legal and ethical oversight of the use of embryos in Ireland.

Conclusion

There is no doubt that the debates on the moral and legal status of the embryo will involve discussions on the beginning of life. ESCR raises series ethical and moral issues but this chapter argues that the Oireachtas has an obligation to clarify the legal status of the embryo and to regulate ESCR in Ireland. The courts should not be left to resolve these issues on a case by case basis. Rather, the status of the embryo and the boundaries of ESCR must be determined by the Oireachtas following a considered public debate. The discussions preceding the introduction of the Protection of Life During Pregnancy Act 2013 show that an informed debate on a topic of this nature is possible. In the wake of the decision of the Supreme Court in *Roche* v. *Roche*, it is clear that another constitutional referendum is not necessary. Instead, the focus should be on the development of a regulatory framework. Policy-makers must not automatically adopt a restrictive approach in face of the moral uncertainty around the embryo. If embryo destructive research is prohibited in Ireland, to be morally consistent, we may also need to ban any therapies that use ESCR. If ESCR is prohibited in Ireland for being immoral, by implication any therapies arising out of this 'immoral conduct' should also be prohibited, otherwise we would be profiting from immoral conduct. A knee jerk reaction that prohibits the research ignores the wider moral and ethical implications of its decision and the long-term impact that a decision would have on the availability and use of future therapies in Ireland must be considered. Finally, it must be clear that this debate is not the same as the abortion debate and the two must not be conflated.

Despite the commitment of the government to regulate ESCR in its Programme for Government (2011) no regulations have been forthcoming. Continuing this legal vacuum gives rise to the possibility of abuse and exploitation of the embryo in Ireland. While the government may not be enthusiastic about beginning a debate on the status of the embryo, Irish policy-makers must confront these challenging ethical considerations and introduce a regulatory framework for ESCR.

Notes

1 I would like to thank Daniel Callahan, Senior Research Scholar and co-founder of the Hastings Center, for a discussion on this point.

2 A hydatiform mole is when an embryo becomes a tumour which will endanger the life of the mother if it is not removed.

3 The term embryo *in vitro* is when the embryo is fertilised outside the woman's body, while the term *in vivo* arises when fertilisation takes place within the woman's body, e.g. in the fallopian tubes.

References

Boyle, K. (1982) 'Pre-empting a delicate issue', *Irish Times*, 5 August.

CAHR (Commission on Assisted Human Reproduction) (2005) *Report of the Commission on Assisted Human Reproduction*. Dublin.

Callus, T. (2011) 'Ensuring operational compliance and ethical responsibility in the regulation of ART: the HFEA, past, present, and future', *Law, Innovation and Technology*, 3(1): 85.

Cohen, C. (2007) *Renewing the Stuff of Lie: Stem Cells, Ethics, and Public Policy.* Oxford: Oxford University Press.
Congregation for the Doctrine of the Faith (2008) *Instruction Dignitas Personae on Certain Biological Questions.* Rome.
CRG (Constitution Review Group) (1996) *Report of the Constitution Review Group.* Dublin.
Department of Health (2005) *Review of the Human Fertilisation and Embryology Act: A Public Consultation.* Dublin.
Department of Health and Security (1984) *Report of the Committee of Inquiry into Human Fertilisation and Embryology.* London.
Editorial (2004) 'The promise of stem cells', *Nature Neuroscience*, 7: 1013.
Evans, D. (ed.) (1996) *Conceiving the Embryo: Ethics, Law and Practice in Human Embryology.* The Hague: Martinus Nijhoff Publishers.
Fitzgerald, K. (2003) 'Human embryonic stem cell research: ethics in the face of uncertainty', in N. Snow (ed.), *Stem Cell Research: New Frontiers in Ethics and Science.* Notre Dame: Notre Dame Press, pp. 131–40.
Ford, N. (1988) *When Did I Begin?* New York: Cambridge University Press.
Goldstein, L. (2008) 'Political issues in the stem cell debate: the view from California', in K. Renwick Monroe, R. Miller J. and Tobis (eds), *Fundamental of the Stem Cell Debate.* Berkley: University of California Press, pp. 95–107.
Grobstein, C. (1981) *From Chance to Purpose.* Massachusetts: Addison-Wesley Publishing Company.
Gunning, J. and English, V. (1993) *Human IVF: A Case Study on the Regulation of Medical Innovation.* Aldershot: Dartmouth.
Harris, J. (1985) *The Value of Life: An Introduction to Medical Ethics.* London: Routledge & Kegan Paul .
Holm, S. (2002) 'Going to the roots of the stem cell controversy', *Bioethics*, 16: 493.
ICB (Irish Council for Bioethics) (2008) *Ethical, Legal and Scientific Issues Concerning Stem Cell Research.* Dublin.
Johnson Kukla, H. (2001–2) 'Embryonic stem cell research: an ethical justification', *Georgetown Law Journal*, 90(2): 503.
Koops, B., Lips, M., Prins, C. and Schellekens, M. (2006) *Starting Points for ICT Regulation.* The Hague: Asser Press.
Latham, R. (2009) 'The once and future debate on human embryonic stem cell research', *Yale Journal of Health Law and Policy*, 9: 483.
Locke, J. ([1689] 1959) *An Essay Concerning Human Understanding.* Collated and annotated by A.C. Fraser. New York: Dover Publications.
Lockwood, M. (1985) 'When does life begin?', in M. Lockwood (ed.), *Moral Dilemmas in Modern Medicine.* Oxford: Oxford University Press, pp. 9–31.
Meyer, M. and Nelson, L. (2001) 'Respecting what we destroy: reflections on human embryo research', *The Hastings Centre Report*, 31(1): 16.

O'Kelly, E. (2014) 'Stem cells: one man's principles are another man's pain', *Irish Independent*, 2 February.

O'Sullivan, C. (2014) 'Failure to legislate "will hurt research"', *Irish Examiner*, 28 January.

Parens, E. (2000) 'What has the President asked of NBAC? On the ethics and politics of embryonic stem cell research', in National Bioethics Advisory Commission, *Ethical Issues in Human Stem Cell Research: Volume II Commissioned Papers*. Maryland, pp. I-1–12.

Petit, E. (2010) 'An ethics committee for patent offices?', in A. Plomer and P. Torremans (eds), *Embryonic Stem Cell Patents: European Patent Law and Ethics*. Oxford: Oxford University Press, pp. 305–22.

Poplawski, N. and Gillett, G. (1991) 'Ethics and embryos', *Journal of Medical Ethics*, 17(2): 59.

Programme for Government (2011) *Government for National Recovery 2011–2016*. Dublin.

Rawls, J. (1993) *Political Liberalism*. New York: Columbia University Press.

Robertson, J. (1999) 'Ethics and policy in embryonic stem cell research', *Kennedy Institute of Ethics Journal*, 9(2): 109.

Semb, H. (2005) 'Human embryonic stem cells: origins, properties and applications', *APMIS*, 113(11–12): 743.

SFI (Science Foundation Ireland) (2010) 'Research using human embryonic stem cells'. Available at: www.sfi.ie/funding/grant-policies/research-using-human-embryonic-stem-cells/ (accessed 4 June 2015).

Siegel, A. (1999) 'Locating convergence: ethics, public policy and human stem cell research', in *National Bioethics Advisory Commission Report: Volume I Commissioned Papers*. Maryland.

Singapore Bioethics Advisory Commission (2002) *Ethical, Legal and Social Issues in Human Stem Cell Research, Reproductive and Therapeutic Cloning*. Singapore.

Singer, P. and Dawson, K. (1988) 'IVF technology and the argument from potential', *Philosophy and Public Affairs*, 17(2): 87.

Smith, D. (2006) 'Stuck in the middle', *Hastings Centre Report*, 36(1): 32.

St John-Stevas, N. (1964) *Law and Morals*. New York: Hawthorn Books.

Sunstein, C. (1990) *After the Rights Revolution: Reconceiving the Regulatory State*. Cambridge: Harvard University Press.

Teklenburg, G., Salker, M., Heijnen, C., Macklon, N., Brosens, J. (2010) 'The molecular basis of recurrent pregnancy loss: impaired natural embryo selection', *Molecular Human Reproduction*, 16(12): 886.

TCD (Trinity College Dublin) (2009) *Policy on Good Research Practice*. Dublin.

UCC (University College Cork) (2008) *Code of Practice for Research Using Embryonic Stem Cell Lines*. Cork.

Varmus, H. (2010) *The Art and Politics of Science*. New York: Norton & Co.

11

Children in clinical trials in Ireland: addressing the gaps in the legal framework

Katherine Wade

Introduction

Clinical trials are an important facet of clinical research as they lead to the development of new drugs, devices and treatments for human illness and disease. In order to develop suitable medicines and treatments for children, it is often essential to carry out clinical trials with them. Since children differ physiologically and developmentally from adults, results of research with adults cannot always be used effectively in paediatric care. In addition, certain diseases and conditions, such as the complications associated with prematurity, affect only children, thereby necessitating research with them. However, the conduct of clinical trials with children raises ethical concerns. The need to acquire evidence-based knowledge on the safety and efficacy of paediatric medicines and treatments must be balanced against the need to protect individual children from harm in the research process (Gill, 2004).

Despite this, the issue of clinical trials with children has received relatively little attention as the focus of either regulatory efforts or academic inquiry in the Irish context. This means that there are gaps in the law and a lack of clarity in relation both to the law and the standards for ethical oversight. Some areas which need further clarity include provisions for child assent and parental consent, the process of risk–benefit assessment and the requirements for research that does not offer the child the prospect of direct benefit (non-therapeutic trials).[1] This chapter will focus on the latter issue, namely the requirements for the protection of children in non-therapeutic clinical trials. This remains one of the most contentious issues in this field and, thus, the legal and ethical requirements in this regard require detailed examination. To this end, this chapter first gives a general overview of the current legal framework regarding clinical trials in Ireland. It then focuses on the law in relation to non-therapeutic clinical trials with children. It is argued that the lack of clarity in Irish law in this area must be addressed in order to provide sufficient protection for children. A clear and transparent system of regulation is also important for parents and those who design, conduct and approve research, to ensure they have a clear understanding of their obligations with respect to children in this context.

Clinical trials in Ireland: the current legal framework

The main legal instrument in the area of clinical trials in Ireland is the European Communities (Clinical Trials on Medicinal Products for Human Use) Regulations, 2004 (EC Regulations 2004). This implements the Clinical Trials Directive 2001 (Directive 2001/20/EC). This framework is in the process of being replaced by EU Regulation No. 536/2014 on Clinical Trials (EU Regulation 2014). Since this is a Regulation (rather than a Directive), it will be directly binding in member states, without the need for implementing legislation and will be fully in force in 2016. Both the EC Regulations 2004 and the EU Regulation 2014 set out requirements for the conduct of clinical trials with investigational medicinal products (IMPs).[2] Such trials involve, for example, the administration of a new drug to compare it with an existing one, or the addition of a drug to a standard treatment regime. Other types of clinical trials which do not involve IMPs are not regulated by a domestic legal instrument.[3] These include interventional clinical trials testing surgical procedures, radiological procedures, devices, behavioural treatments, process-of-care changes and preventive care. Examples of such trials in children include examining different techniques which measure cardiac function and comparing cardiopulmonary bypass combined with a heart-lung machine (ECMO) to standard ventilator treatment. Clinical trials can also be non-interventional, wherein drugs and treatments are observed for efficacy and safety after marketing authorisation has been approved.

While clinical trials which do not involve IMPs are not regulated by a domestic legal instrument, there is a range of different ethical instruments which give guidance in the area. These include the World Medical Association Declaration of Helsinki: Ethical Principles for Medical Research Involving Human Subjects, 2013 (Declaration of Helsinki 2013) and the Council for International Organisations of Medical Sciences, International Ethical Guidelines for Biomedical Research Involving Human Subjects, 2002 (CIOMs Guidelines 2002). Guidance can also be drawn from human rights instruments developed by the Council of Europe, in particular the Convention on Human Rights and Biomedicine (Oviedo Convention 1997) and the Additional Protocol Concerning Biomedical Research (Additional Protocol 2005). However, Ireland has not ratified either of these instruments and therefore they are not legally binding in Ireland. This means that while clinical trials with IMPs are governed by legal requirements, clinical trials which do not involve IMPs are governed only by non-binding ethical guidance.

However, it is submitted that since clinical trials which do not involve

IMPs pose risks to the health of subjects they should also be governed by law. Both types of clinical trials require a robust legal framework setting out protective safeguards for all research participants, including children. This could be achieved by the introduction of a Clinical Research Act covering all clinical research in Ireland. The requirements of the EU Regulation 2014 could be mostly replicated in this Act for interventional clinical trials which do not involve IMPs. This would ensure a clear legal framework and provide equal protection to all children involved in clinical trials in Ireland. It would also mean clarity for Research Ethics Committees (RECs), in that they would be required to assess research protocols by reference to one set of legal standards.

There are also some inadequacies in the current framework for clinical trials with IMPs in Ireland as contained in the EC Regulations 2004 and EU Regulation 2014. These pertain to issues relating to child assent, parental consent and REC approval. However, the remainder of this chapter will focus on the issue of the lack of clarity in the law regarding clinical trials which do not offer the prospect of direct benefit to the child (non-therapeutic clinical trials). The inadequacies of the current Irish law regarding this type of clinical trial are addressed and recommendations for reform are made. This includes measures which can be taken to improve the process of research approval by RECs for clinical trials with children. The recommendations aim to strike a balance between promoting research with children and safeguarding them from unacceptable levels of harm in clinical trials. They also seek to ensure legal clarity for those who apply the law, such as researchers and REC members, in order to provide a consistent level of protection for children in clinical trials in Ireland.

Non-therapeutic clinical trials with children

Non-therapeutic clinical trials with human subjects include Phase I clinical trials, which involve administering a medicinal product to a group of healthy individuals after evidence of its potential efficacy has been gathered from animal trials. Such trials generally assess toxicity and absorption (Institute of Medicine, 2004: 72). Phase II trials can also be non-therapeutic since such trials test toxicity and efficacy in larger groups of people. Often drugs might not have to go through a Phase I trial with children. If the drug is already used in adults or is in a later phase with adults, dose requirements and toxicity information may be studied in children, by carrying out Phase II or Phase III trials with them (Institute of Medicine, 2004: 72–4). In these latter trials, it is usually hoped that they might result in some direct benefit for the children in the trial. However, since some diseases only affect children, or present so differently in them, it is often necessary to carry out Phase I trials of IMPs with children (Institute of Medicine, 2004). For interventional clinical trials which do not involve IMPs, non-therapeutic trials can include new preventative or diagnostic measures or surgical procedures.

The importance of non-therapeutic research with children

If all non-therapeutic research were disallowed, this would mean that much useful research could not be conducted, leading to the underdevelopment of paediatric medicine. There is a growing consensus that to exclude children from clinical research disadvantages them as a group and is therefore unethical (Sauer, 2002; McIntosh, 2004; Roth-Cline and Nelson, 2013). Such exclusion would mean that children would continue to experience the impact of diseases which might have become curable if research were carried out (Kent et al., 2007).

In this regard, the exclusion of children from research has led to unlicensed (this refers to using a drug for indications for which its use has not been approved) and off-label (this refers to administering a drug for an approved indication, but administering it in such a way that has not been approved) use of drugs with them (Choonara, 2004; Ramet and van den Anker, 2007). This means that once a drug has been approved in adults or older children, it is often used in younger children without sufficient information about its safety and efficacy in this population (Baer and Nelson, 2006). Studies in the past 20 years have shown that such practices are widespread in Europe and the United States. For example, a review of studies of off-label prescribing in paediatrics between 1990–2006 showed that the number of subjects receiving at least one off-label or unlicensed drug prescription ranged from 80–93% (Cuzzolin et al., 2006). Neonates are particularly affected by these practices (Conroy et al., 1999; 't Jong et al., 2001; Conroy and McIntyre, 2005; Kimland and Odlind, 2012). A recent study in an Irish Neonatal Intensive Care Unit showed that many neonates, particularly those who were premature, are given off-label and unlicensed treatments (Kieran et al., 2014). The use of off-label drugs is a particular concern for child health and has been shown to cause adverse effects (Choonara, 2004; European Medicines Agency, 2004; Neubert et al., 2004).

The United States Institute of Medicine (2004: 27) contends that '[e]xtrapolation and unsystematic "experimentation" ... may expose children to risk while simultaneously failing to generate a trustworthy knowledge base for future care'. This argument has also been adopted by Regulation (EC) No. 1901/2006 of the European Parliament and of the Council, which aims to promote the development of new medicines with children. It states that '[a]ny concerns about conducting trials in the paediatric population should be balanced by the ethical concerns about giving medicinal products to a population in which they have not been appropriately tested'.[4]

Lack of clarity in Irish law

In relation to the permissibility of non-therapeutic clinical trials with children in Irish law, EC Regulation 2004, Schedule 1, Part 4 sets out that 'some direct benefit for the group of patients involved in the clinical trial is to be obtained from that trial'. As Cave (2010) argues, this statement would appear to rule out research which does not have the prospect of direct benefit, since non-therapeutic research never seeks to benefit the group in the research, but rather future generations. This would seem to be the case, unless the word 'benefit' is interpreted as encompassing 'indirect benefits,' such as extra monitoring (Cave, 2010: 20–2). Similarly, if the term 'group of patients' is interpreted as referring to children, *in general*, who are afflicted with a certain disease or condition, this might also mean that there would be no requirement for direct benefit to the individual children in the trial (Cave, 2010: 18). However, as currently stated, the meaning of the provision remains unclear.

Article 32(1)(g) of EU Regulation 2014 states that the following conditions must be met for a clinical trial with an IMP to be carried out with minors:

> There are scientific grounds for expecting that participation in the clinical trial will produce:
> (i) a direct benefit for the minor concerned outweighing the risks and burdens involved; or
> (ii) some benefit for the population represented by the minor concerned and such a clinical trial will pose only minimal risk to, and will impose minimal burden on, the minor concerned in comparison with the standard treatment of the minor's condition.

EU Regulation 2014 is certainly clearer than the EC Regulations 2004 regarding the permissibility of non-therapeutic clinical trials involving IMPs with children. Article 32(1)(g)(ii) permits research where there is 'some benefit for the population represented by the minor concerned'. This means that clinical trials with IMPs can be conducted on individual children even if there is no prospect of direct benefit to them. It is sufficient that there is a benefit to the population they represent, i.e. children in the same age category. This position is also adopted in other European and international instruments, including the Oviedo Convention 1997 (Art. 17(2)), the Additional Protocol 2005 (Art. 15(2)), and the Declaration of Helsinki 2013 (para. 28).

The clarity provided in EU Regulation 2014 is a welcome development. It is clear that a trial which does not offer the prospect of a direct benefit to the individual child can be carried out. This is an appropriate position, provided adequate safeguards are put in place, as discussed further below. In light of the arguments set out above, it is difficult to justify an outright legal prohibition on clinical trials which do not offer the individual child the prospect of direct benefit. It is important that some Phase I and II trials with medicinal products, devices and procedures are conducted with children in order to tailor medical care to their needs. However, in setting the regulatory requirements in the area, the prospect of possible advances for children as a group must be balanced against the protection of individual children from harm (Miller and Kenny, 2002). An appropriate framework for clinical trials with children must strike a balance between promoting the development of suitable drugs and treatments for them, while providing adequate safeguards for research participants.

One of the main safeguards in non-therapeutic trials with children relates to defining a threshold of acceptable risk.[5] It was set out above that the term 'minimal risk and minimal burden' is used in EU Regulation 2014, the Oviedo Convention 1997, the Additional Protocol 2005 and the Declaration of Helsinki 2013. The following section explores European law regarding the manner in which this phrase should be defined. It is argued that in order to provide an adequate system of protection for children in clinical trials, clear guidance should be set out in law regarding the definition of this risk threshold. In addition, guidance must be given to RECs as to the application of this standard in practice.

Minimal risk and minimal burden

The requirement that non-therapeutic trials with children should incur only 'minimal risk and minimal burden' is present in EU Regulation 2014. However, the Regulation contain little guidance as to how such a phrase might be interpreted. It states that the trial must contain 'minimal risk and minimal burden *in comparison with the standard treatment of the minor's condition*' (emphasis added). The phrase in italics provides little guidance. For example, making a comparison to 'standard treatment' in order to determine acceptable risk levels in trials where there may be a *benefit* for the child is understandable. If the new drug or treatment poses risks which are comparable to those in the standard treatment received by the child, this risk level may be appropriate. However, in determining acceptable risk levels for trials which *do not* offer the prospect of direct benefit to the child, this phrase is inappropriate. This is because 'standard treatment' for a sick child could incur high risks. Using such a definition for the threshold of risk in non-therapeutic trials may allow for comparably high risks in such trials. Regarding research with children, allowing high levels of risk for the good of others is particularly problematic. Thus, it is submitted that the phrase 'in comparison with the standard treatment of the minor's condition' does not provide sufficient guidance on assessing the threshold of risk to be permitted in the context of clinical trials which do not offer the prospect of direct benefit.

A definition of 'minimal risk and minimal burden' is provided in Article 17(1) of the Additional Protocol 2005. This states that '[f]or the purposes of this Protocol it is deemed that the research bears a minimal risk if, having regard to the nature and scale of the intervention, it is to be expected that it will result, at the most, in a very slight and temporary negative impact on the health of the person concerned'. Article 17(2) defines burden in the same way and states that research carries a minimal burden 'if it is to be expected that the discomfort will be, at the most, temporary and very slight for the person concerned'. Simonsen (2012) notes some problems with this definition. First, he argues that the use of the wording 'to be expected' is problematic. This is because the risks of research are usually remote and are certainly not expected in the ordinary meaning of the word (Simonsen, 2012: 196–7). In other words, the language used does not correlate well with the definition of risk which is related to 'probability and magnitude of harm' (Simonsen, 2012: 196). Second, he argues that the reference to 'only very slight and temporary negative impact' is very restrictive, since most research would include even a very remote or theoretical chance of severe complications and enduring harm (Simonsen, 2012: 197).

It is submitted that the definition of 'minimal risk and minimal burden' in the Additional Protocol 2005 is nonetheless useful. Simonsen's criticism regarding the term 'expected' could be addressed by omitting the term from the definition. The Protocol could simply state 'minimal risk refers to, at the most, a very slight and temporary negative impact on the health of the person concerned'. The same recommendation should apply to the definition of minimal burden. In relation to Simonsen's second criticism, it is indeed true that there are unknown risks in all research. Nonetheless, some threshold of risk must be set in non-therapeutic trials. Referring to the remote chance of severe and enduring complications in the definition of minimal risk would be contrary to the aim of providing a restrictive safeguard by which to measure the acceptability of non-therapeutic trials with children.

Furthermore, the definition in the Additional Protocol 2005 avoids many of the complications which have arisen in other attempts to define the concept. For example, in the United States, minimal risk is defined as 'the probability and magnitude of harm or discomfort anticipated in the research are not greater in and of themselves than those ordinarily encountered in daily life or during the performance of routine physical or psychological examinations or tests' (45 CFR 46.102(i) (US Department of Health and Human Services Regulations) and 21 CFR 50.3(k) (Food and Drug Administration Regulations)). This definition raises many difficulties and has been the subject of sustained debate. The difficulties relate to the arbitrariness of comparing research risks to risks in daily life or routine examinations or tests. For example, while society might deem it acceptable for children to be exposed to the risks of playing sports due to the attendant benefits, this does not necessarily mean it would consider it acceptable to expose children to comparable risks for the purposes of *research*, particularly if there is no benefit for them (Wendler et al., 2005). The same is the case for routine tests and examinations. As Freedman et al. (1993) note, a splenectomy or a pancreatic biopsy is defined as minimal risk in medical literature, but may be justified because of the necessity of the procedure in the patient population.

Additionally, daily life and routine tests can differ widely depending on the child's situation. As Glass and Binik (2008) note, the risks faced by children in countries which are experiencing war or famine, for example, are considerably greater than those living in peaceful and developed countries. Similarly, for a sick child routine tests and examinations might include higher risks than those of a normal child. Thus, it could mean that it would be acceptable to expose sick children or children who live in dangerous environments to higher levels of risk than healthy children living in safe environments, in the context of non-therapeutic trials (Glass and Binik, 2008).

The definition in the Additional Protocol 2005 avoids such difficulties, because it does not compare the concept of minimal risk for non-therapeutic trials to risks encountered in other situations. It simply sets out criteria for that which can be considered minimal risk. For an intervention to be considered minimal risk under the Additional Protocol, the possible 'negative impact on the health of the person' must be first 'very slight' and, second, 'temporary'. Thus, if the intervention fails one or both of these tests, it cannot be considered minimal risk. If it is thought that the drug or intervention poses a significant negative impact and/or an impact which might be long-lasting, the trial cannot proceed. In addition, there must *also* only be a minimal burden. This means that not only must the *risks* be very slight and temporary, the same standard applies to the discomforts which may be caused by the trial.

While the definition in the Additional Protocol is free of some the difficulties which have occurred in the Unites States context, it could be argued that the definition simply replaces the word 'minimal' with the term 'very slight', which again requires elucidation. However, in this regard, it must be noted that another aspect of defining minimal risk in the European framework involves the inclusion of examples. The Explanatory Report to the Additional Protocol (para. 100) (Explanatory Report) sets out some concrete examples of interventions which pose a 'minimal risk and minimal burden'. Examples of such interventions include obtaining bodily fluids without invasive intervention, e.g. taking saliva or urine samples or cheek swab; at the time when tissue samples are being taken, for example during a surgical operation, taking a small additional tissue sample, taking a blood sample from a peripheral vein or taking a sample of capillary blood; and minor extensions to non-invasive diagnostic measures using technical equipment, such as sonographic examinations, taking an electrocardiogram following rest, one X-ray exposure, carrying out one computer tomographic exposure or one exposure using magnetic resonance imaging without a contrast medium.

As Simonsen (2012: 199) notes, 'concrete examples contribute to the ascertainment of the standard of minimal risk and burden by establishing palpable and familiar benchmarks'. Regarding the provision of examples in the United States, Kopelman (2000) argues that more work should be done on the development of examples of the risks of harm associated with common interventions, and that this should be done in an open way, through public consultation. This is a positive recommendation that should also be made in the European context. It must also be noted that the examples currently given in the Explanatory Report do not refer to risk levels, discomforts or side-effects which are thought to be acceptable for trials with IMPs. Thus, further guidance needs to be developed in setting acceptable risk in this context. This could refer to the level of information which should be available from pre-clinical testing for example.

However, it must be stressed that a subjective element in the determination of the trial is always necessary. The Explanatory Report states that the procedures on the list of examples may not always entail minimal risk or burden, and assessment on an individual basis must always be carried out. For example, a clinical trial may involve a number of the interventions on the list, which, taken collectively, could entail greater than minimal risk and minimal burden. In addition, regard must be had to the particular characteristics of the group in the trial. For example, the risk of a blood draw for a very premature baby might be greater than for a term neonate. Thus, while lists of interventions which are considered to entail minimal risks certainly provide RECs with useful guidance, they should only be used as a 'supplement to, rather than a substitute for' the informed judgement of RECs (Miller and Weijer, 2000: 8).

This chapter has argued that the definition of minimal risk and the list of examples contained in the Additional Protocol 2005 and its Explanatory Report are positive in terms of providing guidance to RECs in assessing non-therapeutic trials with children. However, it must be noted that Ireland has not ratified the Oviedo Convention or the Additional Protocol 2005. Thus, the definition and guidance contained therein are currently not binding in Ireland. It is submitted that ratification of these instruments is required. It was argued at the outset of this chapter that Ireland should introduce legislation covering all other forms of clinical research. The Council of Europe framework for minimal risk and burden should be replicated in this Act and should apply to all non-therapeutic interventional clinical trials with children in Ireland.

The role of research ethics committees

RECs play a central role in terms of striking the balance between ensuring ethical research is permitted and protecting children in clinical trials. The Council of Europe framework regarding the limits of risk in non-therapeutic clinical trials with children should be included in guidance for RECs. This could be done in the forthcoming legislative reform of RECs governance in Ireland, whereby the Health Information and Quality Authority (HIQA) will be charged with providing operational guidance to all RECs (Madden, 2011: 603).[6] RECs should be provided with the Council of Europe definition of minimal risk and minimal burden, and the list of examples as set out above, including additional guidance for Phase I trials with IMPs. Additionally, dedicated training regarding the definition and its utilisation should be provided to all REC members by HIQA. This would help to ensure standardised approval processes for all clinical trials with children in Ireland.

There are other measures regarding the composition of RECs that should be addressed in order to ensure that RECs provide effective protection for children in clinical trials. For example, both the EC Regulations 2004 (section 13(7)) and the EU Regulation 2014 (Article 10(1)) require the inclusion of paediatric expertise for the approval of clinical trials with children. It is also submitted that healthcare professionals from subspecialties, such as neonatology and paediatric oncology, for example, should be included in RECs for the approval of studies in these areas. These measures are important in ensuring that research proposals receive expert examination from those who are familiar with some of the interventions or drugs in the trial and aware of the physiology of children. In this regard, it would be useful to have one specialist REC in Ireland for the approval of clinical trials with children (Felzmann et al., 2010: 88).

Conclusion

Clinical research involving children raises many legal and ethical challenges. The area of clinical trials, in particular, exposes children to risks to their health and well-being, since it involves the use of drugs, procedures and devices to test their efficacy. Clinical trials which offer no prospect of direct benefit to the child are particularly contentious. Such research is difficult to justify since it exposes children to risks for the good of others. However, disallowing such research would lead to serious impacts for the health of children as a group. Thus, in the legal regulation of this area, a balance must be struck between the interests of the group and the interests of individual children.

This chapter has argued that the framework provided in the Council of Europe instruments reflects an appropriate balance between these competing ethical imperatives. The restrictive definition of minimal risk as a 'very slight and temporary negative impact on the health of the person concerned' contained in the Additional Protocol 2005 is appropriate in this context. Since children's autonomy is developing, they require heightened protection in the context of clinical research. This is particularly the case for neonates and young infants, who are not in a position to express their opinions in relation to research involvement. Involving children in research which has no benefit for them, particularly if the risks involved are serious, can amount to using them as a means to fulfil society's end. Allowing for more than a minimal level of risk for the good of others amounts to 'instrumentalisation of these persons contrary to their dignity' (Explanatory Report to the Oviedo Convention, 1997: para. 111).

In order to ensure the protection of the child, it is also important that RECs have adequate guidance regarding the meaning of minimal risk and minimal burden. In this regard, they should be provided with guidance on the Council of Europe's framework for minimal risk and minimal burden and receive training regarding its utilisation. While the Council of Europe framework is particularly useful in providing concrete examples of minimal risk and minimal burden for researchers and RECs, more work is required regarding the development of additional examples, in particular in the context of trials with investigational medicinal products.

In order for this framework to apply in the Irish context, the Oviedo Convention and its Additional Protocol must be ratified by Ireland. In addition, the Convention's definition of minimal risk and minimal burden and the examples in the Explanatory Report should be included in new Irish legislation applying to all interventional clinical trials with children. This framework must also be used in developing guidance and training for researchers and RECs in Ireland. Taking such steps to clarify Irish law and policy on non-therapeutic trials with children would go a long way in moving towards a robust and transparent system of protection for children in clinical trials in Ireland.

Notes

1 There is much debate over labelling trials as 'therapeutic' or 'non-therapeutic', since trials can involve interventions which do offer the subject direct benefit and those which do not (Verdun-Jones and Weisstub, 1998). Notwithstanding these problems, for reasons of brevity, the term 'non-therapeutic trial' is used to refer to research which *overall* does not offer the prospect of direct medical benefit to an individual child in a trial.

2 This is defined as a 'medicinal product which is being tested or used as a reference, including as a placebo, in a clinical trial' Article 2(2) (5), EU Regulation 2014.

3 One exception to this is that clinical trials which involve medical devices must meet additional requirements set out in the Directive 93/42/EEC Concerning Medical Devices as transposed into Irish law by the European Communities (Medical Devices) Regulations 1997, S.I. No. 252 of 1994. However, these cover safety and quality requirements and do not cover additional provisions regarding the conduct of clinical trials involving devices with children.

4 Article 7, Regulation (EC) No. 1901/2006 of the European Parliament and of the Council of 12 December 2006 on Medicinal Products for Paediatric Use and Amending Regulation (EEC) No. 1768/92, Directive 2001/20/EC, Directive 2001/83/EC and Regulation (EC) No. 726/2004.

5 The interpretation of the term 'benefit' is also central to the protection of children in clinical trials. A full discussion of this is outside the scope of this chapter. Benefit is understood in this chapter as direct medical benefit.

6 The Health Information Bill is expected to be published in late 2015. See Government Legislation Programme, Autumn Session 2014 (17 September, 2014).

References

Additional Protocol to the Convention on Human Rights and Biomedicine, concerning Biomedical Research, Strasbourg, 25. I. 2005.

Baer, G.R. and Nelson, R. (2006) 'Ethical challenges in neonatal research: summary report of the ethics group of the newborn drug development initiative', *Clinical Therapeutics*, 28(9): 1399.

Cave, E. (2010) 'Seen but not heard? Children in clinical trials', *Medical Law Review*, 18(1): 1.

Choonara, I. (2004) 'Unlicensed and off-label drug use in children: implications for safety', *Expert Opinion. Drug Safety*, 3(2): 81.

Conroy, S. and McIntyre, J. (2005) 'The use of unlicensed and off-label medicines in the neonate', *Seminars in Fetal and Neonatal Medicine*, 10(2): 115.

Conroy, S., McIntyre, J, and Choonara, I. (1999) 'Unlicensed and off-label drug use in neonates', *Archives of Disease in Childhood: Fetal Neonatal Edition*, 80(2): F142.

Convention for the Protection of Human Rights and Dignity of the Human Being with regard to the Application of Biology and Medicine: Convention on Human Rights and Biomedicine, Oviedo, 4. IV. 1997.

Cuzzolin, L. Atzei, A. and Fanos, V. (2006) 'Off-label and unlicensed prescribing for newborns and children in different settings: a review of the literature and a consideration about drug safety', *Expert Opinion. Drug Safety*, 5(5): 703.

European Communities (Clinical Trials on Medicinal Products for Human Use) Regulations, 2004, S.I. No. 190 of 2004.

European Medicines Agency (2004) *Evidence of Harm from Off-label of Unlicensed Medicines in Children*, EMEA/126327/2004.

Explanatory Report to the Additional Protocol to the Convention on Human Rights and Biomedicine, concerning Biomedical Research (CETS NO. 195).

Felzmann, H., Sixsmith, J., O'Higgins, S., Ní Chonnachtaigh, S. and Nic Gabhainn, S. (2010) *Ethical Review and Children's Research in Ireland*. Dublin: Office of the Minister for Children and Youth Affairs.

Freedman, B., Fuks, A. and Weijer, C. (1993) 'In loco parentis minimal risk as an ethical threshold for research upon children', *Hastings Center Report*, 23(2): 13.

Gill, D. (2004) 'Ethical principles and operational guidelines for good clinical practice in paediatric research. Recommendations of the Ethics Working

Group of the Confederation of European Specialists in Paediatrics (CESP)', *European Journal of Pediatrics*, 163(2): 53.

Glass, K.C. and Binik, A. (2008) 'Rethinking risk in paediatric research', *Journal of Law and Medical Ethics*, 36(3): 567.

Institute of Medicine (2004) *Ethical Conduct of Clinical Research Involving Children*. Washington, D.C: National Academies Press.

Kent, A., Oosterwijk, C., Schyns, T. and Poortman, Y. (2007) 'Paediatric medicines: a view from patient organisations', in K. Rose and J.N. van den Anker (eds), *Guide to Paediatric Clinical Research*. Basel: Karger, pp. 13–24.

Kieran, E.A., O'Callaghan, N. and O'Donnell, C.P.F. (2014) 'Unlicensed and off-label drug use in an Irish neonatal intensive care unit: a prospective cohort study', *Acta Paediatrica*, 103(4): e139.

Kimland, E. and Odlind, V. (2012) 'Off-label drug use in pediatric patients', *Clinical Pharmacological and Therapeutics*, 91(5): 796.

Kopelman, L. (2000) 'Children as research subjects: a dilemma', *Journal of Medicine and Philosophy*, 25(6): 745.

Madden, D. (2011) *Medicine, Ethics and the Law*, 2nd edn. Dublin: Bloomsbury Professional.

McIntosh, N. (2004) 'Ethical principles of research with children', *Current Paediatrics*, 14(6): 489.

Miller, P.B. and Weijer, C. (2000) 'Moral solutions in assessing research risk', *IRB: Ethics and Human Research*, 22(5): 6.

Miller, P.B. and Kenny, N.P. (2002) 'Walking the moral tightrope: respecting and protecting children in health related research', *Cambridge Quarterly of Healthcare Ethics*, 11(3): 217.

Neubert, A., Dormann, H., Weiss, J., Egger, T., Criegee-Rieck, M., Rascher, W., Brune, K. and Hinz, B. (2004) 'The impact of unlicensed and off-label drug use on adverse drug reactions in paediatric patients', *Drug Safety*, 27(13): 1059.

Ramet, J., and van den Anker, J.N. (2007) 'The European Academy of Paediatrics (EAP/CESP) and its demand for more clinical research', in K. Rose and J.N. van den Anker (eds), *Guide to Paediatric Clinical Research*. Basel: Karger, pp. 5–12.

Regulation (EC) No. 1901/2006 of the European Parliament and of the Council on medicinal products for paediatric use and amending Regulation (EEC) No 1768/92, Directive 2001/20/EC, Directive 2001/83/EC and Regulation (EC) No 726/2004, [2006] O.J. L 378/1.

Regulation (EU) No. 536/2014 of the European Parliament and of the Council of 16 April 2014 on clinical trials on medicinal products for human use, and repealing Directive 2001/20/EC, [2014] O.J. L 158/1.

Roth-Cline, M.D., and Nelson, R.N. (2013) 'Ethical and practical considerations in conducting neonatal research', in A.E. Mulberg, D. Murphy, J. Dunne and

L. Mathis (eds), *Pediatric Drug Development: Concepts and Applications*, 2nd edn. West Sussex: Wiley-Blackwell, pp. 73–82.

Sauer, P.J. (2002) 'Research in children: a report of the ethics group of CESP', *European Journal of Pediatrics*, 161(1): 1.

Simonsen, S. (2012) *Acceptable Risk in Biomedical Research: European Perspectives*. Dordrecht: Springer.

't Jong, G.W., Vulto, A.G., De Hoog, M., Schimmel, M., Tibboel, D. and van den Anker, J.N. (2001) 'A survey of the use of off-label and unlicensed drugs in a Dutch children's hospital', *Paediatrics*, 108(5): 1089 .

Verdun-Jones, S.N. and Weisstub, D.N. (1998) 'Drawing the distinction between therapeutic research and non-therapeutic experimentation: clearing a way through the definitional thicket', in D.N. Weisstub (ed.), *Research on Human Subjects: Ethics, Law and Social Policy*. Oxford: Pergamon, pp. 111–36.

Wendler, D., Belsky, L., Thompson, K.M. and Emanuel, E.J. (2005) 'Quantifying the federal minimal risk standard: implications for pediatric research without a prospect of direct benefit', *Journal of the American Medical Association*, 294(7): 826.

IV

OVERSIGHT OF DECISION-MAKING

12

Governance failures and organisational ethics: perspectives from the Neary and Halappanavar cases

Heike Felzmann

Introduction

While the majority of the professional healthcare ethics literature and in particular professional guidance documents focus primarily on individual accountability and responsibilities of healthcare professionals towards patients, colleagues and the public, the significance of the organisational context for ethical behaviour is considered much less frequently. Yet, in official reports on high profile Irish cases, such as the Lourdes Hospital Inquiry on the Neary case (Harding Clark, 2006) or the Health Information and Quality Authority (HIQA) report on University Hospital Galway (UHG) and the care of Savita Halappanavar (HIQA, 2013), the significance of the organisational context for individual professional decision-making and the success or failure of professional action has been clearly outlined (see also McCarthy, Chapter 1). After an outline of the significance of systemic factors in both of those cases, I will draw on literature from organisational clinical ethics and business ethics to provide a framework for thinking about the wider ethical responsibilities of healthcare organisations. I will outline how organisational structures are directly implicated in the facilitation of ethical actions by members of the organisation. Going even further, these structures could be conceptualised as the organisational equivalent to individual character traits that, if implemented correctly, may achieve the consistent orientation of organisational actions towards the realisation of ethical practice.

The Neary case: individual incompetence perpetuated by structural insufficiencies

Dr Neary was an obstetrician in the Our Lady of Lourdes Hospital in Drogheda who had performed an unusually high number of peripartum hysterectomies for which, in many cases, no clinical justification was available. In this case, there is no doubt about who was responsible for the performance of those unethical interventions, and therefore this case could be perceived as a paradigm case of the individual rogue professional who acts incompetently and with little regard to standards of practice and ethics. However, on a closer look, it is also an instructive case with regard to the importance of the wider context (for example, in relation to the gender aspect, as outlined by McCarthy et al., 2008) as well as specific questions regarding the governance of clinical practice.

In the investigation on the case it became apparent that individual staff members from different professional backgrounds had had concerns about his practices throughout the years (Harding Clark, 2006: 33), but that no effective action to address these concerns ever followed. On the one hand Neary's personality might have had an impact on how such concerns were being dealt with. As the report describes: 'Dr Neary had a strong personality with very strong views on many subjects and his demeanour and mood had a major influence on the unit' (Harding Clark, 2006: 12). General fear regarding job insecurity among existing staff was perceived as a further factor in the silencing of dissent (Harding Clark, 2006: 38, 41). In addition, a strict Catholic ethos underpinned obstetric and gynaecological services and strictly limited interventions like tubal ligations, potentially incentivising solutions in the area of fertility management that appeared compatible with Catholic ethos. As the inquiry describes, there was ample indication that given the strict Catholic ethos in this hospital and elsewhere, in some cases hysterectomies were performed in place of sterilisations. Accordingly, a higher incidence of such hysterectomies might have been perceived as potentially planned, 'compassionate hysterectomies', resulting from a doctor's greater willingness to bypass the strict Catholic ethos of the hospital, rather than from incompetence.

Most importantly, however, the organisational structures that were in place made the independent identification of problematic practices much less likely. There was no requirement of seeking a second opinion before the performance of hysterectomies, and no review and audit structures or staff education requirements were in place to review practice:

> [T]he Maternity Unit had a rigid and definite policy that only allowed clinical patient management to be reviewed if a patient complained. The Review Group found that senior midwives and medical staff had not noted the high rate of hysterectomies, nor had they asked the consultants the reasons for this high incidence. They noted that there was no audit, no regular meetings, no discussions nor any clinico-pathological conferences and no evidence of organised training programmes. In this atmosphere it was difficult for any member of staff to express clinical concerns. (Harding Clark, 2006: 12)

During the process of investigation into the case it emerged that the wider clinical practices in Drogheda differed significantly from other hospitals in Ireland, and abnormalities were not just restricted to Dr Neary:

> The medical culture in Drogheda was different and, in particular, a mode of clinical management was adopted that led to this difference … There was substantial evidence of a curious internal and external culture of isolation and absence of consultation within Our Lady of Lourdes Hospital. (Medical Council report on the Neary case, reported in Harding Clark, 2006: 15–16).

Facilitating this particular culture was an extraordinarily low level of staff turnover where the same staff worked together for decades with remarkably little influx of staff from the outside (Harding Clark, 2006: 41). Staff training under those conditions 'produced suitable nurses who fitted their mould – hardworking, respectful, Catholic nurses who were well trained, knew their place, trusted the consultants and suspended their critical or questioning faculties. They were trained to certain tasks – and to those tasks only' (Harding Clark, 2006: 41).

Overall, the Inquiry clearly considered the systemic aspects of the case to be more relevant than the issue of personal incompetence:

> This is not a simple story of an evil man or a bad doctor, nor is it a story of wholesale suppression of facts. The facts were there for all to see. There was no attempt to hide the procedures or pretend they were something else … It is the story of a doctor who, at critical points during his training, was inadequately supervised. He came to work in a unit which lacked leadership, peer review, audit or critical capacity. It is the story of a doctor with a deep fault line, which was recognised early but never corrected. It is a story of a committed doctor with a misplaced sense of confidence in his own ability. It is a story of deep misunderstanding and misapplication of clinical independence. (Harding Clark, 2006: 34–5)

What this indicates is that the focus on individual professional accountability, while an important factor, nevertheless does not ask the right questions about why so many women were allowed to be harmed over several decades by one doctor in Drogheda.

The Halappanavar case: the 'systems failures' aspect

Savita Halappanavar died in University Hospital Galway in October 2012 from septicaemia, after having been diagnosed with an impending miscarriage a week earlier. She had to wait for several days after her membranes had ruptured to deliver naturally instead of receiving an abortion, as she had requested. A termination at this stage would most likely have prevented the infection that killed her from taking hold in the first place. Initially, public debate centred around the assumption that personal religious convictions of those caring for her in University Hospital Galway impacted on her care, as there had been reports that she had been refused a termination on the grounds that Ireland was a Catholic country. More generally, there was also the concern that the Catholic inspired constitutional protection of the 'unborn' led to fatal decisions on her care. Over the following months, however, when three official investigations into her death (the Coroner's Report, MacLoughlin, 2013; HIQA, 2013; HSE, 2013) showed the extent of clinical failures, the public narrative moved towards the assumption that clinical failures rather than Catholic convictions had led to her death. The following reflections should not be taken as evidence that Catholicism was irrelevant for the course of events, but the primary focus is on the exploration of systemic factors.

All three inquiries into Savita Halappanavar's death found that there were significant deficiencies in the clinical care received, across different professional groups and different levels of seniority and experience. As the HIQA report stated, there was a general lack of provision of basic, fundamental care, for example, not following up on blood tests, failure to recognise that Savita Halappanavar was at risk of clinical deterioration, and a failure to act on or escalate concerns to an appropriately qualified clinician when she was showing the signs of clinical deterioration (HIQA, 2013: 10). In the report, the specific failures identified in relation to her care are, however, considered in the context of wider structures, both locally and nationally, that should support and facilitate the realisation of such practices. The range and scope of wider, systems-related concerns becomes apparent in the long list of specific concerns that HIQA outlines under ten different major headings. They are too far ranging and numerous to be discussed in detail within the scope of this chapter, but provide the reader of the report with a differentiated understanding of the multiple organisational dimensions that underlie the delivery of services to a patient. The report vividly conveys the extent to which deficiencies of an organisational nature have a significant effect on professional practice irrespective of the individual competence of the professionals caring for her.

According to the HIQA report, the individual clinical failures took place in a context where local governance arrangements with regard to numerous aspects of patient care, staff planning and implementation of clinical best practice were not sufficient to ensure safe patient care. One core concern was the implementation of best practice in relation to sepsis management for general and maternity patients. Despite significant patient numbers overall requiring ICU or HDU care for serious sepsis (HIQA, 2013: 13), sepsis management policies were ill defined and practically insufficient. Relevant sepsis screening instruments were not in use or insufficiently implemented, and training was not rolled out effectively to staff at all levels, resulting in at least half of the medical doctors, who would be the key professional group for the effective implementation of clinical sepsis management, not having received relevant internal training (HIQA, 2013: 13). The extent of the governance failures in respect of sepsis management is illustrated in the following passage:

> The Hospital had a guideline in place for the management of 'Suspected sepsis and sepsis in obstetric care'. However, the clinical governance arrangements were not robust enough to ensure adherence to this guideline. In addition, clinical

> staff had not received specific sepsis training in relation to the application of this policy and/or the specific management of a maternity patient with sepsis. The Hospital did not have in place effective arrangements to ensure that patient care was documented or that those caring for patients were fully informed of a patient's condition and treatment plan. The arrangements for the handover of patient care between the maternity clinical teams were not always effective and were not in line with best available evidence. (HIQA, 2013: 11–12)

An additional significant structural concern was related to staffing, and the report highlighted both specific local deficits and wider national shortcomings. In relation to local conditions, among several other serious concerns the report pointed out that 'the casemix of patients accommodated on St Monica's Ward [where Savita Halappanavar was being cared for] and their care needs were significantly diverse and complex. However, there was no evidence that the organisation of the workforce took account of the complexity and diversity of the patient casemix on St Monica's Ward' (HIQA, 2013: 13). On a national level, a comparable absence of important measures of effective workforce planning was evident on a larger scale: '[o]ne … concern is the lack of evidence of any national review, or national population-based needs assessment, undertaken to demonstrate the appropriate allocation of resources, including multidisciplinary workforce arrangements, for the provision of maternity services in Ireland' (HIQA, 2013: 17–18). On the basis of these observations, the report states in no uncertain terms that '[t]he HSE must review its workforce arrangements for maternity services nationally to ensure maternity teams are made up of sufficient numbers of staff with the right mix of skills and deployed effectively both during core and on-call hours' (HIQA, 2013: 19).

These specific shortcomings proved to be symptoms of a wider problem, namely the nature of governance arrangements throughout the Irish healthcare system. The governance of the local hospital group in Galway was described in the report as both overly complex and overly reliant on heavily over-tasked individual professionals. HIQA expressed concern especially 'at the complexity of [the overall hospital governance] structures and the large numbers of committees in place, with a number of these involving the same members, many of whom also have full-time clinical responsibilities' (HIQA, 2013: 15). The discussion of national governance in relation specifically to the maternity system confirmed a picture of inconsistent approaches and some troubling instances of structural disconnect, for example, 'limited connectivity between the HSE's National Clinical Care Programme for Obstetrics and Gynaecology and the HSE office responsible for nursing and midwifery services', likely to impact negatively on the possibility of the 'development of overall models of maternity care' (HIQA, 2013: 18). The significant variability in governance arrangements across maternity units in Ireland was a particular area of concern that led HIQA to conclude that 'where such inconsistencies in governance structures exist, and given the Authority's concerns in relation to the lack of accessible, consistent and reproducible data relating to the quality of the various maternity services found during this investigation, it is impossible to assess the performance and quality of the maternity service nationally' (HIQA, 2013: 17). It recommends a thorough review and implementation of a standardised, evidence-based, effective model of maternity care across Ireland.

One particular area of concern for HIQA was the local and national ability to monitor practice and implement change based on up-to-date information and international best practice within the system. They expressed concerns with regard to the absence of adequate data collection, the lack of proactive approaches to monitoring and the lack of implementation of national and local policies and recommendations. The report found that eight of the 19 maternity units in the country did not provide any annual clinical reports, despite those having been strongly recommended in a previous inquiry; only five units had fully implemented the recommendations from another previous inquiry into an earlier death from maternal sepsis at another Irish hospital. In relation to sepsis reporting, it appeared that no nationally agreed definition of sepsis and no uniform reporting criteria were in place, leading to a situation where there was 'no agreed national dataset of quality and safety measures for maternity services in Ireland and no consistent approach to reporting clinical outcomes' (HIQA, 2013: 20), making monitoring of the safety and quality of services impossible.

Similar deficiencies were evident in the national response to the identification of systemic deficiencies in previous inquiries:

> The lack of a nationally coordinated approach to the implementation of the recommendations of the HSE inquiry into the death of Tania McCabe, the lack of local governance arrangements to ensure that recommendations as applicable to their particular service are implemented, and the ambiguity regarding who has the overall ownership of and responsibility for implementing the National Clinical Care Programmes again raises a fundamental and worrying deficit in our health system. This is the inability to implement change and apply system-wide learning from adverse events across the system in a timely and appropriate manner, in order to prevent the recurrence of patient safety events that may cause harm, or worse, to future patients. (HIQA, 2013: 22)

This litany of organisational shortcomings conveys a picture of significant dysfunction, not just within University Hospital Galway itself, but also in the wider Irish health service, at all stages of service planning and delivery. This degree of structural disconnect, lack of coherence and seeming overall paralysis in the face of need for change constitute significant impediments to the delivery of healthcare to Irish patients, no matter how competent and conscientious individual health professionals in the service may be.

Organisational clinical ethics, ethical climate and the facilitation of individual ethical behaviour

While traditionally organisational aspects in healthcare ethics have been comparatively neglected in comparison to considerations of individual accountability, there is a small but growing body of literature on organisational ethics, including increasing empirical research on organisational ethics (Suhonen et al., 2011). In the area of organisational ethics, particular attention is paid to the question how organisations can facilitate ethical behaviour and what organisational aspects are detrimental to ethical practice. Organisational ethics as relevant to the discussion in this chapter is debated in two distinct bodies of literature, the clinical ethics literature on the one hand and the business ethics literature on the other hand, both of which point to similar phenomena and issues.

In the clinical ethics literature the interest in organisational ethics frequently arises out of the experience of clinical ethicists who realise the importance of organisational factors for the success or failure of their clinical ethics activities. Accordingly, the question of the integration of specific clinical ethics services and other modes of facilitating individual ethical practice into the wider organisational context take centre stage. Singer et al. (2001) consider clinical ethics to be only one, albeit important, component of the wider goal of realising an ethically responsible organisation: '[o]rganisational ethics is an exercise in collective accountability. It has to do with persons acting together on behalf of some institutional goal. It is concerned with defining an ethic, implementing that mission, and allocating responsibility at all levels of institutional life for preserving the fidelity to the mission'.

Singer et al. consider the integration of clinical ethics into the wider culture of quality improvement in healthcare organisations to be essential. In this context, MacRae et al. (2008) draw on Silverman's reflections on systems thinking and argue similarly that wider systemic factors that facilitate or hinder ethical practices within the healthcare organisation as a whole should be foregrounded:

> According to Silverman, systems thinking 'is concerned with the key interrelationships, structures, and processes that control and monitor behaviour ... With systems thinking, the focus is not on individuals as objects of improvement, but rather, on examining interrelationships, communications, ongoing processes, and underlying causes of behaviour with an eye towards changing interactions or redesigning the system to produce different behaviours.' In the healthcare arena, systems thinking has been increasingly evident . . . (MacRae et al., 2008: 313)

They regret the limited progress that has been made so far in relation to the integration of systems thinking into clinical ethics and see its main potential advantage in the comprehensive integration of ethical goals into practices of the organisation, including a pervasive sense that being ethical matters and that effective supports are in place for staff aiming to do 'the right thing'. The concept of an 'ethical climate' is a particularly prominent concept in that context. Chen et al. (2007) specify the role and importance of a positive ethical climate as follows:

> First, a positive ethical climate embodies a set of shared values that reflect societal norms for what the organization should value; how it should prioritize its mission, vision, and goals; and how the organization and the individuals associated with it should behave. Second, a positive ethical climate is one in which the mission and vision of the organization inform expectations for professional and managerial performance and in which the mission and vision are implemented in the actual practices of the organization, in part because the mission and vision reflect shared values. Third, a positive ethical climate is one in which all individuals associated with the organization feel safe in discussing and debating ethically important issues and the values and beliefs that underlie their decisions and actions. (2007: S14)

One of the problems that these authors identify is that perhaps less attention is being paid to organisational ethics in healthcare than in other organisational fields. Drawing on related concepts from the, in this respect, more developed business ethics literature may therefore further advance the debate. For example, Kayes et al.'s (2007) reflection on the notion of 'organisational integrity' may serve to further build an understanding of the notion of ethical climate. One of the core features of an organisation with integrity is that 'the language of ethical decision-making is used' (Kayes et al., 2007: 63) and the ethical aspects of decisions of members of the organisation are acknowledged in their own right and respected, rather than being subordinated to other types of concerns. However, the use of such language is also substantially supported by 'structural supports and procedures that facilitate ethical decision-making' (Kayes et al., 2007: 63). In the healthcare ethics context, these could be dedicated clinical ethics committees or consultation structures, but they may also take a different shape, depending on the subject matter and needs arising in the organisation. It is particularly important that there are clear channels to air and discuss problems without penalty, for example by drawing on outside service providers. A constructive ethical climate is also supported by a 'culture of openness, responsibility, and commitment to multiple [organisational] goals' (Kayes et al., 2007: 63), rather than being expected to conform to a single, potentially ethically restricted understanding of the goals of an organisation. The needs of different stakeholders within and outside the organisation would be recognised in such a climate. When an effective ethical climate is established, staff have reason to perceive themselves as a recognised and valuable part of the organisation and to see their own and the organisation's interests as at least partly aligned.

In such a situation an organisation would have achieved a form of functioning that is indeed 'ethically trustworthy'. Mason (2004), in his discussion of the specific defects of the organisational culture underlying NASA's fateful decisions in relation to the Challenger disaster, highlights the importance of three different key factors for the achievement of organisational trustworthiness, focusing especially on the need to be open, transparent and self-critical. His account of the background to the Challenger disaster highlights the challenges with adequate management of power structures and constructive use of dissenting voices. In trustworthy organisations the following characteristics would apply:

> 1 Knowledge and expertise is valued highly and encouraged to flow to the points in the organization where it is needed at the time it is needed. Contrary or annoying news is embraced. …
> 2 As many operations as feasible must be made open and transparent. Silence, confidentiality, cover-up, over protection of rights, and efforts to protect a reputation instead of telling the full truth are [largely] eliminated … Potential and actual conflicts of interest are identified, reported and eliminated.
> 3 Countervailing powers are encouraged, and independent oversight and audit of all operations is established, so that vested interests are exposed and controlled. Valuable information is not suppressed. (Mason, 2004: 139)

Application to organisational failings in Ireland

How do the reflections in the preceding section apply to the organisational failings identified in the Neary and Halappanavar reports? Organisational ethics as conceptualised here focuses strongly on facilitating ethical behaviour by individual members of the organisation and identifying obstacles to the realisation of specific ethical behaviours. This conceptualisation of organisational ethics seems to match especially some of the problems identified in the Neary case where specific concrete ethical behaviours by individuals should have occurred but were discouraged or prevented by organisational factors. Not only was the ethical requirement of informed consent for an intervention with as serious and far-ranging consequences as hysterectomy not implemented, but Dr Neary never had to account for this serious omission until the official investigations were undertaken. Most significantly, there was little evidence that the requirements for assuring professional competence and taking effective steps to address incompetence or unsafe practices, which are recognised explicitly in most professional ethics codes, were being taken seriously by staff in the Lourdes Hospital. The organisation did not implement any recording, monitoring or auditing measures that could have ensured that staff members' actions could have been opened up to scrutiny.

Structures and implicit expectations that were in place also created a noxious ethical climate in which loyalty and conformity, 'knowing one's place' and 'not interfering', were considered more important than staff taking action to ensure that unsafe practices were addressed. The fear of the consequences of taking action and crossing the wrong person was highlighted strongly in the Inquiry. Similarly, the absence of requirements of consultation and second opinions was a sign of a misunderstanding of the ethical balance between professional autonomy and professional accountability, pushing the scales towards an exaggerated and not ethically bound understanding of clinical independence of consultants.

And ultimately, the effect of religious norms led to the engagement in practices that were not clinically indicated in order to achieve a religiously proscribed goal while pretending interventions were based on clinical necessity. This duplicity in turn led to a climate in which aberrant obstetric practices could easily be explained by other motivations and a general acceptance that official presentations might hide a different reality. While the management of the hospital strongly denied that any such practices took place, numerous witnesses to the inquiry confirmed that there was a tacit understanding that hysterectomies might be a religiously acceptable way of preventing further pregnancies for women.

However, while an organisation's ethical climate and its level of support for ethical practices are significant factors, ethical requirements on organisations extend much more widely. While it is important that organisations specifically facilitate their members in realising individual ethical practice, the practices of organisations more generally should also be open to ethical scrutiny themselves.

Virtuous organisational character and ethical practice in healthcare

The previously introduced notions of organisational integrity and organisational trustworthiness already point in the direction of considering features of ethical organisations that they share with moral agents. In the following I will draw on work by Geoff Moore who in a series of papers has applied a neo-Aristotelian framework to the analysis of organisational practices. Moore relies on MacIntyre's (1985) work on the relation of virtues, practices and institutions and works with them in the conceptualisation of the virtuous character of organisations. While the realisation of practices such as medicine is dependent on the existence of 'institutions', MacIntyre highlights that in institutions the pursuit of external and internal goods are in constant intrinsic tension:

> Institutions are characteristically and necessarily concerned with … external goods. … Nor could they do otherwise if they are to sustain not only themselves, but also the practices of which they are the bearers. For no practices can survive for any length of time unsustained by institutions. Indeed so intimate is the relationship of practices to institutions and consequently of the goods external to the goods internal to the practices in question that institutions and practices characteristically form a single causal order in which the ideals and the creativity

> of the practice are always vulnerable to the acquisitiveness of the institution, in which the cooperative care for common goods of the practice is always vulnerable to the competitiveness of the institution. In this context the essential feature of the virtues is clear. Without them, without justice, courage and truthfulness, practices could not resist the corrupting power of institutions. (Maclntyre, 1985: 194)

Moore highlights the corruptive potential of organisations that might cause employees who are intent on realising a practice, such as healthcare, to lose faith in the organisation's ability to sustain the practice, when 'the dominance of the pursuit of external goods threatens to eclipse the exercise of the virtues within the practice' (Moore, 2002: 25). Moore highlights the importance of the notion of craftsmanship, stating that 'craftsmen will always hold to the principles of their craft, and while accepting that efficiency and economy are goods (among others), will also always attempt to find, indeed to create or re-create, within their work what it means to be in a practice' (Moore, 2005b: 248). Moore refers here to the facilitation of the individual realisation of craftsmanship in organisations, its potential of playing a 'part in the humanizing of business from within', and the importance of resisting 'the corrupting power of institutions' (Moore, 2005b: 249).

However, Moore goes further and also claims that the virtue ethics framework could be directly applied to organisations. He argues that organisations are sufficiently similar to human agents for it to make sense to ascribe agency, responsibility and character to them, and that we can judge organisations more or less like we do moral agents. While by no means uncontroversial, the assumption of corporate intentionality and moral agency has been endorsed by a number of authors in the field, including French and Garrett. For example, French considers a corporation's internal decision structure to be equivalent to a person's agency, insofar as it 'accomplishes a subordination and synthesis of the intentions and acts of various biological persons into a corporate decision', where the whole is greater than the sum of its parts (French, in Moore, 1999: 332). Garrett states that:

> [c]orporations are moral agents because the reciprocal adjustment of individual intentions and plans that take place in such organisations yields a corporate intentionality that is more like human intentionality than it is like the efficient causality that might be attributed to blindly operating social wholes such as markets. (Garrett, in Moore, 1999: 334)

In keeping with these assumptions, Moore defines institutional character as 'the seat of the virtues necessary for a corporation to engage in practices with excellence' (Moore, 2005a: 669). He follows Aristotle's and MacIntyre's descriptions of virtue as dispositions to deliberate and act in certain ways meeting standards of excellence. Virtue requires a certain degree of internal consistency, an accurate understanding of situations in which action is called for, and accurate judgement in choosing the best course of action that avoids the pitfalls of morally deficient action. Moore draws on MacIntyre's further elaboration of his definition of virtues as 'those dispositions which will not only sustain practices and enable us to achieve the goods internal to practices, but which will sustain us in the relevant kind of quest for the good, by enabling us to overcome the harms, dangers, temptations and distractions which we encounter' (MacIntyre, in Moore, 2005b: 246). While these dispositions might be somewhat more malleable in the institutional context than in individuals (Moore, 2005a: 675), the principle nevertheless remains the same.

Virtues are only developed through a prolonged process of engagement in relevant fields of action and require ongoing fine-tuning and active adaptation to circumstances. Establishing an organisational virtue requires establishing solid and reliable structures that can serve as equivalent to human virtues, structures that can embody value-oriented decision-making and the effective execution of actions to realise such goals. Different organisational structures need to be integrated seamlessly, so as not to cause inconsistent actions towards incompatible goals, but instead an overall integrated approach to the good organisational life. This integrated approach, however, should not be insulated from outside concerns, as Moore points out in his remarks on the danger of compartmentalisation (Moore, 2005a: 671); the same fundamental ethical norms should govern institutional decision-making and everyday life. Accordingly, virtuous organisations need to be appropriately open to relevant ethical concerns from any of its members and enable 'the questioning of the hitherto unquestioned' (Moore, 2005a: 674).

Given the complexity of corporate character, the implementation of corporate virtue can fail in different respects. Moore focuses primarily on the specific possibility of corruption of internal goods by the predominance of external goods in the corporate sphere; he sees a particular need for 'a power-balanced structure that prevents systemic biases … to ensure that the views and desires of particular constituencies are not privileged over those of others' (Moore, 2005a: 673). He is also aware of the potential impact of the wider social context on the organisation, and highlights that a virtuous organisation needs 'to resist the corrupting power of organisations with which it in turn relates … [including] the whole range of business, political and social institutions with which the organisation may engage' (Moore, 2005a: 676).

However, it is apparent from his discussion that any structural impediment to the establishment of excellence in the realisation of the internal practice can be considered ethically problematic. Moore particularly highlights the significance of appropriate internal systems and processes for the implementation of virtuous practice. He claims that '[t]he task of creating the virtuous organisation is essentially managerial' (Moore, 2005a: 677); the establishment of governance structures is especially essential and it is advisable to embed 'organizational virtue in such things as governance structures, rather than relying solely upon individual agents to preserve it' (Moore and Beadle, 2006: 386). This includes in particular the distribution of 'both decision-making authority and decision criteria within institutions' (Moore and Beadle, 2006: 377) and 'decision-making systems and processes that enable rational critical dialogue' (Moore and Beadle, 2006: 375).

Conclusion

In relation to both of the Irish cases presented in this chapter, the reflections in the previous section would indicate that the wide range of governance failures identified in the reports could be understood as ethical failings. What the organisations failed to achieve in both cases was an appropriate realisation of virtuous practice within their organisation. By embodying structures that were not primarily oriented towards the realisation of the internal good of the provision of excellent healthcare, but other distracting goals like loyalty to religious values or particular institutional traditions, as in the Neary case, the organisation failed in its ethical responsibility. The problematic structures and impact of the wider social environment were particularly evident in the silencing of alternative voices and the prevention of critical dialogue about the core values of the organisation. In the Halappanavar case, the primary failing seemed to be less the orientation towards alternative, but distracting goals, but perhaps more the incompetent realisation of practices to achieve this goal, especially in relation to a lack of coherence of organisational actions. The establishment of relevant action structures was neglected, for example regarding clinical handover, or assignation of specific clinical responsibilities. Dysfunctional structures were implemented at different levels, for example the assignment of a particularly challenging patient mix to St Monica's ward without corresponding workforce allocation for this ward, or at a macro level the UHG top governance level arrangements for staff with highly demanding dual roles but no specific arrangements in place to manage these. In some cases only half measures were implemented, for example early warning sign monitoring methods were only partly rolled out, sepsis management guidelines were not circulated and were unclear, and sepsis management training was officially mandated but widespread non-compliance had no consequences. The lack of data collection and monitoring made organisational self-assessment and improvement impossible. All these deficiencies disrupted the effective achievement of their patients' health, the internal good that the institution was meant to achieve.

As this chapter has aimed to establish, the understanding of two important Irish healthcare ethics scandals requires attention to the organisational aspects of ethical practice. It has been argued that this does not just refer to the facilitation of ethical practice for individual healthcare professionals within organisations, but that ethical analysis should also address the nature of organisational governance itself, and that virtue ethics might provide conceptual resources to describe these issues as ethical issues of significance.

References

Chen, D., Werhane, P. and Mills, A. (2007) 'Role of organization ethics in critical care medicine', *Critical Care Medicine*, 35(2) (Suppl): S11.

Harding Clark, M. (2006) *The Lourdes Hospital Inquiry: An Inquiry into Peripartum Hysterectomy at Our Lady of Lourdes Hospital, Drogheda*. Dublin: The Stationery Office.

HIQA (Health Information and Quality Authority) (2013) *Investigation into the Safety, Quality and Standards of Services Provided by the Health Service Executive to Patients, Including Pregnant Women, at Risk of Clinical Deterioration, Including those Provided in University Hospital Galway, and as Reflected in the Care and Treatment Provided to Savita Halappanavar*. Dublin.

HSE (Health Service Executive) (2013) *Final Report: Investigation of Incident 50278 from Time of Patient's Self-referral to Hospital on the 21st of October 2012 to the Patient's Death on the 28th of October, 2012*. Dublin.

Kayes, C., Stirling, D. and Nielsen, T. (2007) 'Building organizational integrity', *Business Horizons*, 50: 61.

MacIntyre, A. (1985) *After Virtue*. London: Duckworth.

MacLoughlin, C. (2013) *The Coroner's Report of the Inquest on the Death of Savita Halappanavar*. Clifden

MacRae, S., Fox, E. and Slowther, A. (2008) 'Clinical ethics and systems thinking', in P. Singer and A. Viens (eds), *Cambridge Textbook of Bioethics*. Cambridge: Cambridge University Press, pp. 313–21.

Mason, R. (2004) 'Lessons in organizational ethics from the Columbia Disaster: can a culture be lethal?', *Organizational Dynamics*, 33(2): 128.

McCarthy, J., Murphy, S. and Loughrey, M. (2008) 'Gender and power: the Irish hysterectomy scandal', *Nursing Ethics*, 15(5): 643.

Moore, G. (1999) 'Corporate moral agency: review and implications', *Journal of Business Ethics*, 21(4): 329.

Moore, G. (2002) 'On the implications of the practice-institution distinction: MacIntyre and the application of modern virtue ethics to business', *Business Ethics Quarterly*, 12(1): 19.

Moore, G. (2005a) 'Corporate character: modern virtue ethics and the virtuous corporation', *Business Ethics Quarterly*, 15(4): 659.

Moore, G. (2005b) 'Humanising business: a modern virtue ethics approach', *Business Ethics Quarterly*, 15(2): 237.

Moore, G. and Beadle, R. (2006) 'In search of organizational virtue in business:

agents, goods, practices, institutions, and environment', *Organization Studies*, 27(3): 369.

Singer, P., Pellegrino, E. and Siegler, M. (2001) 'Clinical ethics revisited', *BMC Medical Ethics*, 2:1. Available at: www.biomedcentral.com/content/pdf/1472-6939-2-1.pdf (accessed 11 June 2015).

Suhonen, R., Stolt, M., Virtanen, H. and Leino-Kilpi, H. (2011) 'Organizational ethics: a literature review', *Nursing Ethics*, 18(3): 285.

13

Psychiatric admission in Ireland: the role of country of origin

Brendan D. Kelly

Introduction

Mental disorder has a lengthy relationship with national law in most jurisdictions (Shorter, 1997; Scull, 2005), including Ireland (Robins, 1986; Kelly, 2008). This relationship has always been conflicted and contested: in 1684, Nathaniel Lee, an exuberant Restoration playwright, was diagnosed with mental disorder and involuntarily detained at Bethlem psychiatric hospital, just north of London. Lee disagreed violently with his committal, but found himself in a minority: 'They called me mad, I called them mad, and damn them, they outvoted me' (Porter, 2002: 88).

Involuntary detention and treatment for mental disorder have been a feature of most societies throughout the course of history, regardless of whether or not there was formal mental health legislation permitting it (Shorter, 1997). Ireland's current mental health legislation (the Mental Health Act 2001), like that of other countries, permits involuntary admission and treatment in certain, defined clinical circumstances. In 2012, there were 18,173 admissions, voluntary and involuntary, to Irish psychiatric units and hospitals, yielding an overall admission rate of 396.1 per 100,000 population per year (Daly and Walsh, 2013). Almost 11% of these admissions were involuntary, a slight increase from the previous year (9.5%). This also represented a slight increase in the *rate* of involuntary admissions from 39.4 per 100,000 population in 2011 to 41.9 in 2012.

Across all admissions, including both voluntary and involuntary admissions, the most common diagnosis was depressive disorder (30%). The schizophrenia group of disorders was the second most common diagnosis among all admissions (20.5%) and the most common among involuntary admissions (43%). Notwithstanding these clinical correlates of involuntary admission, however, there is a paucity of evidence about the *non-clinical* correlates of involuntary admission in Ireland. This chapter examines one such potential correlate, country of origin, which has a demonstrated relationship with involuntary admission in certain other countries (Lay et al., 2011), but, until recently, was not comprehensively studied in Ireland (Ng and Kelly, 2012; Kelly et al., 2015).

This topic is an important one for several reasons. From a legal perspective, any deprivation of liberty is a significant interference with observance of the right to liberty, and it is essential that any such deprivation is legal, proportionate and used in a fashion that is clearly justifiable. From the perspective of medical ethics, it is essential that psychiatrists and other mental health workers accord not only with appropriate legislation governing involuntary admission and treatment, but also with medical ethical standards, especially when using psychiatric diagnosis and treatment as the basis for deprivation of liberty. In addition, involuntary treatment is a recognised component of mental health services in Ireland and elsewhere, and, for that minority of patients who require involuntary treatment, it is essential that they have access to such treatment in a fashion that is not only consistent with relevant law and medical ethical standards, but also with the goals and directions of mental health policy.

For these reasons, the research team that I lead at University College Dublin, Ireland has performed a series of studies of clinical and non-clinical correlates of admission status in an inner-city inpatient psychiatry unit for adults in Dublin (Ng and Kelly, 2012; Kelly et al., 2015). This research team comprises myself, medical doctors undergoing postgraduate training in psychiatry, and undergraduate medical students doing electives in psychiatry. The studies' findings pertain to the inpatient psychiatry unit at which I also work as a consultant psychiatrist and where I lead a clinical team comprising myself, medical doctors undergoing postgraduate training in psychiatry, psychiatric nurses, a clinical psychologist, a social worker, an occupational therapist and undergraduate medical students doing electives in psychiatry. The findings from our studies form the basis for this chapter and largely shape the discussion and conclusions presented, in the context of the broader literature on this topic.

Migration and mental disorder

Migration is associated with altered patterns of psychological distress, mental disorder and access to treatment (Kelly and Feeney, 2007). The consequent, complex relationship between country of origin and involuntary admission status in Ireland is best explored by looking at, first, the relationship between migration and mental disorder and, second, psychiatric admission patterns among individuals born in Ireland and those not born in Ireland.

Migration has significant effects on health, with migrants showing higher rates of both physical (Gleize et al., 2000) and mental disorders compared to native populations (Gavin et al., 2001; Kelly, 2003). In the United Kingdom,

Irish, Caribbean and Pakistani immigrants have significantly increased rates of suicidal thoughts and deliberate self-harm (Nazroo, 1997). Asian and Egyptian immigrants have increased rates of bulimia and anorexia nervosa (Bhugra and Jones, 2001). Schizophrenia is six times more common in African-Caribbeans living in the United Kingdom compared to the native population (Harrison, 1990) and up to four times more common among migrants to the Netherlands (Selten et al., 1997).

Asylum-seekers present particular challenges to mental health services as they come from a variety of cultural backgrounds and often have sharply diminished social support. Many have experienced human rights abuse, torture or displacement in their homeland (Silove et al., 2000; Ryan et al., 2009). As a result, post-traumatic stress disorder affects 46.6% of all refugees in, for example, Oslo (Lavik et al., 1996). Research on this topic in Ireland is still quite limited, but there has been some work done since rates of inward migration increased in the late 1990s: between 1995 and 2000, approximately 250,000 persons migrated into Ireland, and the aggregate figure for immigrants over this five-year period represented some 7% of Ireland's entire population (MacÉinrí, 2001).

One chart-review study at St James's Hospital, Dublin (Kennedy et al., 2002) showed that the mental health needs of migrants in Ireland were indeed high, comparable to those of migrant populations in other countries. Foley-Nolan et al. (2002) studied the mental health of 210 immigrants in Cork and Kerry and found that some 70% of respondents had generally poor psychological health and, of these, only 4% had seen a counsellor and 2% had seen a psychiatrist.

The need for more detailed knowledge of the mental health needs of individuals resident in Ireland but not born here has been highlighted repeatedly in the psychiatric literature (Gavin et al., 2001; Clare, 2002; Feeney et al., 2002; Kelly, 2004). The clinical needs of asylum-seekers in Dublin in particular were highlighted by the Inspector of Mental Health Services in 2005 (Inspector of Mental Health Services, 2005: 390). Similarly, the national mental health policy, *A Vision for Change* (Expert Group on Mental Health Policy, 2006: 48), also highlighted this group, noting that the mental health needs of specific groups such as refugees, asylum-seekers and 'other immigrant populations will be addressed by the provision of comprehensive mental health services that are based on care planning taking all the needs of the individual into account'.

How does this altered pattern of mental health need among migrants and non-native populations translate into access to mental health care and, specifically, rates of involuntary admission? Overall, research from countries other than Ireland suggests that being a member of a non-majority ethnic group increases risk of involuntary detention and treatment. In New Zealand, involuntary admission is associated with Maori rather than European ethnicity (Wheeler et al., 2005). In Switzerland, involuntary admission is associated with being a 'foreign national', even after controlling for gender, age, diagnosis and severity of mental disorder (Lay et al., 2011). In the United Kingdom, black and minority ethnic patients are 3.3 times more likely to be detained compared to the general population (Singh et al., 2007). The reasons for this are unclear; suggested explanations include patient-related factors (e.g. increased rates of mental disorder), illness-related factors (e.g. increased severity) and service-related factors (e.g. misdiagnosis or racial stereotyping).

Comparing rates of involuntary admission among particular groups (e.g. migrants) across different European countries is a deeply challenging task, however, not least because overall involuntary admission rates vary considerably across Europe (Salize and Dressing, 2004), with rates as low as 12.4 per 100,000 population in Italy and as high as 232.5 in Finland (Fiorillo et al., 2011). These substantial differences likely reflect a variety of factors including different laws across countries (Dressing and Salize, 2004) and different traditions of mental health care (Amaddeo et al., 2007). Whatever their underpinnings, these cross-national differences greatly complicate the interpretation of cross-national comparisons of psychiatric admission rates among particular groups, such as ethnic minorities or migrants (Riecher-Rössler and Rössler, 1993).

Further complexity stems from the fact that not all individuals of minority ethnicities are migrants to their host countries, so cross-national comparisons need to be interpreted with great caution. For example while black and minority ethnic patients in the United Kingdom are 3.3 times more likely to be detained than the general population (Singh et al., 2007), many of these individuals (e.g. those with origins in the West Indies or Bengal) may be the second or third generation of their families to live in the United Kingdom and, as a result, are no longer migrants. This reduces direct comparability between these findings from the United Kingdom and studies of migrants or individuals in minority ethnic groups in other countries, such as Ireland, where inward migration is a relatively new phenomenon. In addition, many studies of migrants or individuals in minority ethnic groups do not distinguish between recently arrived migrants, forced refugees, newly established minority ethnic groups, long-established minority ethnic groups, migrant workers, holidaymakers, and various other kinds of possible groupings.

Notwithstanding these interpretative issues, it is relatively clear from the literature that being a migrant or belonging to a minority ethnic group has a significant effect on patterns of mental disorder and help-seeking, with especially compelling evidence of increased risk of schizophrenia among certain migrant groups (Harrison, 1990; Selten et al., 1997). This phenomenon is difficult to explain, as incidence of schizophrenia is not increased in these migrants' countries of origin (Hickling and Rodgers-Johnson, 1995). It is notable, however, that the increase in risk of schizophrenia among migrants shows an inverse relation with the size of the migrant group (i.e. the larger the migrant group, the smaller the increase in risk), suggesting that social isolation or stressors may play a role (Boydell et al., 2001). This kind of social stressor may persist, at least to a certain extent, in second-generation migrants who did not themselves migrate but still may have increased risk of schizophrenia in the United Kingdom (Harrison et al., 1997).

Admission patterns among individuals born in Ireland and not born in Ireland

Given that the demographic and clinical variables associated with involuntary admission in Ireland are incompletely understood, and that there are virtually no data on this topic as it relates specifically to residents who were not born in Ireland, our research group designed a research programme to develop a better understanding of diagnostic and demographic correlates of involuntary psychiatric admission status in Dublin's north inner-city, looking specifically at individuals resident in our area who were born in Ireland and those who were born elsewhere.

The first study in this research programme examined all admissions under the Mater Catchment Area Adult Psychiatry Service, at St Aloysius Ward in the Mater Misericordiae University Hospital, Dublin over a 36-month period (from January 2008 to December 2010) (Ng and Kelly, 2012) and again over a 30-month period (from January 2011 to June 2013) (Kelly et al., 2015). St Aloysius Ward is a 15-bed acute adult psychiatry inpatient unit which forms part of a community mental health service provided collaboratively by the Mater Misericordiae University Hospital, Health Service Executive and St Vincent's Hospital (Fairview).

This inpatient unit provides inpatient psychiatric care to an inner-city catchment area of 33,000 people. Adjusting for deprivation, as recommended in the national mental health policy, *A Vision for Change* (Expert Group on Mental Health Policy, 2006), yields a deprivation-adjusted population of 43,000 (utilising a multiplier of 1.3 which applies to this area) (Kelly and Teljeur, 2004; Mental Health Commission, 2006). Ireland's mental health system lends itself well to the kind of analysis presented in this chapter because it is organised in such a fashion that all public (non-fee-paying) psychiatry admissions of individuals resident within this geographical catchment area *must* occur in this admission unit. The high level of deprivation in this area means that rates of admission to private (fee-paying) hospitals are negligible, further enhancing the completeness of these studies

Over the course of the first study (January 2008 to December 2010), there were 446 admissions to this inpatient unit, of which 67 (15.0%) were involuntary (Ng and Kelly, 2012). This was higher than the national proportion of involuntary admissions (8.1%) (Daly and Walsh, 2010) but the same as that reported in another psychiatry service in Dublin's inner-city (15.7%) (Nwachukwu et al., 2010). This high proportion of involuntary admissions may be explained, at least in part, by high rates of social deprivation, unmet forensic mental health need and homelessness in this area, all of which impact on patterns of psychiatric presentation and admission (O'Neill et al., 2002; Expert Group on Mental Health Policy, 2006; Mental Health Commission, 2006; O'Neill et al., 2007).

These data, however, focus on the *proportion* of admissions that were involuntary (15.0%) compared to the national *proportion* (8.1%). Looking at proportions can be misleading because some mental health services may admit only patients who are very ill, thus generating a misleadingly high proportion of involuntary admissions compared to other mental health services. For example, Service A may admit a total of 100 patients per year, of whom 10 are involuntary, so that the proportion of admissions that is involuntary in Service A is 10%. Service B, covering a similar catchment area, may have much better community treatment facilities and thus admit only a total of 10 patients per year, of whom 2 are involuntary, so that the proportion of admissions that is involuntary in Service B is 20%. This may create the impression that Service B is more custodial than Service A, whereas the opposite is the case. To resolve this issue, it is useful to look at *rates* of involuntary admission per 100,000 population rather than the proportions of admissions that are involuntary.

On this basis, between January 2008 to December 2010, the inpatient unit in this study had an annual admission rate (adjusted for deprivation) of 345.7 admissions per 100,000 population per year, which was lower than the national rate (476.3) (Daly and Walsh, 2010). The involuntary admission rate was 51.9 per 100,000 population per year, which was higher than the national rate (38.5). There was no relationship between admission status and gender, age, employment or marital status, i.e. in the inpatient unit studied, there was no statistical association between admission status and factors such as gender or marital status, with males as likely to be involuntary patients as females, and single persons as likely to be involuntary patients as married persons.

One of the key purposes of this research was to examine the role, if any, of country of origin in determining overall and involuntary admission status. In the first study, the most common country of origin was Ireland (86.1%), although some 42 different countries were represented, from five different continents: Europe (other than Irish) (7.6% of all admissions), Africa (3.8%), America (1.1%), Asia (1.1%) and Australasia (0.002%). Country of origin was significantly associated with admission status: among individuals born outside Ireland, 33.9% of admissions were involuntary, compared to 12.0% among individuals born in Ireland. Regrettably, in this first study it was not possible to calculate *rates* of involuntary admission per 100,000 individuals born in Ireland and born elsewhere, owing to the absence of population data about the number of residents in this area who were born inside and outside of Ireland.

Notwithstanding this limitation, further analysis indicated that diagnosis was related to admission status: over one third (37.5%) of admissions with schizophrenia were involuntary compared to 1.4% of admissions with alcoholic disorders (Ng and Kelly, 2012). In addition, diagnosis was related to country of origin: 53.2% of admissions of individuals from outside Ireland were with a diagnosis of schizophrenia, compared to 18.5% of admissions of individuals from Ireland. As a result, it appeared that the high proportion of admissions that were involuntary among individuals born outside Ireland was attributable to an increased likelihood of such individuals being diagnosed with schizophrenia, compared to those born in Ireland. This was confirmed by multi-variable analysis which demonstrated that diagnosis, rather than country of origin, was the *only* independent predictor of admission status.

Despite this finding, it was apparent that country of origin merited further investigation, not least because it was related to a diagnosis of schizophrenia and, thus, involuntary admission, but also because this first study had focused on the *proportion* of admissions that were involuntary and could not calculate *rates*, which would be more informative. Fortuitously, a national census was performed in Ireland in 2011 and data were released in such a fashion as to permit calculation of the number of individuals resident in this catchment area who were born in Ireland and the number of individuals born elsewhere.

These new census data facilitated a second study, examining admissions over a 30-month period from January 2011 to June 2013 (Kelly et al., 2015). Over this period, there were 518 admissions, of which 70 (13.5%) were involuntary. Again, this was higher than the national proportion of involuntary admissions (9.5%) (Daly and Walsh, 2012) but lower than the proportions in the first study (Ng and Kelly, 2012) and in another psychiatry service in Dublin's inner-city (15.7%) (Nwachukwu et al., 2010). As in the first study, involuntary admission was associated with a diagnosis of schizophrenia and being born outside Ireland: among individuals born outside Ireland, 32.5% of admissions were involuntary compared to 9.9% among individuals born in Ireland (Kelly et al., 2015). These results were very similar to those in the first study (Ng and Kelly, 2012) except that on multi-variable analysis in the second study, country of origin, and *not* diagnosis, was the sole significant independent predictor of admission status.

Owing to the new census data, it was possible to expand the second study to explore *rates* of involuntary and voluntary admission per 100,000 population in this catchment area among those born outside Ireland and those born in Ireland. Interestingly, this analysis showed that *rates* of involuntary admission were slightly but not dramatically higher among individuals born outside Ireland (deprivation-adjusted rate: 76.5 involuntary admissions per 100,000 population per year) compared to those born in Ireland (65.4). Unexpectedly, the most dramatic difference between the two groups lay in rates of *voluntary* admission, which were dramatically lower among individuals born outside Ireland (158.5) compared to those born in Ireland (596.2).

Reasons for this low uptake of *voluntary* inpatient psychiatric care among individuals born outside Ireland may include different patterns of help-seeking behaviour, especially for mild or moderate mental illness (which generally would not result in involuntary admission), in this group. This explanation is supported by evidence from other countries that ethnicity (Ghali et al., 2013) and country of origin can have significant effects on pathways to care (Tarricone et al., 2012). Further quantitative and qualitative studies are needed in Ireland to clarify whether this is also the case in Ireland and explain in greater depth the relatively low rates of voluntary admission among individuals born outside Ireland.

Overall, the findings from these two studies are consistent with the idea that schizophrenia is a particular problem in individuals born outside Ireland and living in Dublin's inner-city. It is already known that 70% of migrants in Ireland have poor psychological health (Foley-Nolan et al., 2002) and, in 2007, the Health Service Executive, in its *Inter-Cultural Health Strategy 2007–2012*, acknowledged that 'many asylum seekers and refugees may suffer from a significant burden of mental health problems' (Health Service Executive, 2007: 42) and 'mental health services should be resourced to provide services to other ethnic groups' (Health Service Executive, 2007: 87). The data presented in this chapter now demonstrate the extent and nature of this issue in relation to schizophrenia within this population in Dublin's inner-city.

These findings are also strongly consistent with international studies that associate high rates of involuntary admission with specific diagnoses (especially schizophrenia) (Riecher et al., 1991; Salize and Dressing, 2004; Mulder et al., 2008) and socio-economic deprivation (Riecher et al., 1991; Bindman et al., 2002; Webber and Huxley, 2004). This effect is now also demonstrated in Ireland, and it is also now clear that the increased proportion of admissions that is involuntary among individuals born outside Ireland is explained by a higher rate of schizophrenia diagnoses among those admitted (Ng and Kelly, 2012). The most interesting feature of these results, however, is that the excess of involuntary admissions among individuals born outside Ireland is relatively modest when compared to the dramatically lower rate of *voluntary* admission among this group. This merits both further reflection and study, especially in relation to pathways to mental health care among individuals who are not born in Ireland.

Conclusion

The role of country of origin in relation to psychiatric admission status is interesting both internationally and in Ireland. Data presented in this chapter demonstrate that schizophrenia is a particular problem in individuals born outside Ireland and living in Dublin's inner-city, and that this is associated with involuntary admission (Ng and Kelly, 2012; Kelly et al., 2015). These data also support international studies that associate high rates of involuntary admission with specific diagnoses (especially schizophrenia) and socio-economic deprivation.

The most interesting feature of these results, however, is that the excess of involuntary admissions among individuals born outside Ireland is relatively modest and that the rate of voluntary admission among this group is dramatically lower than that among individuals born in Ireland. This is possibly related to differing pathways to mental health care among individuals born outside Ireland, especially in relation to mild or moderate mental disorder which would not normally result in involuntary admission. This also suggests that the balance of human rights concerns for a majority within this group may lie with difficulties accessing voluntary mental health care rather than denial of liberty as a result of involuntary detention.

Further research is needed in a number of areas relating to country of origin and rates of voluntary and involuntary psychiatric admission. In the first instance, variations in detention rates across countries merit close examination and significant efforts are already underway in this regard, most notably with the collaborative, multi-site EUNOMIA study ('European Evaluation of Coercion in Psychiatry and Harmonization of Best Clinical Practice') (Fiorillo et al., 2011). Second, future research could usefully focus on certain, apparently non-clinical correlates of involuntary admission status, such as socio-economic deprivation (Bindman et al., 2002). While there is some evidence that this relationship is independent of clinical diagnosis (Riecher et al., 1991), and that lack of social support is especially significant (Webber and Huxley, 2004), more research is needed. Third, there is a need for deeper research into the relationships between migrant status, ethnicity and rates of involuntary admission (Wheeler et al., 2005; Lay et al., 2011). Data presented in this chapter suggest that at least part of the excess of involuntary admission among individuals born outside Ireland appears to be attributable to clinical diagnoses (i.e. increased proportion diagnosed with schizophrenia) but further work is needed to gain a more fine-grained understanding of this in the Irish context: do non-clinical factors (e.g. culture, language) affect diagnostic practices, and thus admission status, in this group? Does the social situation of migrants in Ireland affect expressions of psychopathology, leading to altered patterns of help-seeking and, perhaps, access to services? Why is there such a relatively low uptake of voluntary inpatient psychiatric care among individuals born outside Ireland?

Methodological issues are important in this context. The analyses presented here, for example, divided the catchment area population into two groups: those born in Ireland and those born elsewhere (Ng and Kelly, 2012; Kelly et al., 2015). This rather blunt division was used in order to compare findings with national census data, which divided the population into these two groups. Future research, however, needs to distinguish more carefully between various different kinds of minority groups, including recently arrived migrants, forced refugees, newly established minority ethnic groups, long-established minority ethnic groups, and various other groupings within host countries. All of these groups have very different personal, social and cultural experiences of host countries and are likely to present with different constellations of physical and mental health problems (Ryan et al., 2009); these differences should be carefully reflected and explored in future work.

The role of differing mental health laws also merits greater attention in future studies. While Ireland's mental health laws were revised relatively recently and are today in greater accordance with international human rights standards (Kelly, 2011), there is still a need for more study of the effects of mental health laws on involuntary admission rates and social justice (Sen, 2009) both within and between countries. There is a particular dearth of data relating to mental health laws and involuntary admission practices in the developing world, and it is to be hoped that future cross-national initiatives will include a broader variety of societies in their analyses, so as to provide a more nuanced and complete picture of the experiences of the detained mentally-ill around the world.

Regarding clinical care, there has been an awareness of the high rate of mental health need among migrants in the catchment area of these studies for many years, and in 2007 a dedicated Cultural Psychiatry Service was established to map and meet this need. This collaborative project has clinical, research and educational components. Preliminary reflections on migration and mental health need in Ireland, as well as the merits and demerits of dedicated Cultural Psychiatry Services, are presented by Kelly (2009).

At national level, it is apparent that differences in patterns of help-seeking suggested in this chapter could usefully be considered in future planning exercises in Ireland's mental health services. In particular, increased emphasis on the cultural competence of healthcare providers would be a good first step in recognising and addressing the differing health needs and practices of individuals from different ethnic groups and cultural backgrounds.

References

Amaddeo, F., Becker, T., Fioritti, A., Burti, L. and Tansella, M. (2007) 'Reforms in community care: the balance between hospital and community-based mental health care', in M. Knapp, D. McDaid, E. Mossialos and G. Thornicroft (eds), *Mental Health Policy and Practice Across Europe*. Berkshire, England: McGraw-Hill/Open University Press, pp. 235–49.

Bhugra, D. and Jones, P. (2001) 'Migration and mental illness', *Advances in Psychiatric Treatment*, 7(3): 216.

Bindman, J., Tighe, J., Thornicroft, G. and Leese, M. (2002) 'Poverty, poor services, and compulsory psychiatric admission in England', *Social Psychiatry and Psychiatric Epidemiology*, 37(7): 341.

Boydell, J., van Os, J., McKenzie, K., Allardyce, J., Goel, R., McCreadie, R.G. and Murray, R.M. (2001) 'Incidence of schizophrenia in ethnic minorities in London: ecological study into interactions with environment', *British Medical Journal*, 323(7325): 1336.

Clare, A. (2002) 'Immigration: new challenges for psychiatry and mental health services in Ireland', *Irish Journal of Psychological Medicine*, 19(1): 3.

Daly, A. and Walsh, D. (2010) *Activities of Irish Psychiatric Units and Hospitals 2009*. Dublin: Health Research Board.

Daly, A. and Walsh, D. (2012) *Activities of Irish Psychiatric Units and Hospitals 2011*. Dublin: Health Research Board.

Daly, A. and Walsh, D. (2013) *HRB Statistics Series 20: Activities of Irish Psychiatric Units and Hospitals 2012*. Dublin: Health Research Board.

Dressing, H. and Salize, H.J. (2004) 'Compulsory admission of mentally ill patients in European Union member states', *Social Psychiatry and Psychiatric Epidemiology*, 39(10): 797.

Expert Group on Mental Health Policy (2006) *A Vision for Change: Report of the Expert Group on Mental Health Policy*. Dublin: The Stationery Office.

Feeney, L., Kelly, B.D., Whitty, P. and O'Callaghan, E. (2002) 'Mental illness in migrants: diagnostic and therapeutic challenges', *Irish Journal of Psychological Medicine*, 19(1): 29.

Fiorillo, A., De Rosa, C., Del Vecchio, V., Jurjanz, L., Schnall, K., Onchev, G., Alexiev, S., Raboch, J., Kalisova, L., Mastrogianni, A., Georgiadou, E., Solomon, Z., Dembinskas, A., Raskauskas, V., Nawka, P., Nawka, A. Kiejna, A., Hadrys, T., Torres-Gonzales, F., Mayoral, F., Björkdahl, A., Kjellin, L., Priebe, S., Maj, M. and Kallert, T. (2011) 'How to improve clinical practice on involuntary hospital admissions of psychiatric patients: suggestions from the EUNOMIA study', *European Psychiatry*, 26(4): 201.

Foley-Nolan, C., Sheahan, A. and Cahill, D. (2002) *A Better World – Healthwise: A Health Needs Assessment of Immigrants in Cork and Kerry*. Cork: Southern Health Board.

Gavin, B.E., Kelly, B.D., Lane, A. and O'Callaghan, E. (2001) 'The mental health of migrants', *Irish Medical Journal*, 94(8): 229.

Ghali, S., Fisher, H.L., Joyce, J., Major, B., Hobbs, L., Soni, S., Chisholm, B., Rahaman, N., Papada, P., Lawrence, J., Bloy, S., Marlowe, K., Aitchison, K.J., Power, P. and Johnson, S. (2013) 'Ethnic variations in pathways into early intervention services for psychosis', *British Journal of Psychiatry*, 202(4): 277.

Gleize, L., Laudon, F., Sun, L.Y., Challeton-de Vathaire, C., Le Vu, B. and de Vathaire, F. (2000) 'Cancer registry of French Polynesia: results for the 1900–1995 period among native and immigrant population', *European Journal of Epidemiology*, 16(7): 661.

Harrison, G. (1990) 'Searching for the causes of schizophrenia: the role of migrant studies', *Schizophrenia Bulletin*, 16(4): 663.

Harrison, G., Glazebrook, C., Brewin, J., Cantwell, R., Dalkin, T., Fox, R., Jones, P. and Medley, I. (1997) 'Increased incidence of psychotic disorders in migrants from the Caribbean to the United Kingdom', *Psychological Medicine*, 27(4): 799.

Health Service Executive (2007) *National Intercultural Health Strategy, 2007–2012*. Dublin.

Hickling, F.W. and Rodgers-Johnson, P. (1995) 'The incidence of first contact schizophrenia in Jamaica', *British Journal of Psychiatry*, 167(2): 193.

Inspector of Mental Health Services (2005) *Report of the Inspector of Mental Health Services 2004*. Dublin.

Kelly, B.D. (2003) 'Globalisation and psychiatry', *Advances in Psychiatric Treatment*, 9(6): 464.

Kelly, B.D. (2004) 'Mental health policy in Ireland, 1984–2004: theory, overview and future directions', *Irish Journal of Psychological Medicine*, 21(2): 61.

Kelly, B.D. (2008) 'The Mental Treatment Act 1945 in Ireland: an historical enquiry', *History of Psychiatry*, 19(73): 47.

Kelly, B.D. (2009) 'Health services, psychiatry and citizenship in a globalizing world: a perspective from Ireland', *Health Policy*, 93(1): 48.

Kelly, B.D. (2011) 'Mental health legislation and human rights in England, Wales and the Republic of Ireland', *International Journal of Law and Psychiatry*, 34(6): 439.

Kelly, B.D., Emechebe, A., Anamdi, C., Duffy, R., Murphy, N. and Rock, C. (2015) 'Custody, care and country of origin: demographic and diagnostic admission statistics at an inner-city adult psychiatry unit' *International Journal of Law and Psychiatry*, 38: 1.

Kelly, B.D. and Feeney, L. (2007) 'Coping with stressors: racism, migration', in D. Bhugra and K. Bhui (eds), *Textbook of Cultural Psychiatry*. Cambridge: Cambridge University Press, pp. 550–60.

Kelly, A. and Teljeur, C. (2004) *A New National Deprivation Index for Health and Health Services Research: Short Report*. Dublin: Small Area Health

Research Unit, Department of Public Health and Primary Care, Trinity College Dublin.
Kennedy, N., Jerrard-Dunne, P., Gill, M. and Webb, M. (2002) 'Characteristics and treatment of asylum seekers reviewed by psychiatrists in an Irish inner city area', *Irish Journal of Psychological Medicine*, 19(1): 4.
Lavik, N.J., Hauff, E., Skrondal, A. and Solberg, O. (1996) 'Mental disorder among refugees and the impact of persecution and exile: some findings from an outpatient population', *British Journal of Psychiatry*, 169(6): 726.
Lay, B., Nordt, C. and Rössler, W. (2011) 'Variation in use of coercive measures in psychiatric hospitals', *European Psychiatry*, 26(4): 244.
MacÉinrí, P. (2001) *Immigration into Ireland: Trends, Policy, Responses, Outlook*. Cork: Irish Centre For Migration Studies.
Mental Health Commission (2006) *Community Mental Health Services in Ireland: Activity and Catchment Area Characteristics 2004*. Dublin.
Mulder, C. L, Uitenbroek, D., Broer, J., Lendemeijer, B., van Veldhuizen, J.R., van Tilburg, W., Lelliot, P. and Wierdsma, A.I. (2008) 'Changing patterns in emergency involuntary admissions in the Netherlands in the period 2000–2004', *International Journal of Law and Psychiatry*, 31(4): 331.
Nazroo, J. (1997) *Ethnicity and Mental Health*. London: Policy Studies Institute.
Ng, X.T. and Kelly, B.D. (2012) 'Voluntary and involuntary care: three-year study of demographic and diagnostic admission statistics at an inner-city adult psychiatry unit', *International Journal of Law and Psychiatry*, 35(4): 317.
Nwachukwu, I., Crumlish, N., Heron, E.A. and Gill, M. (2010) 'Irish Mental Health Act 2001: impact on involuntary admissions in a community mental health service in Dublin', *The Psychiatrist*, 34(10): 436.
O'Neill, A., Casey, P. and Minton, R. (2007) 'The homeless mentally ill: an audit from an inner city hospital', *Irish Journal of Psychological Medicine*, 24(2): 62.
O'Neill, C., Sinclair, H., Kelly, A. and Kennedy, H. (2002) 'Interaction of forensic and general psychiatric services in Ireland: learning the lessons or repeating the mistakes?' *Irish Journal of Psychological Medicine*, 19(2): 48.
Porter, R. (2002) *Madness: A Brief History*. Oxford: Oxford University Press.
Riecher, A., Rössler, W., Loffler, W. and Fatkeheuer, B. (1991) 'Factors influencing compulsory admission of psychiatric patients', *Psychological Medicine*, 21(1): 197.
Riecher-Rössler, A. and Rössler, W. (1993) 'Compulsory admission of psychiatric patients – an international comparison', *Acta Psychaitrica Scandinavica*, 87(4): 231.
Robins, J. (1986) *Fools and Mad: A History of the Insane in Ireland*. Dublin: Institute of Public Administration.
Ryan, D.A., Kelly, F.E. and Kelly, B.D. (2009) 'Mental health among persons

awaiting an asylum outcome in western countries', *International Journal of Mental Health*, 38(3): 88.

Salize, H.J. and Dressing, H. (2004) 'Epidemiology of involuntary placement of mentally ill people across the European Union', *British Journal of Psychiatry*, 184(2): 163

Scull, A. (2005) *The Most Solitary of Afflictions: Madness and Society in Britain, 1700–1900*. Yale: Yale University Press.

Selten, J.P., Slaets, J.P. and Kahn, R.S. (1997) 'Schizophrenia in Surinamese and Dutch Antillean immigrants to The Netherlands: evidence of an increased incidence', *Psychological Medicine*, 27(4): 807.

Sen, A. (2009) *The Idea of Justice*. London: Allen Lane.

Shorter, E. (1997) *A History of Psychiatry*. New York: John Wiley and Sons.

Silove, D., Steel, Z. and Watters, C. (2000) 'Policies of deterrence and the mental health of asylum seekers', *Journal of the American Medical Association*, 284(5): 604.

Singh, S.P., Greenwood, N., White, S. and Churchill, R. (2007) 'Ethnicity and the Mental Health Act 1983', *British Journal of Psychiatry*, 191(2): 99.

Tarricone, I., Stivanello, E., Ferrari, S., Colombini, N., Bolla, E., Braca, M., Giubbarelli, C., Costantini, C., Cazzamalli, S., Mimmi, S., Tedesco, D., Menchetti, M., Rigatelli, M., Maso, E., Balestrieri, M., Vender, S. and Berardi, D. (2012) 'Migrant pathways to community mental health centres in Italy', *International Journal of Social Psychiatry*, 58(5): 505.

Webber, M. and Huxley, P. (2004) 'Social exclusion and risk of emergency compulsory admission. A case-control study', *Social Psychiatry and Psychiatric Epidemiology*, 39(12): 1000.

Wheeler, A., Robinson, E. and Robinson, G. (2005) 'Admissions to acute psychiatric inpatient services in Auckland, New Zealand: a demographic and diagnostic review', *New Zealand Medical Journal*, 118(1226): U1752.

14

Protecting rights in mental health law: the relationship between the courts and mental health tribunals

Darius Whelan

Introduction

Mental health law, and in particular the law concerning involuntary detention, has been a subject of protracted debate in Irish society. The European Court of Human Rights (ECtHR) held in *Winterwerp* v. *The Netherlands* (1979–80) 2 EHRR 387 that, except in emergency cases, the decision to detain a 'person of unsound mind' must be supported by objective medical expertise, the mental disorder must be serious enough to warrant compulsory confinement, and the validity of confinement must be based on the persistence of the disorder (at para. 39). Article 5(4) of the European Convention on Human Rights (ECHR) does not necessarily require that all detentions be automatically reviewed, as long as a detained person has the right to take proceedings by which the lawfulness of his or her detention shall be decided speedily by a 'court' (which includes independent tribunals). Ireland's Mental Health Act 2001 requires that all involuntary admissions for mental disorder be reviewed within 21 days by a three-person mental health tribunal (MHT). The tribunals review both procedural and substantive aspects of the person's detention. Under section 18 of the 2001 Act, they also have the power to waive or 'cure' a procedural defect which may have occurred, provided the defect does not affect the substance of the order and does not cause an injustice.

The tribunal system became operational in 2006, and there are hundreds of hearings each year.[1] Inevitably, there has been a significant amount of litigation about the exact parameters of the tribunals' powers and the relationship between the tribunals and the courts. This litigation has been an important opportunity for the courts to establish principles and standards for the tribunals. As a person's liberty is at stake, it would be expected as a matter of policy that courts would subject the tribunal process to very strict scrutiny. However, there is strong evidence that the Irish courts are, in general, extremely deferential to the decisions of MHTs. The courts' approach raises serious questions about their commitment to the rights of persons detained under mental health legislation.

In this chapter, the focus will be on key written judgments of the High Court and Supreme Court where the courts have in some way reviewed a decision of a mental health tribunal. The issues will be considered under five headings: an examination of the remedies of applications under Article 40 and judicial reviews; the MHTs' power to review procedural matters; the power to waive procedural irregularities; statements from the courts concerning the importance of MHTs following procedures correctly; and the relevance of the ECHR and the UN Convention on the Rights of Persons with Disabilities (CRPD). Detailed accounts of the Mental Health Act 2001 and case-law interpreting it may be found in literature by authors such as Keys (2002), O'Neill (2005), Whelan (2009) and Casey et al. (2010). An Expert Group has recently recommended various reforms to the 2001 Act (Expert Group on the Review of the Mental Health Act 2001, (2015)).

Despite some statements to the contrary, the general picture which emerges is that the courts have not engaged in robust supervision of mental health tribunals. Instead, the general tenor of the case-law has been to endorse decisions of tribunals to affirm detentions, and to limit access to the courts to the most extreme violations of procedural rights. This is a disappointing outcome, in light of the supposed rights-based focus of the Mental Health Act 2001.

Remedies: applications under Article 40 and judicial reviews

The focus of this chapter will be on cases which took the form either of an application under Article 40 of the Constitution or a judicial review. These remedies have distinct features which significantly impact on the courts' role. An application under Article 40 of the Constitution (which is also known as a habeas corpus application, although there are technical differences) is an inquiry by the High Court into the lawfulness of a person's detention. The onus is on the detaining authority to justify the detention and if it is not justified, the person must be released.[2]

As mental health tribunals are public bodies, their decisions may alternatively be challenged by way of a judicial review application in the High Court. This is a more flexible remedy than an application under Article 40 as issues other than the current legality of the detention may be considered. For example, the person may seek a declaration that one of the actions which took place in the chain of events was unlawful, or that a particular section of the 2001 Act is repugnant to the Constitution or incompatible with the ECHR. The grounds for judicial review are mainly procedural and the courts will generally steer away from consideration of the merits of the decision.

In cases concerning the 2001 Act, the courts have applied four limitations on the availability of these remedies. First, in the key Supreme Court case of *E.H.* v. *Clinical Director of St Vincent's Hospital* [2009] IESC 46, para. 50, it was held that an application under Article 40 should only be brought if 'the best interests of the patient so demand' (see further Whelan, 2012). This limits the availability of the remedy and has had a chilling effect on potential challenges to detention. Given that 'best interests' in this context appear to be equated with medical best interests, the case represents a remarkable prioritisation of medical considerations over legal ones. It has been commented that courts tend to be deferential to medical opinion (Teff, 1994: xxiii–iv) and this may be seen as a further example of this phenomenon (see further Whelan, 2009; Irish Human Rights Commission, 2010; Lynn, 2010; Murray, 2010).

Second, in *T.O'D.* v. *Kennedy* [2007] IEHC 129, Charleton J commented that if there are procedural issues with a detention, the 'ordinary remedy' is to bring these matters before the tribunal. He said that the High Court in exercising its jurisdiction under Article 40 of the Constitution has a much more limited function in simply declaring, at any particular point in time, whether someone is or is not lawfully detained. It can review the MHT's decisions but he did not see that this would be either appropriate or necessary if the statutory scheme was followed. He said that he 'would expressly hold that if at a time when the High Court considers an application for habeas corpus, a period of unlawful detention has been cured validly by a decision of the mental health tribunal under section 18(1) of the Mental Health Act 2001 that [*sic*] the remedy is no longer available'. This view would appear to unduly restrict the availability of the remedy of an application under Article 40, placing unwarranted weight on the decision of a MHT as to which procedural defects are sufficiently minor to be waived.

Third, the courts have repeatedly held that there is no 'domino effect' in applications under Article 40. If there is an unlawfulness at an earlier stage of detention, it may be 'cured' by a subsequent lawful detention. For example, in *R.L.* v. *Clinical Director of St Brendan's Hospital* (Supreme Court, *ex tempore*, 15 February 2008), the Supreme Court held that even if there had been breaches of section 13 of the 2001 Act (regarding removal of the person to the hospital), this would not render what is on the face of it a lawful detention on foot of an admission order invalid (at 5–6). The courts have contrasted this with a criminal matter, where different reasoning might apply, and previous matters which have a causal relationship with the present detention might need to be considered.[3] However, if a stage in the statutory procedure for involuntary admission is omitted completely, a different outcome may result. In *S.O.* v. *Clinical Director of Adelaide and Meath Hospital* [2013] IEHC 132 there had been a failure to comply with the requirement that a doctor should examine the person before making a recommendation that the person be admitted under the Act and Hogan J therefore ordered that the person's subsequent admission was unlawful.

Fourth, O'Malley J noted in *D.H.* v. *Clinical Director of St Patrick's Hospital* (High Court, *ex tempore*, 18 June 2012) that, as judicial review is a discretionary remedy, the court might in some cases take into account the powers of the MHT in deciding whether to exercise the court's discretion. Her suggestion seemed to be that on occasions the court might refuse the remedy of judicial review due to the existence of the MHT's parallel 'sort of mini judicial review jurisdiction of its own' (at 2). On the other hand, O'Malley J also stated in that case that, where personal liberty is at stake, she would be 'reluctant to close the door to the person seeking the protection of the High Court' (at 2).

The MHT's power to review procedural matters

The function of the MHT hearing is to review the person's detention and decide whether to confirm or revoke the relevant admission or renewal order. According to section 18 of the Act, to affirm the order, the MHT must be satisfied that:

1. the person is 'suffering from a mental disorder' *and*
2. *certain procedures* have been complied with, or, 'if there has been a failure to comply with [these procedures], that the failure does not affect the substance of the order and does not cause an injustice'. (section 18(1)(a))[4]

The MHTs therefore are clearly required to consider procedural matters, which is in sharp contrast to the powers of the first tier tribunals in England, which may not consider procedural issues (section 72 Mental Health Act 1983, England and Wales, as amended). However, only certain procedural matters may be reviewed by MHTs. A difficult issue is whether the lack of power to review certain procedural sections leads to a breach of the ECHR.

Article 5(4) of the ECHR states that a detained person has the right to take proceedings by which the lawfulness of his or her detention shall be decided speedily by a 'court' (which includes independent tribunals). It can be argued that MHTs must have the power to review, without restrictions, both the substantive and procedural aspects of the person's detention. The primary authority for this argument is *Brogan* v. *United Kingdom* (1989) 11 EHRR 117, a case concerning detention under the Prevention of Terrorism Act 1984, where it was held that arrested or detained persons are entitled to a review hearing upon the procedural and substantive conditions which are essential for the 'lawfulness', in the sense of the ECHR, of their deprivation of liberty. Thus, an Article 5(4) 'court' reviewing detention (which includes mental health tribunals) must be able to review both procedural and substantive grounds for a person's detention. This was confirmed in *Nikolova* v. *Bulgaria* (2001) 31 EHRR 3, a case concerning an appeal against a remand in custody on a criminal charge. There are possible counter arguments which may be made, by referring for example to the fact that an application under Article 40 of the Constitution could be used to 'fill in the gaps' in the powers of MHTs (see Whelan, 2009: para. 9-16).[5]

An attempt of sorts was made to raise this issue in *C.C.* v. *Clinical Director of St Patrick's Hospital (No.1)* [2009] IEHC 13, but the judgment only considers one aspect of the issue. It was argued that MHTs ought to have power to release a person if section 13 of the 2001 Act, concerning removals to hospitals, was breached, even though section 13 is not one of the listed procedural sections which may be reviewed by the tribunal. The applicant relied on *Storck* v. *Germany* (2006) 43 EHRR 6, in which it was held that Article 5(1) of the ECHR lays down a positive obligation on the state to protect the liberty of its citizens, and that the state cannot absolve itself from responsibility by delegating its obligations in such matters to private bodies. McMahon J rejected this argument, referring to the fact that the MHT had offered an adjournment to the applicant. He continued:

> Had the applicant availed of the adjournment it would have given the applicant's solicitor the opportunity of making the same request to those who had power of release including presumably the clinical director. If the applicant got no satisfaction from the clinical director then the applicant could have commenced proceedings against the clinical director's refusal under Art.40.4 of the Constitution. A claim, however, that the State failed under the Convention to protect the applicant's right to liberty, because the Tribunal did not have the power under the Act, is not sustainable for the simple reason that the applicant did not have the correct target for his complaint. (at 27)

This only deals with one aspect of the case-law on Article 5 – the fact that a state cannot delegate its responsibility to protect citizens' liberty to private bodies. There had been no tribunal or court review of the person's first stay in the clinic in the *Storck* case, and so the case has very little relevance to the question of the scope of such a review if such a review takes place.

The power to waive procedural irregularities

As stated earlier, MHTs have the power, under section 18 of the 2001 Act, to waive a procedural irregularity under certain listed sections if 'the failure does not affect the substance of the order and does not cause an injustice'. In a series of cases, mainly clustered in the period from April to July 2007, the courts interpreted section 18 inconsistently. The details of these cases may be found elsewhere (Whelan, 2009: 9-24–9-38) but the main points will now be reviewed, before turning to some more recent case-law. Interestingly, two of the 2007 cases[6] concerned procedural compliance with sections 23 and 24 of the 2001 Act, which concern re-grading of persons from voluntary to involuntary status, even though technically a MHT does not have power to consider compliance with those sections. As technically the tribunals did not have jurisdiction to consider these sections, the comments of the High Court in those cases may also, technically, not be binding on future courts.

In the 2007 cases, there were clearly two schools of thought: some cases held that section 18 could only be used to excuse minor failures of an insubstantial nature, while others held that tribunals could excuse virtually any procedural defect, unless it was in reckless disregard of the statutory scheme. Statistically speaking, there was more support for the first school. O'Neill J held in *W.Q.* v. *Mental Health Commission* [2007] IEHC 154 that only failures of an insubstantial nature which did not cause an injustice could be excused. In that case, he held that it was not permissible for a renewal order to be signed by a psychiatrist from outside the hospital, who was not involved in care and treatment, but was brought in for the purposes of review. This approach was expressly followed by Mac Menamin J in *J.B.* v. *Director of the Central Mental Hospital (No.2)* [2007] IEHC 201, a case where it was found that the person was in lawful detention even though the renewal order was signed by a psychiatrist who was not on the staff of the hospital in which the person was detained. Similar reasoning was used by O'Higgins J in *Q.* v. *Governor of St Patrick's Hospital* (High Court, *ex tempore*, 21 December 2006) where he held that one cannot do violence to the section and a tribunal cannot excuse a failure to use sections 23 and 24 in sequence. This approach was also supported indirectly by Hardiman J in *M.D.* v. *Clinical Director of St Brendan's Hospital* [2007] IEHC 183, when he stated that tribunals must contribute to a situation of total compliance with statutory provisions, although admittedly he was focusing on the necessity for the MHT to record its decision carefully rather than on the meaning of section 18.

Charleton J belonged to the second school; in *T.O'D.* v. *Kennedy* [2007] IEHC 129, he stated that section 18 refers to the entirety of the relevant sections, not simply minor matters as to typing, time or procedure and he held that a tribunal could affirm a detention under section 23 which was six days longer than permitted. This reasoning was approved of by Peart J in *J.H.* v. *Lawlor* [2007] IEHC 225, concerning a detention which was 20 minutes longer than permitted, although Peart J did say that each case of delay would have to be considered in its own context and on its own facts. O'Keeffe J also adopted the second school of thought in *A.R.* v. *Clinical Director of St Brendan's Hospital* [2009] IEHC 143, concerning failure on the part of a psychiatrist to tick a box on a renewal form indicating that the person continued to suffer from a mental disorder.

There have been fewer cases since 2007 in which the meaning of section 18 has been considered. In *G.F.* v. *Clinical Director of Acute Psychiatric Unit* [2013] IEHC 309, a doctor had signed a recommendation for admission in which he stated the person's clinical condition but did not tick a box indicating which subsection(s) of section 3 applied to the person's mental disorder. This meant that on a strict reading of the form, the doctor had not recommended the person's admission. The tribunal decided that this was a breach of the Act but it did not affect the substance of the admission order or cause an injustice. Hogan J stated, '[i]n my view, while no procedural error is excluded *ex ante* from the scope of section 18, the task of the Tribunal under this section is essentially to examine whether the substance of the procedural protections was satisfied and to ensure that any non-compliance did not cause an injustice' (at para. 9). He went on to hold that the case was 'really indistinguishable' from the *A.R.* case, and applying that case by analogy, the tribunal was entitled to apply its section 18 powers and affirm the person's detention.

Although section 18 was not specifically mentioned in *D.* v. *Health Service Executive* [2009] IEHC 488, there was an endorsement of the tribunal's decision to consider the report of an independent psychiatrist in circumstances where the independent psychiatrist had (for understandable reasons) not had an opportunity to interview the responsible consultant psychiatrist. The requirement that this interview take place is contained in section 17, which is not one of the listed procedural sections which the tribunal may consider.[7] Peart J noted a submission by counsel that compliance with section 17 could not be considered by the tribunal, but did not return to this issue in his judgment. It is also unclear whether the tribunal explicitly relied on section 18 to 'cure' the lack of interview between the two psychiatrists. Ultimately, Peart J found that 'the defect, if it be that, in the report is not so fundamental as to invalidate the report to the extent that the tribunal could not be entitled to have regard to it' (at 8). In his view the tribunal was entitled to decide as it did and proceed, if it so decided, to affirm the order.

Hogan J enunciated a new principle concerning the meaning of section 18 in the recent case of *P.D.* v. *Clinical Director, Department of Psychiatry, Connolly Hospital* [2014] IEHC 58. A psychiatrist had intended to make a second renewal order for a three-month period on 13 January 2013, but had made two mistakes on the renewal order: she completed the wrong part of the form, filling out the reference to section 15(2) of the 2001 Act rather than section 15(3), and she inserted the wrong date, referring to either 13 or 14 April 2013. The tribunal had waived these irregularities, relying on its power under section 18. Hogan J held that the detention was unlawful, as the renewal order was bad on its face, and therefore this was not a case where the provisions of section 18(1)(a)(ii) came into play at all.

The reasoning applied by the court in this case is noteworthy. Hogan J noted that a critical point is that the tribunal's task is simply to review the earlier admission or renewal order. Even where the tribunal affirms such an order, the decision of the tribunal does not actually supplant or replace the earlier order. The renewal order itself remains the basis for the detention. Section 18 did not come into play at all because it concerns infirmities which might attach to the renewal order by reason of earlier non-compliance with certain key procedural requirements prescribed by the 2001 Act. Hogan J continued:

> This, however, is not quite what has happened here. It is not suggested that there has, in fact, been some *prior non-compliance* with statutory formalities such as might render invalid a renewal order which is *otherwise good on its face*. It is rather a question of whether the order – in this case, the renewal order of 13th January 2014 – is, in fact, good on its face and whether it recites an appropriate legal basis for the applicant's detention. (at para. 8)

Hogan J then discussed an immigration case, *G.E.* v. *Governor of Cloverhill Prison* [2011] IESC 41, in which the Supreme Court held that a notice refusing leave to land in the state was invalid on its face and therefore the applicant's detention was unlawful. Applying these standards, he held that the errors on the face of the document were too significant to admit of any conclusion other than that the renewal order was bad on its face. Hogan J concluded that the clinical director in this case had not clearly established the lawful basis for the detention in the manner required by Article 40 of the Constitution. He commented that the Oireachtas might well consider amending the 2001 Act to enable obvious clerical errors of this kind to be corrected 'by means of a form of slip rule procedure, along, of course, with safeguards and external supervision of any changes to an admissions order or renewal order' (at para. 16).

This is a very significant finding for cases where such an error arises in future. It re-opens the prospect of the courts applying a stricter approach to construction of documentation in detentions under the Mental Health Act, especially where there is an error in the most recent document justifying detention at the time of the tribunal or court hearing. It is notable that Hogan J did not review the previous case-law on section 18, and moved very quickly to immigration case-law regarding the validity of a detention based on a document which is bad on its face. He also did not refer to the best interests principle, or to the *E.H.* case, where it was held that 'mere technical defects' should not give rise to a 'rush to court' (at para. 50). Questions remain open as to whether, if the *G.E.* principle were being applied to some of the 2007 case-law on the meaning of section 18, a different result would have been reached. For example, was the detention in the *T.O'D.* case, which was six days longer than permitted, bad on its face?

Unfortunately, it is not possible to state definitively what the current legal position is regarding the meaning of section 18(1)(a)(ii). There appears to be more support for the view that it can only be used to excuse minor failures of an insubstantial nature, but it is possible that the courts will swing again in the opposite direction. From the perspective of constitutional and human rights, the view that section 18 can only be used to excuse minor failures would be more appropriate, given that the person's liberty is at stake. In a review of the issue in 2011, Amnesty International Ireland recommended clarification of the statutory wording by referring to 'minor failures of compliance which are of an insubstantial nature' (2011: 109). The Expert Group on the Review of the Mental Health Act 2001 (2015: 50) decided not to recommend a change in the wording of section 18, although the emphasis in the group's report was on whether or not a 'slip rule' allowing rectification of errors within 14 days of admission should be introduced.

Statements from the courts concerning the importance of MHTs following procedures correctly

The courts have made some statements to the effect that it is very important that MHTs follow procedures correctly. The most significant example is *M.D.* v. *Clinical Director of St Brendan's Hospital* [2008] 1 IR 632, a case in which the psychiatrist had failed to tick the relevant box on the information notice to notify the person whether he was being detained under an admission order or a renewal order, which was a breach of section 16 of the 2001 Act. The tribunal had affirmed the person's detention. In the High Court, Peart J held (at 640) that the psychiatrist's oversight did not result in any unlawfulness of detention. By the time the case reached the Supreme Court, a second tribunal hearing had been held, which also affirmed the person's detention. While the Supreme Court found the detention to be lawful, Hardiman J considered the question of the role of the tribunal in such a case in more detail. Referring to the tribunal's recording of reasons for its decision, he said that this was an absolutely essential part of the tribunal's functions and neither the psychiatrist nor the tribunal could avoid or frustrate the review simply by the making of an inadequate or insufficient record of the exercise by them of the very considerable powers conferred upon them by statute (at 644).

When the tribunal was filling in the form which recorded its decision, it ticked both the box which indicated that the provisions of sections 9, 10, 12, 14, 15 and 16 had been complied with and the box indicating that if there had been a failure to comply with any such provisions, the failure did not affect the substance of the order and did not cause an injustice. Hardiman J expressed concern that, the psychiatrist having omitted to comply with section 16, the tribunal nevertheless certified that section 16 had been complied with when 'it manifestly had not' (at 649). Hardiman J made the following additional comments regarding the tribunal's decision:

> In my view it was illogical to reach both of these findings. If the first finding was correct, the second was otiose. If the proviso contained in section 18(1)(a)(ii) (that there has been a failure it did not affect the substance of the order or cause an injustice) requires to be invoked, as it did, then that situation will arise only if there has in fact been a failure to comply with some section of the Act of 2001. Moreover, I cannot see how it can be certified, as it was, that if there has been a failure to comply with any such provision then the failure did not affect the substance of the order and did not cause an injustice unless the precise failure in question is identified and its effect ascertained. (at 649)

He also stated that the tribunal consists of three persons, a lay representative, a lawyer and a psychiatrist. It was important that, if it is found that a particular section of the 2001 Act has not been complied with, that fact should be ascertained, recorded and its effect discussed. Only in this way can the mental health tribunal hope to contribute to a situation of total compliance with the statutory provisions (at 649).

Hardiman J's comments are an important expression, at Supreme Court level, of the importance of following procedures correctly. His strong emphasis on the need for tribunals to comply with the Act, and principles of natural justice, in full sends a significant signal to members of tribunals and guides them in the performance of their role.

The relevance of the ECHR and the CRPD

In the case-law on the Mental Health Act 2001 to date, there have only been a small number of references to ECHR case-law, and the courts have generally tended to distinguish the ECHR cases rather than apply them to the issues in the case (on the relevance of the ECHR to mental health law, see Bartlett et al., 2006). A good example here is *E.H.* v. *Clinical Director of St Vincent's Hospital* [2009] IESC 46, where the person sought to challenge her classification as a voluntary patient from 10–22 December 2008, when she arguably lacked capacity to be 'voluntary' and was not free to leave the hospital. Heavy reliance was placed in the legal argument on *H.L.* v. *United Kingdom* (2005) 40 EHRR 32, also known as the 'Bournewood gap' case. However, the Supreme Court held that the *H.L.* case was not relevant as it could not bear on the applicant's detention subsequent to 22 December, thus glossing over the fact that from 10–22 December, the procedural safeguards of the Mental Health Act were not available to the person (for fuller discussion of *E.H.* see Whelan, 2009: 5-32–5-37 and Murray, 2010). Another case where ECHR case-law was distinguished is *P.L.* v. *Clinical Director of St Patrick's University Hospital (No.2)* [2012] IEHC 547.

These decisions have sent a signal to mental health tribunals that, in general, ECHR case-law is not very relevant to their deliberations. This is a matter of concern, as clearly the tribunals, as organs of the state, are required to perform their functions in a manner compatible with the state's obligations under the Convention (section 3 ECHR Act 2003; Kilkelly, 2009; De Londras and Kelly, 2010). This means that, in principle, decisions of the ECtHR in Strasbourg should be taken very seriously by the tribunals. No case concerning the 2001 Act has been brought to the ECtHR since the Act came into force. This is surprising, as if a person were to challenge the Act's provisions concerning voluntary status before the ECtHR, it is likely that such a challenge would succeed.

While the state has not yet ratified the CRPD,[8] the ECtHR has held that the CRPD may be used as an aid to interpreting the ECHR (*Glor* v. *Switzerland*, Application No. 13444/04, Judgment 30 April 2009; *Stanev* v. *Bulgaria* (2012) 55 EHRR 22). Furthermore, Mac Menamin J held in *M.X.* v. *Health Service Executive* [2012] IEHC 491 that the CRPD is a helpful reference point in interpreting constitutional rights. It will be interesting to see, as awareness of the CRPD grows, and as the state moves to its ultimate ratification, whether it will have an impact on the courts' approach to issues of interpretation of the Mental Health Act. For example, the courts may have difficulty in reconciling the prohibition on deprivations of liberty based on disability in Article 14 of the CRPD with the right to detain 'persons of unsound mind' under Article 5 of the ECHR.

Conclusion

The decisions of the courts regarding mental health tribunals have been affected to a great extent by the limitations of the application under Article 40 as a remedy. In applications under Article 40, the courts will not, in general, find that the detention is unlawful if there have been 'mere technical defects' in the process. Judicial review is a more flexible remedy, but most of the applications to date have been brought under Article 40 instead. Lawyers' preference for applications under Article 40 appears to relate to its relatively speedy availability as a remedy, and the possible easier availability of free legal aid for such a case. The courts' reluctance to find detention unlawful is also informed by their paternalistic interpretation of the 'best interests' principle. The *E.H.* case, in requiring legal representatives to consider the person's best interests, has had a chilling effect on litigation.

The courts have not been consistent in their interpretation of the power of the MHTs, under section 18 of the Mental Health Act, to waive procedural irregularities in the process. Some cases suggest that this power should only be used to waive minor irregularities; others suggest that tribunals may 'cure' more significant procedural breaches. In some cases, tribunals have waived procedural irregularities regarding sections which they are not even empowered to consider. More recently, it has been held in the *P.D.* case that if the current order justifying detention is bad on its face, section 18 does not even 'come into play' at all. It may be that a statutory amendment is required to clarify the meaning of section 18.

There have been very few references to the ECHR or the CRPD in the case-law. When the ECHR has been referred to, the courts tend to distinguish the relevant cases so that they are held not to apply. This is an issue of concern as tribunals may take this as a signal that they can conduct their reviews without regard to ECHR case-law when in fact they are statutorily obliged to do so under the ECHR Act 2003.

On the whole, the courts have tended to give very wide latitude to the tribunals in their decision-making, when closer supervision seems warranted. While the Mental Health Act heralded a new era of rights-based mental health law in many respects and was intended to ensure compliance with international obligations, the Irish courts have not embraced this new era and have preferred to hark back to paternalistic reasoning from the 1940s. Further legislative change may assist in re-orientating the courts' perspective more to the rights-based approach, although they may continue to refuse to change what appears to be a deeply entrenched approach even if required to do so by new legislation.

Notes

1 For example, there were 1,896 hearings by the MHTs in 2013 – Mental Health Commission (2014: 43).

2 The courts may use the technique of delayed or 'staggered' release if a person has a serious mental disorder and may require to be detained again – see Whelan, 2009: 2-42–2-44 and also the recent case of *F.X.* v. *Clinical Director of Central Mental Hospital* [2014] IESC 1.

3 *S.C.* v. *Clinical Director of St Brigid's Hospital*, Supreme Court, 13 March 2009, judgment not available, quoted in *E.H.* v. *Clinical Director of St Vincent's Hospital* [2009] IESC 46; [2009] 3 IR 774, at 792.

4 The tribunal must be satisfied 'that the provisions of sections 9, 10, 12, 14, 15 and 16, where applicable, have been complied with'.

5 See also *X.* v. *United Kingdom* (1981) 4 EHRR 188, where it was held that a review by way of habeas corpus procedure in England was not sufficient for a continuing confinement. The court referred to the fact that in habeas corpus cases, the case is considered on the basis of affidavit evidence, and the focus is on enquiring into whether the detention is in compliance with the requirements stated in the relevant legislation and with the applicable principles of the common law. As a result, the habeas corpus proceedings were not in compliance with Article 5(4) of the ECHR.

6 *Q.* v. *Governor of St Patrick's Hospital*, High Court, O'Higgins J, *ex tempore*, 21 December 2006 and *T.O'D.* v. *Kennedy* [2007] 3 IR 689. Another example is *N.B* v. *Clinical Director of Our Lady's Hospital Navan and Others* [2007] IEHC 403.

7 See *W.Q.* v. *Mental Health Commission* [2007] IEHC 154; [2007] 3 IR 755 at 769, where one of the points raised was that a tribunal had not been convened under section 17 to review the person's detention before the renewal order was made. O'Neill J noted that this matter was outside the scope of the tribunal's consideration because section 17 is not listed among the sections in respect of which an MHT is required to consider compliance.

8 For consideration of the relationship between the CRPD and mental health law, see for example Doyle (2010), Fennell and Khaliq (2011), Bartlett (2012), Morrissey (2012) and Szmukler et al. (2014).

References

Amnesty International Ireland (2011) *Mental Health Act 2001: A Review*. Dublin: Amnesty International Ireland.

Bartlett, P. (2012) 'The United Nations Convention on the Rights of Persons with Disabilities and mental health law', *Modern Law Review*, 75(5): 752.

Bartlett, P., Lewis, O. and Thorold, O. (2006) *Mental Disability and the European Convention on Human Rights*. Leiden: Martinus Nijhoff.

Casey, P., Brady, P., Craven, C. and Dillon, A. (2010) *Psychiatry and the Law*, 2nd edn. Dublin: Blackhall Publishing.

De Londras, F. and Kelly, C. (2010) *European Convention on Human Rights Act: Operation, Impact and Analysis*. Dublin: Round Hall.

Doyle, S. (2010) 'The new paradigm for involuntary detention – Article 14 of the UN Convention on the Rights of Persons with Disabilities and the right to liberty of persons with mental disabilities', *Irish Yearbook of International Law*, 4–5: 71.

Expert Group on the Review of the Mental Health Act 2001 (2015) *Report of the Expert Group on the Review of the Mental Health Act 2001*. Dublin: Department of Health.

Fennell, P. and Khaliq, U. (2011) 'Conflicting or complementary obligations? The UN disability rights Convention on human rights and English law', *European Human Rights Law Review*, 6: 662.

Irish Human Rights Commission (2010) *Policy Paper Concerning the Definition of a 'Voluntary Patient' under s. 2 of the Mental Health Act 2001*. Dublin: Irish Human Rights Commission.

Keys, M. (2002) *Mental Health Act 2001*. Dublin: Round Hall.

Kilkelly, U. (ed.) (2009) *ECHR and Irish law*, 2nd edn. Bristol: Jordan Publishing.

Lynn, M. (2010) 'The Mental Health Act 2001: paternalistic or rights-based?', Mental Health Law Conference, University College Cork, 26 February

Mental Health Commission (2014) *Annual Report 2013*. Dublin: Mental Health Commission.

Morrissey, F. (2012) 'The United Nations Convention on the Rights of Persons with Disabilities: a new approach to decision-making in mental health law', *European Journal of Health Law*, 19(5): 423.

Murray, C. (2010) 'Reinforcing paternalism within Irish mental health law – contrasting the decisions in *EH* v. *St Vincent's Hospital and Others* and *SM* v. *The Mental Health Commission and Others*', *Dublin University Law Journal*, 32: 273.

O'Neill, A. (2005) *Irish Mental Health Law*. Dublin: First Law.

Szmukler, G., Daw, R. and Callard, F. (2014) 'Mental health law and the UN Convention on the rights of persons with disabilities', *International Journal of Law and Psychiatry*, 37(3): 245.

Teff, H. (1994) *Reasonable Care: Legal Perspectives on the Doctor–Patient Relationship*. Oxford: Clarendon Press.

Whelan, D. (2009) *Mental Health Law and Practice: Civil and Criminal Aspects*. Dublin: Round Hall.

Whelan, D. (2012) 'Can the right to personal liberty be interpreted in a paternalistic manner? Cases on the Mental Health Act 2001', *Irish Human Rights Law Review*, forthcoming.

15

Patient-centred dying: the role of law

Mary Donnelly

Death is not the opposite of life, but a part of it.
Haruki Murakami, *Blind Willow, Sleeping Woman: 24 Stories*

Introduction

The way we die is a fundamental part of our life story. Yet, most of us dedicate little time to thinking about how we want to die (McCarthy et al., 2010). It seems inevitable in contemporary Ireland that the law will play an increased role in decisions about the end of life. There are several reasons for this. Ongoing technological development and increased medical knowledge, including the emergence of the diagnosis of a 'minimally conscious state'[1] (MCS) in the 1990s, are making end-of-life choices more complex. Frequently, too, these choices are made in an impersonal hospital environment (see Lyons, Chapter 16). Moreover, as the Irish population becomes more diverse, different religious and ethical ethos must be recognised and appropriately accommodated.

A more formalised approach to dying may be inevitable but it is not without difficulties. As noted by the American medical historian David Rothman, 'that dying has become a legal process is not an unqualified sign of progress' (1991: 261). As well as the trauma of legal actions at a very vulnerable time for dying people and those who care about them, there is a broader risk of 'legalism'. As described by Judith Shklar, legalism is the development of an 'ethical attitude that holds moral conduct to be a matter of rule following and moral relationships to consist of duties and rights determined by rules' (1964: 1). Such an impoverished approach to end-of-life care must be guarded against.

This chapter examines the legal context within which decisions about the end of life are made. It argues that an ethical approach to end-of-life care must be centred on the dying person and that finding ways to ensure that this person's voice is heard must be core to the development of legal frameworks. In this respect, the law has, to date, been inadequate. While the law has been effective at hearing (and enabling to be heard) voices which are loud and clear, such as capable adults refusing treatment for religious reasons, where voices are less audible or less distinct, the law has offered less. For the vulnerable person, the person with capacity difficulties, the person who is confused or distressed or disturbed, the law has offered little scope for expression or involvement. This chapter is concerned primarily with this group of people and with exploring how legal frameworks can best ensure that their voices are heard in making decisions about their care at the end of their lives.

The chapter begins by identifying the normative case for a patient-centred approach to end-of-life care. It then explores the ways we currently address and regulate decisions about the end of life in Ireland and identifies the likely impact of changes in the proposed capacity legislation on this. Then, drawing on experiences from the United States and the United Kingdom, it develops arguments regarding the most appropriate decision-making structures within which to consider difficult questions around end-of-life care.

The normative basis for patient-centred dying

If ensuring patient-centred dying is to be adopted as an underpinning goal for the law, it is important to understand why this should be the case. The argument developed here is that a patient-centred approach is more appropriate than an approach focused solely on the ethical principle of sanctity of life and that a patient-centred approach should be based on respect for the principle of dignity (rather than autonomy).

The sanctity of life principle, which derives from the Judeo-Christian tradition, regards life as having an intrinsic value, unrelated to the individual's view of his or her own life. At its most extreme (sometimes described as 'vitalism'), respect for the principle requires that life be preserved at all costs (Keyserlingk, 1979: 12). More commonly, adherents to the principle recognise that it does not require a person 'to administer or undergo a treatment which is not worthwhile' (Keown, 1997: 485). However, crucially, the determination of whether or not a treatment is worthwhile is made not by the individual but on external bases. Thus, Keown argues that a treatment would not be worthwhile 'either because it offers no reasonable hope of benefit or because, even though it does, the expected benefit would be outweighed by burdens which the treatment would impose, such as excessive pain' (1997: 485).

The sanctity of life principle rightly retains ongoing ethical importance. As described by Hoffmann LJ in *Bland* v. *Airedale NHS Trust* [1993] AC 789 at 826, regardless of religious belief, a recognition of the 'intrinsic value of human life' forms 'part of almost everyone's intuitive values'. It is '[o]ur belief in the sanctity of life [which] explains why we think it almost always wrong to cause the death of another human being, even one who is terminally ill or so disabled that we think that if we were in his position we would rather be dead'. However, as Hoffman LJ went on to acknowledge, sanctity of life is 'only one of a cluster of ethical principles which we apply to decisions about how we should live' (1993, at 826). Focusing solely on the sanctity of life fails to address the individual whose life is at stake; it ignores his or her essential subjectivity and accords insufficient weight to his or her views.

In justifying why decisions about end-of-life care should respect the views of the individual, the ethical principle (and legal right) of first recourse will typically be that of autonomy. As described by Ronald Dworkin, 'we allow someone to choose death over radical amputation or a blood transfusion, if that is his informed wish, because we acknowledge his right to a life structured by his own values' (1993: 239; see Campbell, Chapter 4).

Yet simple reliance on autonomy, certainly as it is constructed legally, provides an inadequate foundation for the ethical importance of patient-centred dying. As Daniel Callahan describes, autonomy lacks the 'intellectual strength or penetration' to address difficult ethical questions (2003: 499). Reliance on autonomy offers solutions in the straightforward contest between sanctity of life and individual choice where a person with capacity refuses treatment for religious or other reasons. However, once the principle of autonomy is required to move beyond this, it begins to run into difficulties. Referencing the autonomy of dying people who may well be confused, distressed, disturbed and vulnerable seems somehow to miss the point. This is illustrated by the following account:

> [A] young mother in [her] early 30's had an inoperable tumour at [the] back of her nose and throat. In the end stages, this girl refused pain relief or sedatives. She did not want much medical intervention. It was the most distressing death I ever witnessed ... It was very distressing for her, her family and staff. She was from a very poor social background and had little or no education. Staff tried to assist her as much as possible but it was an awful death for her. (Quinlan and O'Neill, 2008)

Few of us would wish the death described here for ourselves or for those we care about. Yet, the manner of the death met the technical legal requirements regarding autonomy and respect for individual choices.

If respect for autonomy cannot provide a principled basis for patient-centred dying, it is necessary to look beyond this principle. In this respect, the widely debated (and frequently maligned) concept of dignity presents a better fit. The difficulty with dignity is, of course, one of definition. Dignity is 'the shibboleth of all perplexed and empty-headed moralists' (Schopenhauer, 1873: 51) and frequently seen as 'soft and mushy' (Waldron, 2012: 137). It is therefore necessary to identify what is meant by dignity in this context. First, as is now generally accepted, dignity must involve an egalitarian component (Rosen, 2012: 53). Although there is still debate regarding the scope of equality (see, for example, Catholic arguments in respect of abortion/euthanasia), for present purposes, it is relatively uncontroversial that dignity in the context of end-of-life care is not linked to conceptions of capacity or rationality in the same way as autonomy. We all have an equal right to dignity in dying and this is not diminished because we are confused, distressed, disturbed or vulnerable. Second, respect for dignity must take account of individuals' perspectives of what is or is not dignified (Beyleveld and Brownsword, 2002). Thus, respect for dignity has a subjective element and respecting the views of the dying person is an essential part of respecting his or her dignity. Where the person is confused or disturbed or has limited capacity, respect for dignity requires making efforts to determine his or her views, drawing on the resources and knowledge of those who know the person.

The current framework for end-of-life care

The legal framework for end-of-life care in Ireland is fragmented, uncertain and incomplete. The only relevant legislative elements are the prohibition on assisted suicide in section 2(2) of the Criminal Law (Suicide) Act 1993 and the requirement in section 14(1) of the Health Act 2007 (Care and Welfare of Residents in Designated Centres for Older People) Regulations 2009 that '[t]he registered provider shall ensure that the designated centre has written operational policies and protocols for end-of-life care.'. Some, albeit limited, clarity is added by the small number of relevant judicial decisions (see *In Re a Ward of Court* [1996] 2 IR 79; *JM* v. *St Vincent's Hospital* [2003] 1 IR 321; *Fleming* v. *Ireland* [2013] IESC 19). From these, we know that end-of-life care must respect constitutional rights to autonomy, dignity and bodily integrity (whether or not the individual has capacity); that artificial nutrition and hydration (ANH) is not legally distinct from other forms of medical treatment; that a diagnosis of persistent vegetative state (PVS) is not required for the removal of ANH; that decisions in respect of persons lacking capacity must be made in the person's best interests; that advance decisions are, in principle, to be respected; and, that there is no constitutional right to assisted suicide. Beyond this, however, decisions are made in a legal vacuum.

In such an uncertain legal context, ethical guidance assumes even greater significance. The guidance provided by the Irish Medical Council's *Guide to Professional Conduct and Ethics for Registered Medical Practitioners* (2009) is, in many ways, more helpful than Irish law. Under the heading 'End of life care', doctors are advised of their responsibility 'to take care that the patient dies with dignity, in comfort and with as little suffering as possible' (2009: 22.1); that there is no obligation to start or continue a treatment or ANH 'that is futile or disproportionately burdensome, even if such treatment may prolong life' (2009: 22.2); that they must respect the right of patients to refuse medical treatment or request the withdrawal of medical treatment and respect a patient's advance healthcare plans (2009: 22.3); and, that they must take care to communicate effectively and sensitively with patients and their families (2009: 22.4). These obligations should be read together with paragraph 19 of the Guide, which requires that, in assessing what alternative forms of hydration and nutrition are possible and appropriate, account must be taken of the burdens and risks to the patient and of the patient's wishes, if known, and paragraph 34.6, which requires that the patient's past and present wishes be taken into account when making decisions on a patient's behalf. The Guide represents the beginnings of a patient-centred approach to dying. However, it still leaves many questions unresolved (compare, for example, the detailed guidance in the United Kingdom General Medical Council's *Treatment and Care Towards the End of Life*, 2010). The Guide is also limited in terms of requirements for, and advice regarding, a more active approach to listening to patients who are confused, distressed or have limited capacity.

Making decisions in practice

Given the limitations of the legal framework, the more interesting question is how decisions are made in practice. Here, we are in still more uncertain territory. It would be overly optimistic to believe that the lack of case-law suggests a fully functional, ethically appropriate approach. It may suggest, however, that assertive family members have a greater impact on treatment decisions thus avoiding the need for court referrals. Quinlan and O'Neill's study of practitioner perspectives on end-of-life care suggests that, when family members actively request more invasive treatment, this, rather than the dying person's wishes, is prioritised (2008). Given the reality that any potential litigation is much more likely to come from a family member rather than the dying person, relatives have an inbuilt degree of influence and the possibility that litigation risk management rather than ethical imperatives will influence decisions about end-of-life care must be recognised and addressed.

O'Shea et al.'s study (2008) offers important insights into end-of-life care in acute and long stay care settings. The study shows that a significant number of staff described communication methods with dying people which did not let the person know that they were coming towards the end of life. At times, this was in spite of the person's express question (2008: 157). The study also found that there was no evidence of formal end-of-life planning which reflected any engagement with patients (2008: 158). This finding accords with McNamee and O'Keeffe's (2004) study of do-not-resuscitate instructions (DNRs) which found that, although DNRs were generally appropriately documented and made following consultation, this was more often with families rather than patients. These practices may be changing following the publication of the HSE *National Consent Policy* (2013: para. 3.1), which states that the individual's own views and values are centrally important in the decision to record a DNR instruction on a patient's file.

O'Shea et al.'s study also found that, while communication with dying people was clearly limited, there was 'limited criticism of care provided and the end-of-life care experienced by patients appears to be positive when taken as a whole' (2008: 159). It is probable that these responses are primarily from relatives. It is an unavoidable difficulty with researching the dying process that the perspective of the person at the centre will not be heard. Bearing this in mind, however, O'Shea et al.'s finding is important in thinking about how to develop future standards. Decisions about end-of-life care are fundamentally decisions about people. Having a 'better' legal framework and a more formalised decision-making process but greater patient and family distress would seem like poor progress indeed.

Changes to the legal framework

Two changes to the legal framework described above are likely to come into effect when the Assisted Decision-Making (Capacity) Bill is enacted. First, it is probable that the legislation will provide for advance decision-making and second, the legislation will provide a framework for decision-making for people with diminished capacity. Both aspects will impact on decisions about the end of life, introducing greater certainty in some respects but also creating greater legal formality around dying.

The introduction of advance decision-making

The need for legislation allowing for advance decision-making has been recognised by the Irish Council for Bioethics (2007) and the Law Reform Commission (2009) and in February 2014, the Minister for Health announced a Public Consultation on the draft General Scheme for Advance Healthcare Directives which it is intended to incorporate into the capacity legislation.

If the proposals are enacted, they will permit every adult with capacity to refuse (but not to demand) treatment including life sustaining treatment (other than 'basic care'[2]) and this refusal will continue to apply notwithstanding subsequent incapacity. The draft General Scheme suggests a limited possibility of overriding the advance directive on the basis of the conduct of the person when he or she does not have capacity. Thus, the proposed Scheme places a higher value on respect for the precedent (or prior) autonomy of the capable person than on the contemporaneous preferences of the person lacking capacity. By doing this, the proposed legislation avoids some of the difficulties regarding unenforceable advance directives which were identified by critics of the legislative scheme established by the Mental Capacity Act 2005 (MCA) in England and Wales (Maclean, 2008; Samantha, 2009). However, as Allen Buchanan has argued, there are ethically significant differences between respecting precedent and current autonomy (Buchanan, 1988: 279).[3] Given these differences, it is not necessarily always the most appropriate response to allow the clear voice of the past to talk over the more muted voice of the present (Donnelly, 2010: 200).

While not diminishing the ethical significance of how we choose to resolve possible conflicts between an advance directive and the contemporaneous preferences of a person with impaired capacity, it is also important to remember that in most end-of-life contexts, there will be no conflict and the introduction of advance decision-making will provide an important mechanism for people to ensure that their voices can be heard in decisions at the end of life. However, the experience in other jurisdictions suggests that relatively few people will avail themselves of the opportunity to make an advance directive. In England and Wales, take-up on the advance decision-making provisions in the MCA 2005 is 3–4% of the public (House of Lords Select Committee, 2014: 75), with numbers also being low among patients with diagnosed chronic conditions. This is in spite of findings that 82% of the public have strong views about what they want at the end of life. Statistics from the United States also show that fewer than 25% of Americans have completed an advance directive (Johnson et al., 2012). This is in spite of advance directive legislation being in force for over 20 years and a specific statutory obligation on most care facilities to draw the possibility of making an advance directive to the attention of patients (the Patient Self-Determination Act 1990). Among the reasons identified for the low rates of advance directives are a lack of knowledge among healthcare providers about state laws and an associated discomfort in discussing the issue; a reluctance on patients' part to confront their own mortality; and the difficulty with a dialogue around end of life during a period of acute admission (Johnson et al., 2012).

The impact of capacity legislation

The proposed capacity legislation recognises the importance of respecting the 'will and preference' of persons with impaired capacity. In order to achieve this, the proposals provide for forms of supported decision-making (assisted and co-decision-making) where someone, typically a relative or friend, appointed by a person with impaired capacity is afforded legal authority to support the person in making decisions and having these put into effect. In an end-of-life context, this aspect of the proposed framework affords a role to the selected support person, which, in many cases, they already play, albeit without the kind of legal endorsement which the proposed legislation will afford them. By allowing the person to choose their support, the proposed legislation offers a better degree of control to the person than is currently the case when more assertive relatives may drown out not just the patient's voice but also those of relatives or friends with other perspectives on the person's wishes. However, these forms of support will only come into place if the person with impaired capacity chooses to activate the legal framework and it is unclear whether there will be a significant uptake.

A further notable feature of the proposed legislation is that it looks likely to significantly increase the formalisation of the dying process. As the legislation is drafted, a significant number of decisions about life-sustaining treatment will require the court approval of the High Court. Thus, the effect of the legislation, as drafted, is to place the High Court at the centre of decisions about end-of-life care. Yet, as will be argued below, the High Court is rarely the most suitable place to make these kinds of decisions.

Developing an appropriate framework for end-of-life decision-making

David Rothman has noted the irony in the fact that the response to the power imbalance between doctors and patients was the creation of other authority figures in the forms of judges, lawyers, ethicists, advocates and others, commenting that, '[t]o make certain that the patient's voice would be heard and respected demanded the support of a chorus, and as sometimes happens, the chorus can overwhelm the soloist' (1991: 261). Given the inevitability of some degree of formalisation of dying, it therefore behoves us to think about how a more formalised process should work, keeping in the foreground at all times the concern with ensuring patient-centred dying. The discussion below draws on aspects of the experience from the United States and the United Kingdom in order to identify why formal oversight of dying can sometimes be necessary and also to develop the argument that courts of law are not necessarily the most appropriate place for this oversight to take place.

Formalising end-of-life decision-making

Most of the time, the act of dying does not require a legal audience. Patient-centred end-of-life care is far more effectively delivered through enhanced ethical standards; better training for professionals; and initiatives such as the Hospice Friendly Hospitals programme.[4] However, sometimes there is a need for oversight of decisions.

The highly publicised case of Terri Schiavo shows the deficiencies of a wholly privatised decision-making framework. Under United States law, where a person lacks capacity, decisions about end-of-life care are made by a surrogate appointed by the person, and if none has been appointed, by a surrogate according to a designated statutory hierarchy, beginning with a spouse and followed by an adult child; parent; and adult brother or sister. Ms Schiavo had been in a PVS for some eight years following a cardiac arrest. Her husband, who was her surrogate decision-maker, made a decision (on the basis of the statutory test that this is what Ms Schiavo would have chosen) to remove ANH. This decision was opposed by Ms Schiavo's parents, who had strong Catholic religious beliefs, and who also purported to apply the statutory test of what Ms Schiavo would have wanted. Had they been making the decision, Ms Schiavo would continue to have lived. Indeed her parents stated that simply having their daughter alive brought them joy and that they would, if necessary to save their daughter's life, have been prepared to approve the amputation of all her limbs and subject her to further surgery thereafter (Wolfson, 2005). The point here is not that Ms Schiavo's husband was right and her parents were wrong (or vice versa) but that any system whereby decisions about life or death (and the manner of these) are made on the basis of who happens to be at the top of a list of surrogates fails to accord sufficient respect to the individual, treating her ultimately as a means towards an end rather than as an end in herself.[5]

Having a formal mechanism to deal with decisions around the end of life offers other benefits for patients and their families. In a UK-based study, Halliday, Kitzinger and Kitzinger (2015) examined 'legal consciousness' (i.e. awareness of and attitude towards the law) in families where a family member had experienced a catastrophic brain injury and was in an MCS. For some family members, law was seen as a 'sword against the power of the medical profession' (2015: 64). Where there was a dispute regarding welfare, reference to law was seen as empowering. Law was also sometimes seen as a 'tactical weapon to be wielded instrumentally in a personal struggle' (2015: 64). Some relatives (who had made applications to the Court of Protection for the removal of ANH) also expressed their relief at being 'able to pass this life-and-death decision up to a higher decision making forum' (2015: 65). For others, however, law was seen as a barrier, standing in the way of what they saw as the best decisions for their loved one and judicial reluctance to allow the withdrawal of ANH led some family members to express their preparedness to kill their relatives themselves as a way of releasing them. The mixed feelings towards the role of law which this study reveals are reflective of broader questions regarding court-based decisions about end-of-life care. The review of selected case-law from the UK in the next section is instructive in identifying the difficulties with court-based resolutions in this context.

Overseeing dying: the limits of court-based review

In the United Kingdom, the courts took on the task of overseeing dying with some reluctance. In *Airedale NHS Trust* v. *Bland* [1993] AC 789 at 880, Lord Browne-Wilkinson looked regretfully back to the days when 'doctors exercised their own discretion, in accordance with medical ethics, in cases such as these'. Judicial discussion around treatment withdrawal reveals ongoing uncertainty about how to resolve tensions between quality of life and sanctity of life and about the role to be played in this resolution by the patient's voice. The two cases discussed here show these tensions in operation and raise questions about the suitability of courts as the most appropriate place to resolve them.

The decision of the Court of Protection in *W* v. *M* [2011] EWHC 2443 (Fam) concerned an application for the removal of ANH from a woman (M) who had been in an MCS since 2003. Unchallenged evidence was provided by M's (loving and devoted) partner and family that she had specifically indicated that she would not have wished to live in this situation. There was evidence that M was currently in pain, discomfort and emotional distress and was severely restricted in what she could do. However, there was also evidence that M had some positive experiences and that she seemed to enjoy company and listening to conversation. Baker J rejected the application. Describing his approach to M's wishes and feelings (as communicated by her family), Baker J stated (at para. 6) that 'whilst I take those statements into account, they are not binding and in all the circumstances I do not consider they carry substantial weight in my decision'. Instead, he stated, '[t]he factor which does carry substantial weight, in my judgment, is the preservation of life' (at para. 7).

For the present discussion, the relevant matter is not the appropriateness of the ultimate decision but rather the way in which this was reached. It is clear that Baker J made a genuine effort to understand M. He visited her nursing home and the hearing lasted for ten days. This was by no means an unconsidered or careless decision. Yet, the dismissal of the patient's views, as communicated through her partner and family, reflects an underlying difficulty which the law encounters in responding to conditions of uncertainty. It is the function of judges to make legal decisions. In doing this, they will inevitably be drawn towards concepts which they can work with. This explains why courts have been drawn towards the legal right of autonomy which offers straightforward answers to difficult questions (Donnelly, 2010). It also explains the attraction of preservation of life in situations where straightforward respect for autonomy is not possible. Both conceptions offer a degree of concreteness when the patient's voice does not.

The law's difficulty in dealing with uncertainty at the end of life was acknowledged by Lady Hale in *Aintree University Hospitals NHS Foundation Trust* v. *David James and Ors* [2013] UKSC 67. This case also concerned a patient in an MCS who had suffered multiple organ failure following a long illness. The applicant Trust sought declarations permitting the withholding of cardio-pulmonary resuscitation, invasive support for circulatory problems and renal replacement therapy. Lady Hale noted that '[t]he courts have been most reluctant to lay down general principles which might guide the decision [regarding treatment withdrawal]. Every patient, and every case, is different and must be decided on its own facts' (para. 36). She continued:

> [I]in considering the best interests of this particular patient at this particular time, decision-makers must look at his welfare in the widest sense, not just medical but social and psychological … they must try and put themselves in the place of the individual patient and ask what his attitude to the treatment is or would be likely

> to be; and they must consult others who are looking after him or interested in his welfare, in particular for their view of what his attitude would be. (para. 39)

Lady Hale affirmed that the patient's wishes need not always prevail 'any more than those of a fully capable patient must prevail' (para. 45). She also acknowledged that it will not always be possible to ascertain what an incapable patient's wishes are. However, she was clear that 'insofar as it is possible to ascertain the patient's wishes and feelings, his beliefs and values or the things which were important to him, it is those which should be taken into account because they are a component in making the choice which is right for him as an individual human being' (para. 45).

The approach described by Lady Hale is messy. It lacks the kind of precision with which lawyers and legal decision-makers are most comfortable. Yet, if we accept patient-centred dying as the underpinning ethical premise for the law, this offers an ethically more defensible position because it affords a space for patients' voices to be heard.

The lack of precision in the test put forward by Lady Hale raises the question of whether courts are the best place for the kind of nuanced, fact-drenched assessment that is required in attempting to balance the messages from patients' indistinct voices with other relevant factors. Courts are inevitably drawn towards certainty at the expense of nuance. Moreover, although decisions about the end of life involve elements of the law, these decisions cannot be reduced to purely legal terms. There are alternatives to court-based decision-making. One, which is suggested by Huxtable (2012), is the use of clinical ethics committees. Huxtable argues that such committees can encourage 'reliable, reflective and reciprocal negotiations, in which the interests of different participants are acknowledged' (2012: 153). Other forms of alternative dispute resolution could also be considered (Dresser, 2004). Neveloff Dubler and Liebman have developed the concept of bioethics mediation, based around a 'principled resolution' as a mechanism to address contentious ethical issues (2011).[6] Neveloff Dubler argues that 'the notion of a principled resolution combines the strengths of a mediative process that levels the playing field with legal norms and ethical conventions, and uses both as support for forging a consensus' (2011: 179). Clearly, all of these ideas need further development in an Irish context. The important point for the current discussion is that it is possible to construct alternative structures around end-of-life decision-making and that these may better serve the ethical goal of ensuring patient-centred dying.

Conclusion

This chapter has argued that the ethically most appropriate response to increased legal involvement in the process of dying must be the prioritisation of a patient-centred approach to end-of-life care. The chapter has also shown that, while legal oversight of dying is sometimes necessary, there are difficulties with simply utilising law-based reasoning in this area. While an ultimate reference to the court should not (and constitutionally could not) be displaced, it is difficult to justify using the courts as the first point of reference. The lack of spaces other than courts for discussion of individual situations is problematic across many areas of Irish healthcare ethics and law. While some clinical ethics committees do exist, there remains considerable variation in terms of remit, scope and buy-in (Manning and Smith, 2002; McCarthy et al., 2011: 418). This fragmented framework fails to provide any alternative to court review and it provides dying patients with very limited protection from arbitrary decision-making. Developing spaces for discussion and resolution of ethically challenging issues must be a priority for both the dying and the living.

Notes

1 Patients in an MCS may be able to follow simple commands; gesture yes or no; and engage in some degree of purposeful behaviour (Giacino, 2002). There is still limited knowledge of how much awareness patients in an MCS actually have – and there is a continuum of consciousness within this category.

2 This is defined in the draft General Scheme as including but not limited to warmth, shelter, oral hydration, oral nutrition and hygiene measures.

3 Buchanan (1988: 279) identifies three ethically significant differences: first, even if the individual is fully informed when making the advance directive, there may be subsequent developments in terms of prognosis and treatment which cannot have been taken into account; second, the assumption that a competent person is the best judge of their own interests is weakened in the context of choices about future contingencies under conditions where those interests have been radically changed; third, the important formal safeguards which protect against imprudent decisions made in a contemporaneous context may not be present in respect of an advance directive.

4 The programme, which is run by the Irish Hospice Foundation, aims at developing and promoting a culture of care within hospitals which draws on the principles of hospice-based care. One of the products of the programme is the *Quality Standards for End-of-Life Care in Hospitals: Making End-of-Life Care Central to Hospital Care*, 2010.

5 This offends the Kantian Categorical Imperative as stated in the following terms: 'Act in such way that you treat humanity, whether in your own person or in the person of any other, always at the same time as an end and never merely as a means to an end' (Kant, 1785 in Gregor, 1997: 402).

6 A 'principled resolution' is 'a consensus that identifies a plan that falls within clearly accepted ethical principles, legal stipulations, and moral rules defined by ethical discourse, legislatures, and courts, and that facilitates a clear plan for future intervention' (Neveloff Dubler and Liebman, 2011: 14).

References

Beyleveld, D. and Brownsword, R. (2002) *Human Dignity in Bioethics and Biolaw*. Oxford: Oxford University Press.

Buchanan, A. (1988) 'Advance directives and the personal identity problem', *Philosophy and Public Affairs* 17: 277.

Callahan, D. (2003) 'Individual good and common good: a communitarian approach to bioethics', *Perspectives in Biology and Medicine*, 46: 496.

Donnelly, M. (2010) *Healthcare Decision-Making and the Law: Autonomy, Capacity and the Limits of Liberalism.* Cambridge: Cambridge University Press.

Dresser, R. (2004) '*Schiavo*: a hard case makes questionable law', *Hastings Center Report*, 34(3): 8.

Dworkin, R. (1993) *Life's Dominion: An Argument About Abortion, Euthanasia, and Individual Freedom.* New York: Alfred A Knopf.

General Medical Council (2010) *Treatment and Care Towards the End of Life: Good Practice in Decision Making.* London.

Giacino, J.T., Ashwal, S., Childs, N., Cranford, R., Jennett, B., Katz, D.I., Kelly, J.P., Rosenberg, J.H., Whyte, J., Zafonte, R.D. and Zasler, N.D. (2002) 'The minimally conscious state: definition and diagnostic criteria', *Neurology*, 58: 349.

Gregor, M. (ed.) (1997) *Kant: Groundwork of the Metaphysics of Morals* (Cambridge Texts in the History of Philosophy). Cambridge: Cambridge University Press.

Halliday, S., Kitzinger, C. and Kitzinger, J. (2015) 'Law in everyday life and death: a socio-legal study of chronic disorders of consciousness', *Legal Studies*, 35(1): 55.

Health Service Executive (2013) *National Consent Policy.* Dublin.

House of Lords Select Committee (2014) *Report on the Mental Capacity Act 2005: Post Legislative Scrutiny.* London.

Huxtable, R. (2012) *Law, Ethics and Compromise at the Limits of Life.* London: Routledge-Cavendish.

Irish Council for Bioethics (2007) *Is it Time for Advance Care Directives?* Dublin.

Irish Hospice Foundation (2010) *Quality Standards for End-of-Life Care in Hospitals: Making End-of-Life Care Central to Hospital Care.* Dublin.

Johnson, R., Yanfang, Z., Kristin Newby, L., Granger, C. and Granger, B. (2012) 'Reasons for non-completion of advance directives in a cardiac intensive care unit', *American Journal of Critical Care*, 21: 311.

Keown, J. (1997) 'Restoring moral and intellectual shape to the law after *Bland*', *Law Quarterly Review*, 113: 481.

Keyserlingk, E. (1979) *Sanctity of Life or Quality of Life in the Context of Ethics, Medicine and Law.* Ottawa: Law Commission of Canada.

Law Reform Commission (2009) *Report on Bioethics: Advance Care Directives.* Dublin.

Maclean, A. (2008) 'Advance directives and the rocky waters of anticipatory decision-making', *Medical Law Review*, 16: 1.
Manning, P. and Smith, D. (2002) 'The establishment of a hospital clinical ethics committee', *Irish Medical Journal*, 95: 54.
McCarthy, J., Donnelly, M., Dooley, D., Smith, D., Campbell, L. (2011) *End-of-Life Care: Ethics and Law.* Cork: Cork University Press.
McCarthy, J., Weafer, J., Loughrey, M. (2010) 'Irish views on death and dying: a national survey', *Journal of Medical Ethics*, 37: 454.
McNamee, J. and O'Keeffe, S. (2004) 'Documentation of do-not-resuscitate orders in an Irish hospital', *Irish Journal of Medical Science*, 173: 99.
Neveloff Dubler, N. (2011) 'A "principled resolution": the fulcrum for bioethics mediation', *Law and Contemporary Problems*, 74: 177.
Neveloff Dubler, N. and Liebman, C. (2011) *Bioethics Mediation: A Guide to Shaping Shared Solutions Revised and Expanded Edition.* Nashville: Vanderbilt University Press.
O'Shea, E., Murphy, K., Larkin, P., Payne, S., Froggatt, K., Casey, D., Ní Léime, Á. and Keys, M. (2008) *End-of-Life Care for Older People in Acute and Long-Care Stay Settings in Ireland.* Dublin: Irish Hospice Foundation.
Quinlan, C. and O'Neill, C. (2008) *Practitioners' Narrative Submissions.* Unpublished. Dublin: Irish Hospice Foundation.
Rosen, M. (2012) *Dignity: Its History and Meaning.* Cambridge, MA: Harvard University Press.
Rothman, D. (1991) *Strangers at the Bedside: A History of How Law and Bioethics Transformed Medical Decision Making.* New York: Basic Books.
Samantha, J. (2009) 'Lasting powers of attorney for healthcare under the Mental Capacity Act 2005: enhanced prospective self-determination for future incapacity or a simulacrum?', *Medical Law Review*, 17: 377.
Schopenhauer, A. (1837) *The Basis of Morality.* Trans. A.B. Bullock (1903). London: S. Sonnenschein.
Shklar, J. (1964) *Legalism.* Cambridge, MA: Harvard University Press.
Waldron, J. (2012) *The Harm in Hate Speech.* Cambridge, MA: Harvard University Press.
Wolfson, J. (2005) 'Erring on the side of Theresa Schiavo: reflections of the Special Guardian Ad Litem', *Hastings Center Report*, 35(3): 16.

16

Improving end-of-life care in intensive care units

Barry Lyons

First I will define what I conceive medicine to be. In general terms, it is to do away with the sufferings of the sick, to lessen the violence of their diseases, and to refuse to treat those who are overmastered by their disease, realising that in such cases medicine is powerless. (Hippocrates, c.400 BCE)

Politicians must address tough questions about limited resources. How many teachers are you willing to fire in order to have 78-year olds have a procedure which will be invented 5 years from now that adds 4 months to their life? (Gates, 2011)

Introduction

International figures indicate that 95% of critically ill patients (in intensive care units (ICUs))[1] lack capacity (Cohen et al., 2005), and in Ireland generally have not completed an advance healthcare directive (AHD). The mean mortality rate in adult ICUs varies from 10–29% (Society of Critical Care Medicine, 2012) with a European average calculated as 13.5% using data from participating units in 17 countries (Sprung et al., 2003). In Irish ICUs, death follows the withdrawal of non-beneficial artificial life-sustaining interventions in approximately 35% of cases (with an equal number dying after limits have been placed on their treatment). The withholding or withdrawal of interventions generally happens after a course of action has been agreed between clinicians and the patient's family (Collins et al., 2006b). Although there is no formal data yet available, the number of patients who die in this jurisdiction, following the withdrawal of life-sustaining treatment (WLST), is likely to exceed 500 annually (ICSI and JFICMI, 2014).

While presently these deaths rarely become the subject of legal scrutiny, it is notable that (at the time of writing) section 4(2) of the Assisted Decision-Making (Capacity) Bill 2013 states:

> Notwithstanding any other provision in this Act, the High Court, and not the court, shall have jurisdiction relating to every matter in connection with –
> (a) non-therapeutic sterilisation,
> (b) withdrawal of artificial life-sustaining treatment, or
> (c) the donation of an organ,
> where the matter concerns a relevant person who lacks capacity.

While section 53 of the Bill allows informal decision-makers to make healthcare decisions for the person lacking capacity, such decisions cannot include those 'referred to in section 4(2) nor a matter closely connected with a matter referred to in section 4(2)'. It is also to be noted that Head 6(2) of the Advance Healthcare Directives Bill 2013 provides that:

> Where the terms of a valid and applicable advance healthcare directive, and the authority of any patient-designated healthcare representative appointed therein, intersect with the provisions of Section 4(2) of the Assisted Decision-Making (Capacity) Act, effect shall be given to the advance healthcare directive and the authority of the patient-designated healthcare representative in accordance with this Part of the Act.

One reading of all of this is that WLST from an incapacitated individual who does not come under Head 6(2) is a decision over which the High Court will have sole jurisdiction; that, in essence, an application must be made to the High Court before artificial life-sustaining interventions could be withdrawn from an incapacitated patient in an ICU who lacks an AHD (or patient-designated healthcare representative) that dictates the withdrawal of medical interventions. It is unlikely that the legislators intended to encompass all such patients under section 4(2), perhaps aiming solely to include decisions about the proposed withdrawal of artificial nutrition and hydration (ANH) from patients in a permanent vegetative state (PVS) as occurs in other jurisdictions (Department for Constitutional Affairs, 2007: para. 8.18), or to set out the relevant jurisdiction in the event that a court hearing might be required to decide on some matter. Nonetheless, the Bill, as set out, would appear to embrace almost all critically ill individuals. Regardless of the final wording of the legislation, any proposed intervention by the courts should give us pause for thought and provide us with an opportunity to assess current practice and how it might be improved upon.

A process that required High Court authorisation prior to WLST would represent a significant shift in current practice, but is this problematic? Clearly, such an approach would impact upon workload and expenditure. One might also argue that there would be a human cost as it is inevitable that there would be delays in the process, WLST cases competing with all others for the court's attention. This is likely to lead to distress in some families, as legal procrastination would probably result in a prolongation of the dying phase with individuals continuing to receive burdensome yet non-beneficial care while awaiting the court's decision. In addition, there is the potential for ICU beds to become so blocked up that other critically ill patients will be denied intensive care due to the consequent lack of space and resources (Prospectus Report, 2009).[2] One counter argument to all of this is that the state has a legitimate interest in the well-being of its citizens, and that if persons are to die as a consequence of the withdrawal of medical treatment then the intervention of the courts is appropriate to ensure procedural correctness and fairness. In response, it might be proposed that WLST is a medical matter; that engagement with the patient and his or her family's wishes is an important relational aspect of medical treatment that is best carried out by those entrusted with that individual's care; and that interference by the courts with this relationship represents an unwarranted intrusion that would not be welcomed by patients, families or healthcare professionals. This argument, perhaps, could be taken as an indication that all is well in the world of ICU treatment withdrawal, that the process is scientifically and procedurally sound and based on agreed principles and parameters, and that there is a general consensus on this and minimal variability in practice.

None of these arguments is true. There are no settled international boundaries defining what treatments work and when, and at what point, if ever, they should not be provided or be removed. In the majority of cases, there is agreement between the physicians and the family as to what should happen; not always immediately but generally over a period of time. There are, however (sometimes irreconcilable) conflicts that arise between families and clinicians when the former refuse to accept medical recommendations for their loved one's care, even when there is little or no chance of recovery. Such families hold on in hope of a miracle, and so are unwilling to limit therapy. There is also international evidence of variability in practice between and within institutions, and within Irish hospitals there are no established procedural rules for deciding appropriate pathways in the face of any form of conflict.

This chapter will proceed as follows. It will provide an analysis of the state of critical care provision in Ireland, of how the withdrawal or withholding of therapies usually happens, and discuss the evidence for variability. I will argue that the withdrawal of life-sustaining therapies is not simply a medical matter, but one with considerable social and political dimensions. As such, there is a need for public discourse on the subject, as well as the development of a public policy which might be advanced through the dissemination of institutional and national end-of-life policies. Intensive care is extremely expensive and public expenditure on the marginal care it sometimes provides deserves scrutiny. Thus, it is proposed that the answers to the dilemmas that ICU care throws up will not be attained through the courts, but rather the solution is to be found in a social contract on the use of expensive and resource intensive medical technology.

The state of intensive care in Ireland

Critical care is defined as highly specialised treatment provided to patients whose conditions are life-threatening and require constant monitoring and advanced care, usually in specifically designated units (Hirshon, 2013). Its fundamental aim is to support the organ systems of the sickest patients until they recover from the acute severe injury or illness that afflicts them. It is the most resource intensive element of the hospital system, in terms of technology, human resources and money. In the UK, an intensive care bed costs approximately €2150 per day, compared to a ward bed which averages about €275 per day (Prospectus Report, 2009: 47). In 2005, annual US critical care medicine costs ($81.7 billion) represented 13.4% of hospital costs, 4.1% of national health expenditures, and 0.66% of the gross domestic product (Halpern and Pastores, 2010).

One would think then, given both the human and fiscal expense, that intensive care would be meticulously planned and monitored with rigorous accountability and performance management structures. This is not so, however. Adult critical care services, like many other hospital services in Ireland, have developed in a relatively unstructured and unplanned manner (Prospectus Report, 2009: 22). There are currently 37 hospitals providing critical care across the Republic of Ireland, with nine hospitals bearing the bulk of the burden by delivering most of the care in terms of volume and acuity. These units are under significant pressure having insufficient capacity to meet demands. Overall, there are substantial deficiencies in terms of organisational structure, staffing and beds (Prospectus Report, 2009: 12).

So far, not so good. But the Prospectus Report was compiled at the end of a period of unprecedented economic growth in Ireland. The annual budgetary allocation to healthcare has since fallen by over 22%, at a time when the demand for health services is increasing year-on-year, with a consequent upwards trajectory of costs. The Health Service Executive (HSE, 2013b) has identified a growing population with an increasing number of citizens that are elderly, obese or suffering from one or more chronic illnesses, as a major driver of demand and cost.

End-of-life care and resource allocation in the ICU

The Prospectus Report (2009) has identified critical care as being one of the key health service areas that will be subject to increased demand. New ICU treatments are particularly costly and, with rising patient expectations, the question of how these matters might be balanced against a diminishing (or even static) budgetary allocation is one deserving of analysis. Should intensive care receive more funding than other forms of healthcare provision (e.g. primary care), or should we reassess what ICU is trying to achieve? In essence, as Vincent observes, 'hard decisions regarding resource allocation need to be made now' (2013: vii). However, despite resources being limited, demand exceeding supply, and healthcare expenditure continuing to contract, the option of publicly limiting services (especially those with lifesaving potential) remains a political anathema (Crippen, 2013: xii). There has been a failure to engage the wider public in discussions, (i) about the use of expensive technology in the context of individual and societal goals, values and beliefs, (ii) about fair and equitable access to its potential benefits, and (iii) about its cost–benefit ratio in the sense that marginal gains for individuals may threaten the welfare of many because of the costs entailed.

Critical care is not always a particularly cost-effective therapeutic option as, despite treatment with expensive drugs, interventions, technology and one-to-one nurse–patient ratios, many patients still die (Vincent, 2013: vii). One recent paper looking at five ICUs in a US academic healthcare system over a three-month period identified that 20% of patients were receiving what physicians deemed to be 'probably futile' or 'futile' treatment. These patients spent a cumulative total of 464 days getting 'futile' treatment in ICU. Not all the patients died, but the survivors remained in a 'severely compromised health state'. The cost of futile treatment in the study was estimated at $2.6 million (Huynh et al., 2013).

One reason for the sustained provision of such care is that some families insist on the continuation of aggressive interventions until death supervenes. As noted previously, some form of withholding or withdrawing of medical interventions precedes the majority of deaths, despite the hopes, wishes, prayers and expectations of their families. While most ICU patients' relatives accept this as the reasonable removal of excessively burdensome treatment modalities in the face of almost certain mortality, physicians are increasingly reporting familial resistance (Crippen, 2013: viv). A recent American survey found that the proportion of the general population who believe in 'doing everything possible to save the patient' until the end had doubled (from 15% to 31%) over a 20-year period (Pew Research Center, 2013). Another study asked family members of critically ill patients if they would choose to continue treatment for their relative if the chances of survival were < 1%; 32% of surrogate decision-makers said yes (Zier et al., 2009). In essence, few relatives base their beliefs about the patients' prognoses exclusively on the prognostic information provided to them by physicians. Boyd et al. (2010) identified that other factors (such as personal perceptions of the patient's individual strength of character and will to live, and the family's sense of optimism, intuition and faith) sometimes supersede the importance of the physician's prognostication. How we manage the volatile situation of a family requesting everything in the face of a particularly pessimistic clinical prognostication will become increasingly important in the near future. Not only are doctors possibly infringing on their professional obligation not to harm the patient, but the unnecessary use of resources by that patient has a significant impact on the care that others can access.

End-of-life care in Irish ICUs

In Ireland, the withholding or withdrawal of life-sustaining treatments from incapacitated persons has hitherto been lawful when done in the best interests of that individual (*In Re a Ward of Court* [1996] 2 IR 79). The guidance offered by the Irish Medical Council (2009) indicates that doctors have no obligation to start or maintain any treatment modality 'that is futile or disproportionately burdensome, even if such treatment may prolong life'. With regard to resuscitation, the HSE's *National Consent Policy* (2013a) notes that 'where CPR is judged inappropriate, it is good practice to inform those close to the patient, but there is no need to seek their "permission" not to perform CPR in these circumstances'.

To date the only publicly available data on end-of-life care in ICU from Ireland pertains to one piece of research from a single institution. That hospital was a participant in the pan-European ETHICUS observational study, and collected ten months of consecutive data. Because it is the only information that we have, it is worth briefly reiterating it here. The data related to 1,146 patients who were admitted to the ICU between 1999 and 2000. Of these, 126 patients died (mortality rate = 11%) during the study period. The median age of the deceased was 68 years (range 19–86 years), with a slight preponderance of males (58%). Eighty-five patients (69%) had limits placed on their life-sustaining therapy, interventions being withheld in 45 (36%) and withdrawn in 40 (33%). The main reason for limiting life-sustaining interventions was that the patient was unresponsive to maximum therapy. The most common intervention withheld was cardio-pulmonary resuscitation (CPR) (96%), followed by inotropic (supporting the cardiovascular system) drugs (47%) and kidney dialysis (26%). Tracheal extubation (removing the breathing tube that connects the patient's lungs to the ventilator) or disconnecting the ventilator (often colloquially referred to as 'pulling the plug') were relatively uncommon (16.4%). Artificial nutrition (6%) and hydration (2.4%) were even less frequently withdrawn, most likely reflecting the reality that ANH is rarely perceived as a life-sustaining treatment in the critical care context (Collins et al., 2006a).

It is estimated that in excess of 20,000 patients are admitted to an Irish ICU every year. It is unknown whether the single centre figures described above apply to this whole population. There are no national data, and no means of comparing units. In this regard, it is interesting to note that the Health Information and Quality Authority (HIQA, 2013) review of the tragic case of

Savita Halappanavar made recommendations about maternity care that are equally as germane for ICU (see Feltzmann, Chapter 12). It was observed in the report that:

(1) There are a number of data collection sources involved in the collection of … morbidity and mortality data in Ireland, however, there is no centralised and consistent approach to reporting this.
(2) There is wide variation in the local clinical and corporate governance arrangements in place across the … public … hospitals/units nationally. This means that it is impossible at this time to properly assess the performance and quality of the … service nationally.
(3) The Authority believes that, in order to provide assurances that … [patients] are receiving safe, high quality and reliable care … services must collect, monitor and manage quality and safety performance measures to evaluate the performance of their clinicians and the outcomes for patients.

These comments are as pertinent to critical care as they are to maternity services.

Variability in end-of-life care

The notion of inter-unit variability is alluded to in the HIQA report. Research from a number of institutions and countries indicates that not only are there significant disparities between ICUs in how end-of-life care is managed, but there are also substantial divergences between clinicians within the same ICU. The ETHICUS study, a prospective, observational analysis of end-of-life practices in 37 ICUs in 17 European countries, identified that of 31,417 ICU admissions, 4,248 patients (13.5%) died, and of these, 3,086 patients (72.6%) had their treatment limited. Substantial inter-country variability was found in terms of therapeutic limitations and the manner of dying. For example, withholding of therapy took place in 38% of cases overall, but this varied from 16% to 70%, while the incidence of withdrawal of therapy ranged from 5% to 69%. The authors postulated that there might be a number of reasons for this inter-country variability (in addition to differences in case mix) such as regional differences in politics, law, culture and religion and in the values and practices of physicians (Sprung et al., 2003).

However, significant inter-institutional variation may still be observed even within an individual culture. Quill et al. (2014) reviewed data on decisions to forgo life-sustaining therapy (DFLST) in 269,002 patients admitted to 153 ICUs in the US between 2001 and 2009. The study proposed that if patient characteristics that were associated with DFLST were adjusted for, then the rates of DFLSTs should be reasonably consistent across units. However, there was no uniformity and, after appropriate adjustment, the probability of a DFLST being instituted varied nearly six-fold across ICUs. The authors concluded that, most likely, non-patient-centred matters were influential in the decision-making process and that particular aspects of individual ICU 'culture and practice ... influence end-of-life decision-making'. Two other single hospital (one in the UK and one in the US) studies of patients in adult ICUs found an even larger difference (up to 15-fold) in treatment limitation decisions between experienced intensivists (Poulton et al., 2005; Wilson et al., 2013).

In general, it would seem reasonable that the factors most important in making end-of-life decisions would be the patient's values and the healthcare provider's appraisal of that patient's prognosis. Since most ICU patients are incapable of expressing their wishes at the time of their critical illness, ideas about their preferences are sought from their relatives, or from an AHD should they have one completed. However, the paper from Quill would seem to suggest that other influences are relevant. In fact, a myriad of physician-centred factors appear to impact on DFLST including clinician age, gender, geography, religion, personal life support preferences, practice setting, specialty, experience and familiarity with life support (Wilson et al., 2013). These factors might lead to variability in practice, and such variation possibly can lead to significant differences in what the patient might receive. Variability might well happen in end-of-life decision-making in critical care because of uncertainties regarding prognosis, local politics, law and culture, or patient preferences. Perhaps this variability might sometimes be acceptable, or the patient may not be particularly disadvantaged by it. However, when the variability is due to physician preferences, and the level of care provided dependent on whichever clinician is rostered to the bedside on a given day, then this would seem unreasonably arbitrary and contrary to patient-centred care (Wilkinson and Truog, 2013).

There is some empirical support in the literature for the existence of this notion of *doctor-dominated decisions*, especially with regard to value-laden and contentious decisions. This matter has most frequently been explored with regard to religion. Seale (2010) found that physicians who described themselves as non-religious were more likely than others to report having given continuous deep sedation until death, having taken decisions they expected or partly intended to end life, and to have discussed these decisions with patients judged to have the capacity to participate in discussions. The ETHICUS study found that physicians who were Protestant, Catholic or espoused no religion more frequently used withdrawal of life-sustaining treatments than physicians who were Greek Orthodox, Jewish or Moslem (Sprung et al., 2003). Other research has indicated that personality factors including clinicians' emotional responses to death may impact on end-of-life care (Barr, 2007; Black, 2007).

Given the complexity of end-of -life decision-making, it is probably neither possible nor desirable to have an absolutely uniform methodology dictating events. However, although there is no gold-plated moral compass designed to give direction to physicians in cases of ethical uncertainty, nonetheless the guiding principle should be that care is directed by the patient's rather than the physician's values. Doctor-dominated decision-making is ethically problematic, not least because patient wishes are subjugated.

There is no direct evidence of end-of-life treatment limitation variability in Ireland, largely because nobody has examined the matter. Anecdotal evidence indicates that there most likely are significant differences in the withholding or withdrawing of life-sustaining interventions between Irish ICUs, and between clinicians within these ICUs. It does seem improbable that Irish ICUs would be immune to an otherwise widespread problem.

Thus far, this chapter has tried to demonstrate that we have a number of organisational and governance issues in the ICU. It would appear that we are confronted by increasing demands and expectations from an older and progressively less healthy population (and their family members) in the face of ongoing budgetary constraints. In addition, there is a relatively unexamined decision-making process that, sometimes at least, seems to prioritise physician rather than patient perspectives on end-of-life care. On other occasions, family members dominate the discourse and insist that everything possible be done in order to save a life. There is no tradition of Irish doctors using the courts in order to resolve this issue, even though it remains a great source of frustration and moral distress among staff within ICUs.

In view of these issues, how should we respond? It seems reasonable to contend that what is required is a more systematic approach; one which privileges procedures that acknowledge the impossibility and undesirability of treating all critically ill patients aggressively until the bitter end yet gives a fair hearing to those that wish for this; one that provides guidance on when and how treatment limitation might be appropriate, encourages collective and shared decision-making, promotes advance care planning, provides mechanisms for conflict resolution between physicians and families (or between healthcare professionals), and mandates data collection for audit and comparison (Wilkinson and Truog, 2013).

Governance and end-of-life care in the ICU

How might this all work in practice? The solution to all of the difficulties faced by the ICU cannot be answered by a single individual, but perhaps might be better addressed by a broader competence encompassing clinical, legal, moral and fiscal expertise charged with developing mechanisms that support and integrate the differing ethical perspectives of patient care, and to produce guidance on the matter. Despite this non-individualistic mandate, it remains essential that patients' fundamental rights (such as bodily integrity, informed consent, truth-telling and confidentiality) continue to be protected.

Putting together a consensus document that actually guides action admittedly would be challenging. Yet, it is not an outlandish prospect. The Prospectus Report (2009) into ICU provision in Ireland states: 'end-of-life policies must be available to all ICU personnel and must be reviewed annually'. In 2007, the Dublin Coroner's Court also recommended that a hospital should draw up and publish its guidelines on the withdrawal of life-sustaining care as a matter of urgency. Any guidance drawn up would have to deal with specific, yet difficult, questions. For example:

- How do we prioritise who gets into intensive care – is it first come, first served, or are marginal cases rejected even if there is space. Are there age limit cut-offs?
- How much treatment should a marginal case receive before it is withdrawn if non-effective?
- Who should decide about the utility of life-sustaining treatment; should it be a group decision and if so, does there need to be a consensus between healthcare professionals, or is a majority sufficient?
- What weight should be given to the opinions of the dissenting intensivist, surgeon, oncologist or nurse?
- How important are the opinions, beliefs and values of the family?
- What safeguards should be in place to protect the patient from under- or over-treatment?
- How should we resolve disputes when families are intransigent in their wish to continue care but the physicians deem it to be 'futile'? What mechanisms should be used when there is conflict between families and physicians?
- Should third parties be involved to solve problems and resolve conflicts, and what role should the courts have?

In modern healthcare, evidence-based medicine put into practice via guidelines is the main mechanism employed to promote and ensure high quality in patient care (Timmermans and Angell, 2001). Such guidelines might be defined as 'systematically developed statements to assist practitioners and patient decisions about appropriate health care for specific clinical circumstances' (Dodek et al., 2010: 669). Within the ICU the use of guidelines has improved healthcare professional performance with regard to a variety of interventions (Jackson et al., 2010; Kolle and Micek, 2010; Blackwood et al., 2011). So, using protocol-driven care is nothing new to critical care practice, and the limited evidence available indicates that guidelines may improve end-of-life care, including through the implementation of organisational changes and communication plans for engagement with patients and their families (Schneiderman et al., 2003; Treece et al., 2004; Quenot et al., 2012). Perhaps more relevantly, overt hospital policies on 'medical futility' seem to have been helpful in resolving end-of-life conflicts and improving care in other jurisdictions (Joseph, 2011). However, all of this is not as simple as it seems; for any set of guidelines to work effectively there must be buy-in from all participants and identification of any perceived legal, regulatory, ethical or care-oriented impediments (Lemiengre et al., 2014).

Even if there were no such issues, somehow this seems an insufficient response to the difficulties raised by end-of-life care in the ICU. A number of people sit around a table, produce a document, the staff agree with it and all problems are resolved? There is no doubt that institutional guidelines are important and can positively affect behaviour. But this still renders the matter semi-secret, a quiet institutional programme. Changing how decisions are made about critical care denial or withdrawal seems to demand a greater level of public discourse than this. It is extraordinary that in the history of intensive care provision in this state there has been such limited media coverage of this matter, something that seems particularly strange given the level of interest in whether those not yet born live or die at the hands of the medical profession.

A single institutional policy still allows for inter-institutional variability, something which seems no less arbitrary or more desirable than divergence of practice between professionals within a hospital. Doctors currently 'own' how end-of-life care is managed, but it is uncertain that they alone should be entrusted with this responsibility. Furthermore, it seems a particularly onerous burden, and one that should be shared. The proposal that the High Court has sole jurisdiction over the withdrawal of life-sustaining treatment from the incapacitated would remove this concern from the aegis of doctors and place it within the bounds of a more procedurally secure institution. Yet, this would still leave out much of what is variable – including whether or not a person is admitted to the ICU in the first instance, and cases where treatment modalities are withheld rather than withdrawn. More importantly, end-of-life care should be a discussion, not an adversarial event.

Instead, these matters should be the subject of a national policy, one that is formulated with broad social engagement and becomes publicly available. For this to happen, a framework needs to be applied at an administrative level that covers all healthcare institutions; one that includes clinical, fiscal, administrative and social ethical perspectives. Society and institutions, not the individual physician, must create guidelines limiting the availability of therapies. Doctors, then, can continue to fulfil their obligation to do what's best for the individual patient. While there would seem to be a moral duty for them to assist, as experts, in the development of a public policy, their primary duty would remain as an advocate for the patient.

This is not to underestimate the task of developing appropriate public guidelines and rules while there is professional divergence, not to mention the improbability of a societal consensus on controversial moral issues. Yet, the current position is unsustainable. Doctors should not have to fear to make difficult choices because of the possibility of litigation or professional sanction. Patients should be clear on how decisions will be made when they are sickest and least able to protect their own interests. Most people hope that their death would be a calm and dignified passing. They should not have non-beneficial yet burdensome treatment imposed upon them by well-meaning but overly optimistic physicians or families hoping for the miraculous; yet it would seem unreasonable to arbitrarily deny them beneficial care based on anything but their own choice. Rather, patients must be reassured that fair procedures and just distribution of resources underpin the process.

Conclusion

It is usually accepted that all people should receive a certain minimum level of healthcare. It is probably also a matter of general knowledge that healthcare is increasingly expensive, and if allowed would consume almost all of a country's budget. In addition, it might be recognised that as bad as the problem of scarce health resources is today, it will probably worsen in the years to come because of increasing costs and an ageing and increasingly overweight population with many chronic disorders. There may well be a theoretical understanding that increasing costs and a diminishing budget means that there will be a lack of resources to provide all interventions, treatments or care for all people. Equally, it seems reasonable to assume that most people, in theory at least, would rather have a health system that is equitably distributed and adequate for all those that require it rather than the converse. All of this probably stops when it becomes a matter that involves themselves or their family members. This is particularly the case where life-sustaining treatment is at issue. Yet, in order to maintain a fair system, there must be a form of social contract whereby distributive justice is the dominant force.

Evidence indicates that decisions about the appropriate use of scarce resources, particularly in the ICU, will become more prevalent and more difficult in the future. Such decisions should not be left to the jurisdiction, even if informed, of doctors or in the hands of increasingly demanding family members, but rather should be placed squarely in the political process. This would require a considerable shift in our political culture, but is a position that seems as unavoidable as it is appropriate.

Notes

1 Intensive care is synonymous with critical care and the two terms are used interchangeably in this chapter.

2 It is already the case that patients are refused admission because of a lack of resources. The

2009 report into ICU provision in Ireland identified 278 refused admissions to general units in June 2008. When weighted and calculated, this was rounded up to an estimated annual number of refusals of 4292.

References

Barr, P. (2007) 'Relationship of neonatologists' end-of-life decisions to their personal fear of death', *Archives of Disease in Childhood-Fetal and Neonatal Edition*, 92: F104.

Black, K. (2007) 'Health care professionals' death attitudes, experiences, and advance directive communication behaviour', *Death Studies*, 31: 563.

Blackwood, B., Alderdice, F., Burns, K., Cardwell, C., Lavery, G. and O'Halloran, P. (2011) 'Use of weaning protocols for reducing duration of mechanical ventilation in critically ill adult patients: Cochrane systematic review and meta-analysis', *British Medical Journal*, 342: 7237.

Boyd, E.A., Lo, B., Evans, L.R., Malvar, G., Apatira, L., Luce, J.M. and White, D.B. (2010) 'It's not just what the doctor tells me: factors that influence surrogate decision-makers' perceptions of prognosis', *Critical Care Medicine*, 38: 1270.

Cohen, S., , Sprung, C., Sjokvist, P., Lippert, A., Ricou, B., Baras, M., Hovilehto, S., Maia, P., Phelan, D., Reinhart, K., Werdan, K., Bulow, H.H. and Woodcock, T. (2005) 'Communication of end-of-life decisions in European intensive care units', *Intensive Care Medicine*, 31: 1215.

Collins, N., Phelan, D. and Carton, E. (2006a) 'End of life in ICU: care of the dying or "pulling the plug"?', *Irish Medical Journal*, 99(4): 112.

Collins, N., Phelan, D., Marsh, B. and Sprung, C.L. (2006b) 'End-of-life care in the intensive care unit: the Irish Ethicus Data', *Critical Care and Resuscitation*, 8: 315.

Crippen, D. (2013) *ICU Resource Allocation in the New Millennium: Will We Say No?* Dordrecht: Springer.

Department for Constitutional Affairs (2007) *Mental Capacity Act: Code of Practice*. London.

Dodek, P., Cahill, N.E. and Heyland, D.K. (2010) 'The relationship between organisational culture and implementation of clinical practice guidelines: a narrative review', *Journal of Parenteral and Enteral Nutrition*, 34: 669.

Gates, B. (2011) Interview by Charlie Rose. Cited in J. Lemer and E. Crook. 'Healthcare: transparently opaque', *Financial Times*, 21 February.

Halpern, N.A. and Pastores, S.M. (2010) 'Critical care medicine in the United States 2000–2005: an analysis of bed numbers, occupancy rates, payer mix, and costs', *Critical Care Medicine*, 38(1): 65.

Hippocrates (2012) *On the Art of Medicine*. Trans. J.L. Mann. Leiden: Brill.

HIQA (Health Information and Quality Authority) (2013) *Investigation into the Safety, Quality and Standards of Services Provided by the Health Service Executive to Patients, Including Pregnant Women, at Risk of Clinical Deterioration, Including those Provided in University Hospital Galway, and as Reflected in the Care and Treatment Provided to Savita Halappanavar*. Dublin.

Hirshon, J.M. (2013) 'Health systems and services: the role of acute care', *Bulletin of the World Health Organisation*, 91: 386.

HSE (Health Service Executive) (2013a) *National Consent Policy*. Dublin.

HSE (Health Service Executive) (2013b) *National Service Plan*. Dublin.

Huynh, T.N., Kleerup, E.C., Wiley, J.F., Savitsky, T.D., Guse, D., Garber, B.J. and Wenger, N.S. (2013) 'The frequency and cost of treatment perceived to be futile in critical care', *JAMA Internal Medicine*, 173(20): 1887.

ICSI and JFICMI (2014) *Submission to the Department of Health and Children in Response to the Publication of the Advance Healthcare Directives Bill, 2013*. Dublin.

Irish Medical Council (2009) *Guide to Professional Conduct and Ethics for Registered Medical Practitioners*, 7th edn. Dublin.

Jackson, D.L., Proudfoot, C.W., Cann, K.F. and Walsh, T. (2010) 'A systematic review of the impact of sedation practice in the ICU on resource use, costs and patient safety', *Critical Care*, 14: 59.

Joseph, R. (2011) 'Hospital policy on medical futility – does it help in conflict resolution and ensuring good end-of-life care?' *Annals of the Academy of Medicine of Singapore*, 40: 19.

Kolle, M.H. and Micek, S.T. (2010) 'Using protocols to improve patient outcomes in the intensive care unit: focus on mechanical ventilation and sepsis', *Seminars in Respiratory Critical Care Medicine*, 31: 19.

Lemiengre, J., Dierckx de Casterle, B., Schotsmans, P. and Gastmans, C. (2014) 'Written institutional ethics policies on euthanasia: an empirical based organisational-ethical framework', *Medicine Health Care and Philosophy*, 17: 215.

Pew Research Center (2013) *Views on End-of-Life Medical Treatments*. Washington, DC.

Poulton, B., Ridley, S., Mackenzie-Ross, R. and Rizvi, S. (2005) 'Variation in end-of-life decision making between critical care consultants', *Anaesthesia*, 60: 1101.

Prospectus Report (2009) *Towards Excellence in Critical Care: Review of Adult Critical Care Services in the Republic of Ireland*. Dublin: Department of Health and Children.

Quenot, J.P., Rigaud, J.P., Prin, S., Barbar, S., Pavon, A., Hamet, M., Jacquiot, N., Blettery, B., Hervé, C., Charles, P.E. and Moutel, G. (2012) 'Impact of an intensive communication strategy on end-of-life practices in the intensive care unit', *Intensive Care Medicine*, 38: 145.

Quill, C.M., Ratcliffe, S.J., Harhay, M.O. and Halpern, S.D. (2014) 'Variation in decisions to forego life-sustaining therapies in US ICUs', *Chest*, 146(3): 573.

Schneiderman, L.J., Gilmer, T., Teetzel, H.D., Dugan, D.O., Blustein, J., Cranford, R., Briggs, K.B., Komatsu, G.I., Goodman-Crews, P., Cohn, F. and Young, E.W. (2003) 'Effect of ethics consultations on non-beneficial life-sustaining treatments in the intensive care setting: a randomised controlled trial', *JAMA*, 290: 1166.

Seale, C. (2010) 'The role of doctors' religious faith and ethnicity in taking ethically controversial decisions during end-of-life care', *Journal of Medical Ethics*, 36: 677.

Society of Critical Care Medicine (2012) *Critical Care Statistics*. Illinois.

Sprung, C.L., , Cohen, S.L., Sjokvist, P., Baras, M., Bulow, H.H., Hovilehto, S., Ledoux, D., Lippert, A., Maia, P., Phelan, D., Schobersberger, W., Wennberg, E. and Woodcock, T. (2003) 'End-of-life practices in European intensive care units: the ethicus study', *JAMA*, 290: 790.

Timmermans, S. and Angell, A. (2001) 'Evidence-based medicine, clinical uncertainty, and learning to doctor', *Journal of Health and Social Behaviour*, 42: 342.

Treece, P.D., Engelberg, R.A., Crowley, L., Chan, J.D., Rubenfeld, G.D., Steinberg, K.P. and Curtis, J.R. (2004) 'Evaluation of a standardised order form for the withdrawal of life support in the intensive care unit', *Critical Care Medicine*, 32: 1141.

Vincent, J.L. (2013) 'Foreword'. In Crippen, D. (2013) *ICU Resource Allocation in the New Millennium: Will We Say No?* Dordrecht: Springer.

Wilkinson, D.J. and Truog, R.D. (2013) 'The luck of the draw: physician-related variability in end-of-life decision-making in intensive care', *Intensive Care Medicine*, 39: 1128.

Wilson, M.E., Rhudy, L.N., Ballinger, B.A., Tescher, A.N., Pickering, B.W. and Gajic, O. (2013) 'Factors that contribute to physician variability in decisions to limit life support in the ICU: a qualitative study', *Intensive Care Medicine*, 39: 1009.

Zier, L.S., Burack, J.H., Micco, G., Chipman, A.K., Frank, J.A. and White, D.B. (2009) 'Surrogate decision makers' responses to physicians' predictions of medical futility', *Chest*, 136: 110.

Index